Play by Play

ALSO BY JONATHAN KALB

Beckett in Performance

Free Admissions: Collected Theater Writings

The Theater of Heiner Müller

JONATHAN KALB

Play by Play

Theater Essays and Reviews,
1993–2002

LIMELIGHT EDITIONS   NEW YORK

First Limelight Edition   March 2003

Published in the United States by Proscenium Publishers, Inc., New York

Manufactured in the United States of America

Library of Congress Cataloging-in-Publication Data

Kalb, Jonathan.
Play by play : theater essays & reviews, 1993-2002 / Jonathan Kalb.--
1st Limelight ed.
p. cm.
Includes index.
ISBN 0-87910-984-X (pbk.) -- ISBN 0-87910-989-0 (hardcover)
1. Theater--United States--History--20th century. 2. Theater--New
York (State)--New York--Reviews. I. Title.
PN2266.5.K37 2003

2003001210

For Sam

Contents

Illustrations

Preface

THIS BOOK CONTAINS SELECTED THEATER CRITICISM WRITTEN BE-
tween 1993 and 2002, the decade since the publication of my last criticism collection, *Free Admissions*.

About half the present material originally appeared in *The New York
Times, Theater, Salmagundi, American Theatre*, and an essay collection acknowledged below. The other half is from *The Village Voice*, where I wrote
for the theater section from 1987 to 1997, and *New York Press*, where I
wrote a weekly column as the main theater critic from 1997 to 2001. One
salient difference between this book and *Free Admissions* is the altered
viewpoint of a critic who went from attending about fifty shows a year before 1997 (paying for about half of them) to attending more than 150 a
year, including most of the so-called "major" New York openings (worth
about $10,000-15,000 in press tickets). Because the checkered story of my
tenure at *New York Press* is told in the lecture reprinted as this book's first
selection, I'll dwell on it here only to add these few points.

In 1999, a friend observed that she thought my writing was more
compassionate in *New York Press* than it had been at the *Voice*—a remark that puzzled me at the time because I'd just been grumbling about
the fact that the percentage of duds among New York's self-styled A-list
shows was no better than it had been for the much-maligned B-, C-, and
D-lists. Reading now through my reviews from the past decade, however, I see what my friend meant. There is a difference, but what she saw
as compassion seems to me primarily a matter of breathing room. At

New York Press, I had no space pressure, and setting the length of my column gave me more careful control over my tone than I ever had under the gun of compulsory brevity.

Furthermore (and this I *was* aware of at the time), the job of the lead critic, for all its stresses and institutionalized disappointments, left me more sanguine than I'd ever been about the general health of the American theater—not necessarily as a source of deathless new art but certainly as a flourishing professional craft and a crucible of vital artistic ideas and energies. Some people will no doubt chalk up this buoyancy to the free tickets; they have clearly never sat down to write on deadline and discovered how expensive such tickets can be. To me, the key point is variety of experience. The lead critic invariably ventures farther beyond his personal taste and preferences than other theatergoers do and thus acquires a unique overview of the art and its range of risk-taking. That overview is the real privilege of the job.

Actually, I lived a triple life during the past decade. I taught full-time at Hunter College, eventually becoming Chair of the Theater Department, I was a father to two small boys, who colored my vision of theater and everything else more than I can describe, and I wrote a book on the German playwright Heiner Müller between intense bouts of journalism. I'd like to believe there was always fruitful synergy among these undertakings. I know that there sometimes was.

In any case, no criticism collection is ever really a chronicle of an era, or even of an art during a chosen period. A collection is a chronicle of the critic, a record of an intellectual passage that hopefully does illuminate the landscape traveled through but makes no claim to exhaustiveness. There's a built-in contradiction in the form, because any personal chronicle is obviously meant to be read from cover to cover yet everyone knows that collections are sampled like buffets. For my part, I don't mind the sampling. If watching kids has taught me anything, it's that skeptical people will take what they know they like at first but then dip into the unfamiliar when no one's looking. By the same token, my older son assures me that this book's title will induce thousands of football fans, the audiences of tomorrow, to purchase it by mistake.

The 1990s were filled, for me, not only with intensive New York theatergoing but also with melodramatic academic politics linked to the culture wars, tragicomic journalistic politics surrounding the media-age "crisis of criticism," and frequent trips to Germany in a not-quite-futile search for a theater whose vibrancy resided outside these politics. This territory is the subject of *Play By Play*'s opening section, containing three essays on criticism. The remainder of the book is divided by topic, with separate sections devoted to Samuel Beckett and German theater (my permanent obsessions, it appears), Robert Wilson and other admirably quixotic American theater, and a selection of *New York Press* columns whose subject, substance or both seem to me of continuing interest.

If the book has an overarching theme, it is my ongoing inquiry into the specific function and purpose of theater, a fundamentally language-centered art, in an age that is quickly dispensing with print and inextricably devoted to electronically mediated entertainment. For reasons best explained by what follows, I am among those who persist in seeking wisdom about life's more nettled questions in the flarings and sputterings of this art form that millions find ridiculously retrograde. My other continuing inquiry, into the place and function of serious criticism within a compulsively trivializing environment, is really an outgrowth of this theater commitment. Would I still write criticism if somehow, tomorrow, there were no more theater? Probably, but less often, and with a cooler flame.

Apart from some minor tidying, my articles are reprinted here in the same form in which they first appeared. The temptation to revise was nearly overpowering—especially since the newspaper columns were all written under tight deadlines, some overnight—but I resisted it out of reluctance to falsify the original occasions. The main exception is that (as in *Free Admissions*) passages originally cut due to space limitations have been replaced. Thanks, as ever, to Mel Zerman for his faith, generosity, and courage, to Julie Heffernan for her love and editorial wisdom, and to the editors of all the publications for permission to reprint.

September 2002

Critical Mess

The Death (and Life) of American Theater Criticism

Advice to the Young Critic*

I THANK YOU FOR INVITING ME TO SPEAK ABOUT THEATER CRIT-
icism, which is an art (some might call it a vice) I have practiced for
twenty-two years. University lectures on theater criticism aren't
common, in my experience, partly because the subject falls into the
crevices between edgily linked disciplines—literary studies and theater
practice, scholarship and journalism, art and entertainment. There are
also more practical reasons. Theater programs are partial to visits by
working playwrights, actors, directors, and designers, which makes sense
since they are practitioners of flourishing professions. They can be displayed as evidence of the golden future awaiting the best theater gradu-
ates. In the same circumstances I have to be more circumspect; I can
describe successes to you, but if I'm not to distort the truth, I must also
report my discomfort that my art is in danger of extinction.

---

* A lecture to students at Barnard College and New York University, Fall 2002.

3

Now, please don't worry, I'm not planning to whine. I'm aware that the extreme circumstances as I see them sometimes do have a fertilizing effect, just as dung dropped in a trampled pasture occasionally nurtures tufts of new green grass. I address myself today especially to the tougher tufts among you, to offer the benefit of whatever survivalist wisdom I might have. The fact is, though, there is no way to describe the promise, the opportunity, the necessity, or the dignity of the critical act at the current moment without first explaining, and maybe even attempting to alarm you about, the forces arrayed against it.

I consider myself fortunate. I've had real, sometimes enviable opportunities. After several unhappy years as a pre-med, I began writing theater criticism, with no competition, in my college newspaper, *The Wesleyan Argus*—right after seeing Walter Asmus's astonishing production of *Waiting for Godot* at the Brooklyn Academy of Music, which changed my life more than I knew then because it planted the seed of my first book. Later, after graduation, I reviewed for the local newspaper in my college town, *The Middletown Press*, also a formative experience. At the time, 1981, I considered myself a playwright, and I imagined that writing reviews might help me figure out what was wrong with my plays.

What I discovered instead was a fascination with criticism itself; the way my mind worked was better suited to the art of criticism than to playwriting. I don't mind admitting that what most spurred me to begin with, like many others, was the excitement of having my unique, 21-year-old opinion appreciated at long last by a public other than my mother. The editor of *The Middletown Press* soon disabused me on this point. After reading one pan I wrote of a production at The Long Wharf Theatre, he called me into his office to complain, without an iota of irony or hesitation, that my judgment had differed too much from that of *The New York Times*. "It's just...it's just too DIFFERENT," he told me, "your review, it's just too different from what THEY said, and I'm uncomfortable with that."

From *The Middletown Press* I went on to write for many other publications, including, for about ten years, *The Village Voice*. But my luckiest (albeit tainted) chance came much later, in 1997, when I fell into what felt like a time-warp. After a decade of college teaching, during which I devoted less and less energy to journalism and more and more to books and longer articles and essays about theater, I became the main theater critic for *New York Press*—a free weekly rag-if-there-ever-was-one that sees itself as the *Voice*'s chief competition. There, for four theater seasons, I enjoyed working conditions that were to my knowledge unique in the United States: complete freedom to see and say what I wanted, practically zero space pressure (my column was 1,200 to 1,600 words and could run longer if I wanted), and the chance to appear in print about forty times a year while most of the productions I considered were still running.

Despite the fact that it was for only four years, I lasted longer at *New York Press* than any of its previous theater writers, conceiving my columns not merely as reviews but as essays of general interest grounded on current theater events. As to my longevity, I know that it was partly due to keeping out of the right-wing editors' way, never attempting to locate myself within the paper's internal politics or to respond to the provocations of the other columnists (a few of whom I did admire). In any case, I knew I was breathing air inside a Kennedy-era soap bubble, conjured on a whim by hard-boiled Bushies vaguely curious about its potential novelty in the information era. The inevitable prick came in the spring of 2001, when my editor tersely explained that "the theater is boring" and no longer merited space in the paper. I took this with all the sincerity it deserved. Six months after my departure, another critic, a personal friend of the Editor-in-Chief and CEO, began writing occasional theater reviews in *New York Press*, and today, more than a year later, nearly 100 of my columns are still available on the paper's Web site.

I hope it is obvious that my experience at *New York Press* was an anomaly. One measure of the straits to which American theater criticism has come is the likelihood that few among you have read much of it. I know this is true of most Hunter College students, and I assume it's also the case with any group of undergraduates aged 18-25. Of course I know you have seen theater reviews, but the question is whether they are really criticism. "Criticism" is an honorific term. If I were in charge, it would refer only to serious criticism, meaning informed and objective commentary by writers with enough space to describe their subject vividly, set their opinions in illuminating context, and traffic a bit in ideas. It needn't and shouldn't be obscure, but serious criticism teaches while it entertains and offers advice about what to do on the weekend. It steers its readers toward thoughts, insights and associations they hadn't considered before, and is therefore unafraid to be frequently unfashionable.

This sort of criticism was once common in America—in small and large independent journals such as *Dissent, Partisan Review, Commentary, The Saturday Review, The Nation, Theater Arts, Harper's* and *Vanity Fair* but also, for brief periods, in mass-market forums such as *Time, Newsweek* and *The New York Times*. No American theater critic ever had the intellectual cachet of, say, the early 20th-century German critics Alfred Kerr and Herbert Jhering—including George Jean Nathan, who railed against the vacuousness of Broadway in *The Smart Set* (the monthly magazine he co-founded with H.L. Mencken) from 1908 on, or Stark Young, who wrote for *The New Republic* and, for less than a year in 1924-25, *The New York Times*. During that prewar period, American newspaper editors still generally assumed that theater criticism didn't require any special qualifications; reporters were summarily shifted from obituaries or the police blotter to the "drama beat" as needed.

There was a moment during the surge of upward mobility after the Second World War, however, when the American middle class held a handful of serious critics in high esteem. From 1952-56 Eric Bentley, the country's preeminent drama scholar, was the theater critic of *The New Republic*, and from 1961-64 Richard Gilman reviewed regularly for *Commonweal* before moving to *Newsweek*. In 1963, PBS invited the eminent film critic of *The New Republic*, Stanley Kauffmann, to review plays on television. And later in the 1960s—far-fetched as this may seem today—*The New York Times* had something of a sustained epiphany. Within a short period, it hired the short-story-writer and future *New Yorker* staffer Renata Adler as film critic, the uncompromisingly leftist, 30-year-old John Leonard as editor of the book review, and, for eight months in 1966, Stanley Kauffmann as theater critic.

The film scholar Robert Sklar has suggested that this short-lived interest in *Times* critics with sophisticated taste and strong, original visions was partly fed by the confusion of Hollywood studio executives during the cultural upheaval of the 1960s. Faced with an industry-wide financial crisis, the studio execs became temporarily open-minded and eager to hear from anyone, even intellectuals, who might help them interpret the new age and define what the public wanted. Kauffmann—in a 1967 essay called "Drama on the *Times*," which I think is still the most important piece written about theater criticism in America—referred to his *Times* appointment as "a frontier operation." The paper's managers, he wrote, were "dissatisfied with...the old-line newspaper reviewing, couched in glib journalese and buoyed on hollow, dubiously knowledgeable generalities"; they responded to "the social pressure of the cultural explosion" by making a risky decision (soon regretted)—"to give power to what previously had been tolerated only when impotent: serious theater criticism."

Needless to say, no such historical moment is likely to come again soon. September 11 notwithstanding, we live today in an age of astonishing social complacency in which middle class identity is tightly interlaced with a pseudo-rebellious pop culture, and pop culture is disseminated by mass media largely dedicated to discouraging real thinking. There was a short interval of, say, three months, in the fall of 2001 when it did seem as though reality had trumped fabrication in the American psyche, but with the war in Afghanistan so far away (a televised experience for most of us) and the anthrax scare out of the headlines, that moment of sobriety (Bill Moyers called it "a teachable moment") quickly passed. The thrum of American media culture, which provides the crucial illusions of safety and normality, is contingent on a leveling of values, and hence a devaluing of expertise. This is why the sentiment "hey, everyone's a critic" is so commonplace in our post-your-own-Web-site time. No Hollywood executive today would think of consulting a serious critic on any issue, and the same is true of Broadway producers. Why should they, when, to a shocking extent, they can now control the critical voices people hear?

Ours is the era of the "blurb whore," the pseudo-reviewer bribed with perks to say flattering things that can be quoted in ads. This movie-world creature is admittedly rare in the humbler environs of the theater, but its cynical spirit pervades the theater field as well. The corruption of the annual theater awards systems, the shameless journalistic fawning over productions with large budgets, the cozy relationships between high-profile critics and stars: opinions are all clearly for sale, so who can care deeply about anyone's thoughts? "Whatever," "Get over it," "Not even"—all these generational catchphrases capture the essence of the leveling effect, which, curiously enough, was already apparent to Horkheimer and Adorno in the 1940s. "The cult of celebrities," they wrote, "has a built-in social mechanism to level down everyone who stands out in any way. The stars are simply a pattern round which the world-embracing garment is cut—a pattern to be followed by the shears of legal and economic justice with which the last projecting ends of thread are cut away."

In 1999, New York's mayor, Rudy Giuliani—a pair of "shears" *par excellence*—italicized just how broad-based this anti-critical ethos had grown when he attacked the Brooklyn Museum for an art show he didn't like (and never saw). Giuliani never did close down that show (called "Sensation") or the museum, as he threatened, but his victory was nevertheless consummate. Why? Because nearly every public commentator, across the political spectrum, accepted his premise that anyone's opinion of complex artworks, no matter how uninformed, deserves wide attention as long as he claims to be offended.

If you were born in the 1970s or later, then, you may like provocative and demanding theater and even like thinking about it, but you are at a big disadvantage. You have no first-hand experience of an American cultural environment in which the critical enterprise seems to have much clout. Most of the independent weeklies and monthlies that once printed substantial theater essays are gone—outflanked, outcooled, outabbreviated, and undersold by the blitzkrieg of slick, conglomerate-owned rags deliberately designed to blur the distinction between objective commentary and advertising. Most of what passes as criticism today is camouflaged PR and celebrity-worship, snappy consumer reports shoved into tiny spaces lest they seem too "intellectual," and impromptu opinion-mongering by "personal journalists" more interested in themselves than their subjects. We do have a handful of real critics: Michael Feingold in *The Village Voice* and Robert Brustein in *The New Republic*, both of whom have been at their posts for over thirty years, John Heilpern in *The New York Observer*, on occasion John Lahr (who lives in England), and Fintan O'Toole (the Irish former critic of *The Daily News*, who had his fill of tabloid-America and moved back to Ireland). More names could be added. I don't mean to slight anyone by omission.

The point is, though, that no matter what names I added, this would be a small, embattled and aging group. Most of America's best theater writers long ago gave up begging for space from editors indifferent to theater and went off to write books and articles for quarterlies. To be sure, some of these quarterlies are excellent. Where would seriously aspiring young theater writers turn for sustenance and encouragement today and where would innovative practitioners turn for meditative feedback if not to *Theater, Theatre Journal* and *TheatreForum*? There is no mitigating the fact, however, that these publications appear as much as a year after the productions discussed in them have closed. They are no substitute for forums in which inspired and intelligent writers can connect audiences with new theater art that can still be seen.

Any fair discussion of this situation must also touch on the diminished stature of the theater in American society compared to a generation ago. Obviously, theater today is for the most part no longer a mass form but rather a beloved art for a dedicated minority public. Knowledge of the latest hot plays, playwrights, stage actors and directors is not the passport to social advancement that it once was. I, for one, find it puzzling that the editors of today's general-interest magazines typically consider, say, hip young art stars to be hotter topics than any smart young playwright or director. The work of a newly "discovered" playwright like Rebecca Gilman or Kenneth Lonergan is seen by thousands more people than the first few gallery shows of a new art star, so I can only imagine that the bias comes from the fact that art is amenable to the quick, free glance whereas theater is expensive and demands that people really attend. Maybe theater in the media age is an art for a certain time of life, or a certain time of mind, when people can listen. Whatever the reasons, though, editors today regard theater as a specialized interest, and over time the space devoted to it in large-circulation magazines has been slashed almost to nothing. Even in our few surviving intellectual weeklies and monthlies, theater coverage has become for the most part brief, rare and tuned to predetermined editorial keys, a standing reminder of how little the editors know or care about the art.

I will come back to this point, because I think that theater writers, some good ones included, share responsibility for burdening theater with the quaint aura of a marginal cottage industry. Not that there isn't a case to be made. I am an incurable theater-lover, but my own experience of playgoing fifteen nights a month for four years in a row confirmed my longstanding hunch that ninety-five percent of what is produced in New York (and the selection is massive; I was invited to about ten openings a week) deserves the obscurity in which it wallows, or else enjoys a notoriety it hasn't earned. The other side of this observation, however, is that the remaining five percent—a remarkably large portion when you think about the sweeping editorial prejudice against theater—is extraordinarily vigorous and worthwhile. Some of it is as cutting-edge as any art in the Whitney Biennial. What's missing are voices to contextualize it that way for the general public, rather than emptily exaggerating its appeal or trivializing it as snappy cocktail-party chat.

Which theater critics with a large circulation do you know of who regularly pay substantial attention to anything beyond routine questions of popularity, topicality, and trendiness? Which ones can you point to who consider it a duty to bone up on the production histories of classical plays before reviewing them, or who habitually connect new theater work with interesting new books in the theater field, or outside it, or with trends and movements in other arts? For theatrical innovators in America—and I'm thinking of people like Bill Talen, W. David Hancock, Rinde Eckert, Dare Clubb, or the numerous creative offspring of Richard Foreman—critical pay dirt today consists of a single, forcibly abbreviated article in the *Voice*. Innovative foreign artists are even worse off, since they can't even count on open-minded responses, much less knowledgeable ones— I'm thinking particularly of the recent receptions of the Belgian director Ivo van Hove and the Spanish director Calixto Bieito.

Key institutional and political questions of our time have all but no place in our mainstream criticism: for instance, the effect of grant-writing and art foundation policies on artistic choice; the representation of artists as brands; or the urgent subject of this year's TCG Conference, "The Role of Theater in a Digital Culture." I was pleasantly stunned in May, 2002, to see that the usually fluffy Tony Award edition of the *Times Arts & Leisure* section ran a front-page article by Peter Marks, a critic turned feature writer, about the corporatization of Broadway. This article was kinder to producers than I would have been, but Marks deserves credit for the first substantial discussion of a subject at least eight years old in the paper of record. He touched, at least briefly, on corporate Broadway as a reflection of the institutionalization of the American imagination, as a disastrous planning choice for New York City, and as a withering force within the American theater in general. The question is whether the paper's regular critics will now run with his ball and keep these issues meaningfully before the public. If not, those issues will drop into the great American memory hole like everything else that quarrels with the serene assumptions of consumer culture.

Just one more dispiriting point, an important one, before I shift gears. Yet another impediment to good theater criticism today is that criticism in general, because it involves the supposedly old-fashioned practice of value judgment, has been gradually deemphasized, if not repudiated, in universities. Value judgement was inimical to the new ethos of cultural theory that began to dominate humanities curricula in the 1970s, with flag-bearers such as Roland Barthes, Paul de Man and Michel Foucault, and one result was a generalized hauteur that snubbed value judgment as the vulgar province of journalism. More to the point, though, the knowledge of theater history and dramatic literature that one needs to be a good critic has been getting harder and harder to attain in American universities. Historical knowledge is of course crucial to the critic, much more so than to fiction writers such as playwrights, since the critic is obliged to situate art, to identify contexts, to make sense of what it isn't up to the playwright to explain.

Time was, *no* critics acquired this knowledge at universities I'm aware of, but for the past four decades or so, since the proliferation of theater departments, they have been the presumed source. However, given the changes in graduate curricula I've witnessed, and the frustrations of numerous faculty searches I've participated in and learned of, I've grown very worried about the source running dry. In many graduate programs, the teaching of theater history—a unique discipline dedicated to understanding the intricacies of theater language as distinct from all other languages—is being replaced by historiography, and seminars and dissertations focusing on individual artists are being actively discouraged in favor of groupings of artists and theorists with a political spin inevitably born of trendiness. Faced with a dauntingly competitive academic job market, more and more theater graduate students nationally have been gravitating to densely theoretical and thinly interdisciplinary specializations that they think (usually mistakenly) will make them employable, and this has left them with an unforgivably sketchy grounding in the very art that was supposed to be their basic discipline.

Let me emphasize that I'm not defending any established disciplinary boundaries for their own sake. I'm rather pointing out that the art of theater is still plainly flourishing, yet major wings of the academy, due to their own anxieties about self-preservation, are behaving as though it has died. I'm also saying that penetrating and inspired criticism that demonstrates how to read the language of theater well, in all its complexity, is and has always been its own justification—from George Henry Lewes' epoch-encompassing reports of Kean, Rachel and Macready; to Bernard Shaw's dauntless assaults on the popular well-made play; to Herbert Jhering's passionate and nuanced defenses of the prickly young Bertolt Brecht; to Kenneth Tynan's famously acrimonious debate with Eugène Ionesco, which goaded that playwright into making some of his clearest and most memorable statements.

I suspect many of you may feel helpless to change this situation, but there I think you are wrong. You have enormous power over problems of this kind if they bother you enough. For one thing, you are the customers in a multi-billion-dollar educational industry that literally cannot afford to ignore you. Ask loudly enough for anything curricular in a liberal arts environment and I guarantee you it will appear (and "loudly" is the key word here, not "ask"). For another thing, you are tomorrow's graduate students. Your oedipal rage at the vacuums left by your predecessors will define the future—and let no one fool you with false politesse; intellectual history is as propelled by rage as any fine art.

Oscar Wilde once wrote that "Without the critical faculty, there is no artistic creation at all worthy of the name." He also said that "The influence of the critic will be the mere fact of his own existence," and added that "There was never a time when Criticism was more needed than it is now." These statements were made 112 years ago, yet they are, if anything, more true today than then. In a rare despondent moment in 1994, the dance critic of *The New Yorker*, Arlene Croce, wrote that she couldn't "remember a time when the critic [had] seemed more expendable than now." Her despondency was a challenge, though; provoked by what she saw as the unreviewability of "victim art" such as Bill T. Jones' dance-theater work on AIDS, "Still/Here," she cried "foul" in the hope that an angry public might rise to play referee. There really never was a time when good criticism was more needed than it is now, if only because mass culture has now put critical thinking itself at risk.

My dream as a teacher is that my students will all at least become discerning and demanding readers of criticism. And as for those few of you who like to write—you tufts—well, yes, you ought to consider becoming critics yourselves. Not as a public service (certainly a recipe for bad writing) but out of loyalty to yourselves. Oddly enough, as Kauffmann once wrote, criticism is a talent—just like acting, directing, designing and playwriting. It may sound unfashionable in this era of exploded universal assumptions, but some people are actually more perceptive watchers of plays than others. They see more in theater works than others do, and their creative fulfillment is in communicating their insights persuasively to others. To paraphrase Bernard Shaw—a first-rate drama critic during the early years of his playwriting career—either one is a critic or one isn't, and if one is, suppressing it is futile, and squelching it beneath trendy, self-denigrating notions about the equivalency of all opinions is perverse.

I'm aware that all advice is unwise. Nevertheless, here are my promised words of practical advice, offered with all the recklessness of love.

1. Create your own reality.

Our culture holds only one value more dear than money and youth: self-invention. Don't waste time waiting for any established critic to drop dead so you can slip into the vacancy. Chances are, there will never be a vacancy because the publication will bury the theater column with the critic. Or else it will hire the editor's brother-in-law from Topeka. Very few editors today can make distinctions between good and bad theater criticism; they need you to stick their noses in the plate. *New York Press* didn't have a theater writer when I approached them, and I didn't know until much later that they'd ever had one. At the *Voice*, I was told for years that the paper didn't need a second lead critic, but by continually proposing pieces on interesting and important theater events outside New York, I carved out a place for myself there anyway. This fall, I'm delighted to announce, my newest project, *The Hunter On-Line Theater Review* (www.hotreview.org), will begin publication. This will be an on-line forum for reviews, essays and editorials by new and established writers whose work deserves to be called criticism. So if you're good and committed but at a loss where to begin, come and write for me.

2. Convey why the theater is important.

Since the standard assumption today is that it isn't, everyone who disagrees has a shining chance to surprise people. Bear in mind, however, that most readers don't care nearly as much as you do, to begin with, about the difference between, say, the "liveness" of TV and the "liveness" of theater. This is where having an original artistic sensibility becomes crucial. If your critical writing doesn't swell with articulate enthusiasm for what is indispensable about a certain kind of theater, then it stands no chance of seeming indispensable itself. Time was, a critic like

Max Beerbohm, who confessed his indifference to theater but possessed a charmingly urbane style that made people feel like eavesdroppers at exclusive dinner parties, had a place in a society that regarded theater as essential and scarcely less eternal than the British monarchy. No longer. Today's critics must remake the public conversation, not presume to stand above it. They must create, in their own little corners of a glutted environment, a climate in which it seems normal to care. Shaw "manufactured the evidence" (his phrase) that the new drama he envisioned already existed, and the force of his vision helped engender the reality. His example is the preeminent reminder of how the language of criticism can be procreative.

Having said this, however, I hasten to add that no critic has an obligation to be kind to individual productions. The more you publish, the more your so-called friends will harangue you about industry solidarity and regale you with heart-rending tales of poverty and vulnerability. They will ask, in all candor, "Hey, aren't we all on the same side?" Guess what? These people don't really respect your opinion. Their question comes from essentially the same censorious impulse that objected to dissent and criticism of U.S. government policy after September 11—hey, aren't we all patriots?—and it is beneath response. Any art so vulnerable that it needs euphemized reviews to survive ought to be put out of its misery, just as any country that needs to outlaw flag-burning ought to think again about what loyalty means. The bigger question is, as John Donatich, the publisher of Basic Books, recently put it: "How do we battle the gravitation toward happy consensus that paralyzes our national debate?" Or again Wilde says it well: "A critic cannot be fair in the ordinary sense of the word. It is only about things that do not interest one that one can give a really unbiassed opinion, which is no doubt the reason why an unbiassed opinion is always absolutely valueless."

3. Stretch the envelope—Grasp the apparatus.

Brecht wrote in 1930 that "by imagining that they have got hold of an apparatus which in fact has got hold of them [artists] are supporting an apparatus which is out of their control." Brecht was speaking of film, radio and theater practitioners, but his remark is especially true of critics. If you ever gain access to a mass-market publication, I urge you to remember that, whatever the short-term satisfactions, you will be judged strictly in the long run by your conduct in that circumstance. Failing to grasp the apparatus will ensure that it grasps you. I won't preach obligations to you, but I will opine that any writing that tacitly accepts the preconditions of consumer society can not be, properly speaking, critical.

One needn't be a revolutionary. Even small gestures like broaching a subject beyond the crimped purview of pop culture, or clearly explaining an unfamiliar or slightly complex idea, can stretch the envelope noticeably. I see criticism as a form of resistance in an age when the agents of power (big media and politicians) have coopted the language of rebellion to the point where counter-rebellion is often indistinguishable from rebellion. There is a tiny but tremendously important opportunity in the fact that some arts—theater, dance, poetry—aren't usually considered worthy of commodification by the mass media, and my work tries to wedge that window open. Utopian ardor doesn't make me any paragon of honesty, of course. Often enough, I get my fingers jammed in the sash, or grow infuriated when there's nothing but cotton candy outside the window for weeks on end, and then I'm as capable of venom and compromise as everyone else.

The main point to recognize is that questions of personal integrity are inseparable from questions about grasping the apparatus, particularly in high-profile circumstances where critics are made to feel they must make compromises with celebrity-culture to keep their jobs. A fascinating case study is John Lahr, who frequently writes long, flattering celebrity profiles in the same magazine where he is the chief theater critic. Is this inappropriate or dishonest? It certainly deepens the public's confusion over the difference between criticism and promotion. The area is grey, however. The question is analogous to John Leonard's misgivings (to take only the first two examples from his recent screed in *The Nation*) about whether Thomas Friedman should have played tennis with the Secretary of State when he covered the State Department for the *Times*, or whether Brit Hume should have played tennis with President Bush when he

covered the White House for ABC. Most people nowadays would un-
doubtedly say "who cares?" to all these queries—recognizing that access
is power. That is precisely why critics must care, and hold their integrity
more dear than the public does.

4. Give up the goal of power.

You can't avoid *having* power as a critic, but you should give it up as
a goal. The sooner you do this, the happier you'll be. For most people,
theater criticism isn't a profession, it's a calling, and the long-term satisfaction is in moving minds, not tickets. The fact that most of the appro-
bation and opprobrium that one is subject to as a critic has to do with the
movement of tickets can be distracting and confusing, but you must never
take that personally. Both the praise and the blame are about advertising,
not art or ideas. In any case, producers and publicists today know perfectly well that unfavorable reviews are far better than no reviews. In fact,
they're often as good as favorable ones, because so many people don't really read but rather skim headers and headlines on the way to the listings
and personal ads. Simply getting an event covered is the real PR coup
nowadays, even in the anxiety-producing *New York Times*. I mention all
this to lift a potential burden off you before it ever settles in. As Richard
Gilman once said succinctly: "the critic cannot give his loyalty to men
and institutions since he owes it to something a great deal more permanent. He owes it, of course, to truth and to dramatic art."

And here is the subtler point: the essence of theater in our time, I think,
isn't in power but rather the opposite. Vaclav Havel, the playwright
turned statesman, a quintessential outsider turned insider, said in his 1991
memoir *Disturbing the Peace*: "An inseparable part of the kind of theater
I've been drawn to all my life is a touch of obscurity, of decay or degen-
eration, of frivolity. I don't know quite what to call it; I think theater
should always be somewhat suspect." He was onto something fundamental. Broadway and Disney notwithstanding, theater in the new millennium is not about to become any sort of brave new world of perfect
technology or Apollonian hardware; its long-term destiny is to be the toil-
some domain of "meatware" and "wetware" rehearsing our ancient,

ritualistic system-failures, again and again. The artist who understood this best was the "crossover" avant-gardist Samuel Beckett, an unwitting prophet of the media age who has so far withstood its best efforts to brand and trivialize him. "To be an artist," wrote Beckett in 1949, "is to fail, as no other dare fail, that failure is his world and the shrink from it desertion, art and craft, good housekeeping, living."

5. Write journalism—Read beyond it.

Journalistic criticism is bridge-building—bringing unfamiliar ideas to a general audience, connecting demanding art to a reluctant public, reaching across the borders of established institutions, professions and disciplines. No one can cross a bridge that isn't anchored securely on both banks, however. The world has quite enough academics who don't write lucidly enough to hold a general audience, thank you very much, and quite enough journalists who don't know enough to offer anything but stagnant opinions. The rarity are those in the middle, real ambassadors who can play to both sides. So sharpen your writing, work on it at every opportunity, but also keep yourself informed about at least some of what is written for more specialized audiences—and not just in theater. Journalism is seductive, the more so for intelligent and ambitious writers, who can easily wake up decades into their careers and discover that they have squandered their best ideas without having done justice to them. The only protection is to keep one piling in a deeper pool, so to speak.

6. Ground your work in knowledge, not style.

Some of you are no doubt wondering at this point, "What about fun? Don't delight, enjoyment, and entertainment come into the equation at all?" Absolutely. I, for one, get more pure enjoyment out of good theater than I do from most other pursuits, and I try to convey that in my writing. Recently, I had a medical condition that paralyzed half my face for months, and when I went to see Edward Albee's *The Goat* I laughed so hard at one joke that a spasm developed in my deadened cheek and jump-started my healing. I tell you this not just to amuse you, however, but to illustrate where the majority of pseudo-critics begin and end their ruminations: with stories about themselves and their deep feelings that are, at best, pre-critical. So far, I've told you nothing critical about Edward Albee, I've told you about my cheek, a subject hard to construe as momentous or urgent, no matter how amusing you may find it. The point is, the pleasure of deep feeling never needs defending in the United States; the pleasure of good thinking always does.

Here's a practical test you might apply: pick up any newspaper or magazine review and read it with an eye to whether it could be transferred to the *Sunday Styles* section of the *New York Times* without jarring anyone's sensibilities. If the answer is yes, then you have discovered a stylist in critic's clothing. A stylist is someone who thinks the world is all attitude, and that any hip point of view and mode of expression ought to apply equally to clothing, jewelry, furniture, kitchenware, food, bands, clubs, and oh yes, dramatic masterpieces. Reflexive feeling is all, reflection is nil, and most of the time the first-person pronoun is a sort of verbal shill, avoiding responsibility while seeming to accept it ("this is just my opinion"). To place masterpieces in such a person's hands is like leaving a national forest in the care of a theme-park owner. A stylist is a caretaker of recycled culture, a blind monster that feeds on itself. A critic is an independent human being with open eyes, who knows what and where to eat.

7. Be female, at least sometimes.

Obviously, this will come easier to those of you who happen to be women, but not being female is no excuse for never thinking about it. The majority of theater critics have always been men, and even today, when some of our best theater writers are women (Erika Munk, Alisa Solomon, Elinor Fuchs, Una Chaudhuri), there is only one female lead critic (Linda Winer, at *Newsday*) at a major newspaper in the New York area. More women need to get involved in this field, and more men need to tap their repressed female sympathies. I say this not just for the sake of parity but because I suspect our male critics (perhaps myself included) have not always totally understood the work of innovative female artists, especially playwrights. Let me sidestep the nettled question of how to define "female artistic sensibility" and simply state that I believe there is one, and that I see it in Maria Irene Fornes, Joan Schenkar, Erin Cressida Wilson, the experimental Beth Henley of *Impossible Marriage*, and elsewhere. Critical justice has not been done to these authors, and if this is a disgrace, it is also an opening.

8. Don't review everything.

There is a time in your life when you should see everything, and for most of you, it is now. You must fill up your imaginations with the richest possible array of theater art so that you needn't ever rely on anyone else's assessment of excellence, astonishment, mendacity or mediocrity. Money is an issue, I realize, but there are many ways around expensive tickets, from ushering, to arranging group outings, to internships at theaters and theatrical organizations. Access aside, however, once you have acquired a solid grounding, it's also essential to recognize when to start being discriminating. Many a fine critic has been destroyed by the strain of constantly seeking new ways to describe the same old inadequacies, or by the intellectual palsy born of a sustained diet of histrionic junk food. Don't be a casualty. Know when and how to save up your two cents until you can afford pearls.

9. Write letters to critics.

The lack of an active give-and-take between critics and their readers in America has everything to do with the editorial prejudice against theater I described before. Since even the most famous critics get far less mail than they would ever admit, respectful responses to them, even disagreements, have a much greater chance of being printed than similar letters to other journalists. So the next time you find yourself grumbling with dismay that a theater event you loved or hated isn't the subject of lively public interest, don't suffer in silence. Reach for your keyboard, and let 'em have it. And remember to address the letter to the editor, not the critic, or else it *will* get stuffed in a drawer.

*   *   *

That's about as much advice as I imagine anyone can bear in a single afternoon, so I'll quit while I'm still standing and leave you with just one last proposition. If, having listened to me, any of you now looks into your heart and finds that you are not on my side; that you don't crave the admiration of those who read; that you have no urge to refine a vision of your own; that you secretly do covet power; or that you actually do revere the stylists, hatchet-men and blurb-whores around you, then I beg of you, please, do us all a favor and write about Hollywood and television instead of theater.

The Critic *In Extremis*

———

MERICA IS NO PLACE FOR A THEATER CRITIC. NOT A GOOD one, anyway. It's not just that the theater here has always resisted serious evaluation more than any other art has. It's also that the ambition to overcome that resistance has never won anyone real literary respectability, regardless of talent, power, or insight. Sheer commitment and love of the art have kept many in the game, as we all know, but in this era of media-saturation and fanatical consumerism, when the public's historically thin understanding of critical thinking in general is even more degraded every day, the effort seems especially futile.

Practically all public speech in our trivializing, vulgarizing, celebrity-worshiping age conspires to confuse us about the difference between criticism and public relations. Just as radio jocks are in the pockets of record companies, and the Oscars and Tonys are voted on by insiders protecting their friends and investments, so too do ubiquitous scribblers of semi-articulate gossip, crypto-advertizement, and snotty, byte-sized consumer reports pass off their uninformed opinion-mongering as continuations of the independent and cultivated tradition of Bernard Shaw, Stark Young, Harold Clurman, and Stanley Kauffmann.

The facts on the ground are plainly grim. Most of the journals that once regularly carried theater essays as broad cultural circumspection have disappeared, and those that remain are edited by men and women who don't think theater is very interesting or important. Ignoring meditative theater writing has become an editorial norm in America. The annual ceremony honoring the winner of the George Jean Nathan Award, the country's only major prize for a theater critic, receives no national news coverage, even when the *New York Times* critic wins it. Analytical surveys posing general questions about contemporary journalistic criticism, such as Maurice Berger's 1998 *The Crisis of Criticism*, steer clear of theater entirely. And new critical books about theater are almost never reviewed in national publications—the one reliable exception being when the author is already a celebrity, preferably in a field other than theater.

'Twas not ever thus. For a brief period after the post-WW II economic boom conferred middle-class identity on just about everyone, a few lucky critics had real national profiles. Writing in respectable intellectual journals like *The Saturday Review*, *Commonweal* and *The Atlantic*, and occasionally in mass-market magazines like *Newsweek*, critics such as Kauffmann, Eric Bentley, Robert Brustein and Richard Gilman cultivated a broad interest in theater as an intellectual subject and a platform for cultural debate. But the now super-confident middle class has, in the meantime, "sidelined" theater as a minority pastime—between one and two percent of Americans go to the theater, a steady statistic for many years—and trend-chasing editors anxious about their jobs are not about to buck that judgement. For well over a generation, serious American theater journalism, no matter how intelligent, artful, or insightfully entwined with larger issues, has withered in obscurity, practiced mainly by a dedicated circle of impassioned and utterly impractical Quixotes.

One of the best of these, Gordon Rogoff, has now laid down his lance. In the closing section of his new collection, *Vanishing Acts: Theater Since the Sixties*, entitled "Endgames," he bids farewell to dramatic criticism: "Now I'm the public at last: I pay for entrance, and consequently I select the doors I might risk entering." Who can blame him? Rogoff wrote for the major respectable journals during precisely that period when they stopped bothering with theater. For a time, he had a regular forum in the *Village Voice* (the source for most of his previous collection, published in

1987, *The Theater is Not Safe*) and at one point was a regular essayist for *American Theatre* (from which many of this new book's pieces are drawn). For the most part, though, like all critics worthy of the name, he followed his powerful, idiosyncratic vision, publishing where he could, chronicling momentous events that were deemed negligible in their time, forcing their momentousness into the light with his lucid, steely prose, his perspicacity, and his breadth of soul.

Rogoff at his best is as sharp and inspired as any of the older, more privileged critics just mentioned. Among the prime examples from *Vanishing Acts* are his superb essays on Tennessee Williams, in which he risks the appearance of sloppy, mellifluous abandon, in loving emulation of his subject, while actually nailing down important and penetrating insights: "like Oscar Wilde, [Williams] was gay before his time but never comfortably and predictably gay in his work. He was simply dissenting from all establishments, writing undisguised real women better than anyone else in our theater, presenting macho men who spent their frantic energy trying to disguise the women in their souls. His biggest crime against traditional expectations may have been that his women were always brighter than his men."

Another invaluable, early essay (from 1965) is on the collaboration of Mozart with his preferred librettist Lorenzo da Ponte, who Rogoff says were "ideally suited to each other." This piece is remarkable for its combined expertise in and sensitivity to both music and drama. "Mask and play, then: Mozart putting a face on drama, covering intrigue with the abstractions of music, shadowing sensuality with sound; da Ponte giving intrigue its first rhythms, its orders, shapes, directions, its concrete humors and impulses; Mozart expressing, da Ponte impressing, both serving the whole, like comedy and tragedy in the best plays, as one: unromantically, beyond the regions of conscious will, both of them imagining, and then conjuring drama for music."

My guess is that Baudelaire had passages like this in mind when he said that criticism "should be partial, passionate and political, that is to say, written from an exclusive point of view, but a point of view that opens up the widest horizons." What always made Rogoff marginal in media-age America, alas, is that he could never help operating from a platform of wide and varied knowledge, which he put to flexible, amusing, and sometimes impudent use. Anti-intellectualism is our society's indispensable anodyne; it safeguards us from feeling the full hollowness of our recycled and simulated culture. One of its advantages, though, is that it also safeguards our drama critics from ever falling into the occupational trap Shaw described, of "allowing [oneself] to be distracted by the vanity of playing the elegant man of letters."

Many of Rogoff's shorter essay-reviews, written under deadline pressure, are also gems. The analysis of Ping Chong's 1986 show *Kindness*; two pieces about Joanne Akalaitis' Kroetz productions ("Amusing to watch while remaining humorless…in love with theatrical immediacy, but they are finally too far removed from Kroetz's immediate realities"); a discussion of David Hare as an "expert playwriting bully" who "craftily push[es] pawns on his pseudopolitical chessboard": all of these should be required reading from now on for anyone writing seriously about these artists.

Even when I strongly disagree with Rogoff, he leaves me glad to know his point of view. In a 1988 review of *Speed-the-Plow*, for instance, he says that David Mamet's "short-winded plays keep playing into the hands of the monsters he's putting down." But Mamet himself almost certainly knows that; he's just experimenting with more ruthless cultural and self-critiques than Rogoff is comfortable validating. Still, who could disagree that "like a latter-day Ben Jonson, [Mamet's] getting his charge from his own verbal reconstruction of the way masculine evil talks to itself"? And how annoyed can one get at a critic capable of writing that "Mamet's guys are trumpets and drums, fabulous riff-makers skimming breathlessly over extended justifications of their uniquely stupid, valueless pseudo-philosophies"?

As with all critics, the pleasure and permanence of Rogoff's writing lie as much in style, quality of energy, and habits of voice as in rectitude of judgement—in the way, for instance, he slips in his personal irritations and political disgust like judicious coughs: "Two actors going literally nose-to-nose in an argument are not automatically a howl, at least to those of us who haven't yet called a truce with canned laughter"; "Maybe it would have been truer to let [Joe in *All My Sons*] fail his suicide like Robert McFarlane or get shipped into a hospital like William Casey."

I do have quibbles with *Vanishing Acts*. The selection of pieces, for one thing, is less consistent than in *Theatre is Not Safe*. Sharp as he usually is, Rogoff can grow woolly when his emotions get the better of him; he should have been advised against including a few misty-eyed, devotional, and otherwise under-strength pieces on Joe Chaikin, Larry Kramer, Tony Kushner and others. He's also sometimes so eager to be seen primarily as a writer, an accomplished crafter of language, that he neglects basic practical matters like clearly explaining the plots of plays, or even (in one case—a piece on Beckett) mentioning what play he is reviewing. This obscurity lessens his power and effect as a teacher, and (as Rogoff knows perfectly well) teaching is a prime justification for criticism like his.

I sometimes wonder, though, whether what one is really encountering in such instances is a basic discomfort with journalism on Rogoff's part, only half-acknowledged during a long career in which he several times gave up reviewing for practical theater work. His moody refusal to think up snappy, seductive lead sentences, beginning instead with secondary or peripheral points as if to ask, "what is the true center of this experience?"; his thrill at plunging headlong into the dense, contemplative pith of his thoughts; his repeated efforts to utilize his copious "insider" knowledge about theater practitioners, turning it to more respectable purposes than gossip, even at the cost of seeming smarmy and exclusionary: all of this bespeaks deep and chronic resistences to his writerly circumstances, which probably helped wear him down in the end.

Whatever the truth of all this, we are lucky to have had him on the scene for the nearly four decades his patience held out. Like *Theatre is Not Safe*, *Vanishing Acts* will eventually take its place beside Kauffmann's *Persons of the Drama*, Gilman's *Common and Uncommon Masks* and a small handful of other criticism collections that stand as indispensable theater history, providing more illuminating and exciting records of the artists and artworks discussed in them than a library of videotapes (far less permanent) could provide. Meanwhile, the American theater will continue on its merry and increasingly institutionalized way (as Rogoff describes in his excellent essay "The Management Game"), never quite dying or quite flourishing as a nationally appreciated art. The real question is whether any records of its follies and achievements written for the general public of the future will be worth preserving.

(2001)

The Critic As Humanist

DURING MY YEARS AS A GRADUATE STUDENT IN CRITICISM at the Yale School of Drama, a more or less irresolvable rift existed between that school and the university's English Department. It was the early 1980s, heyday of deconstruction. We theater types were taught by New York humanists who loudly and publicly expressed their contempt for jargon, their appreciation of individual insight and writerly talent over technique and doctrine. There seemed to be no intellectual ground on which these two sides could even meet to debate their differences. Students tend to distrust such stalemates, and I remember thinking of this one as an exquisite instance of two forms of snobbery—one academic, one professional—each failing to recognize its reflection in the other.

Chestful of earnest heroism, I cast myself as a peacemaking diplomat one spring, spent a fortune on books by Bloom, Miller, de Man and others not found on drama school syllabi, and applied for a job teaching English Composition, on the mistaken assumption it would earn me entree beyond the high Gothic walls surrounding the university proper. No rapprochement ever arose, surely in part because that fortune lavished on literary theory had done little to change my attitudes toward theater criticism, but also because no one on the English side ever cared a whit

for my mission. No hard feelings. Really, no feelings or thoughts of any
sort concerning the episode followed me as I began my critical career. I
had put it behind me like a bit of adolescent sexual experimentation until
Jody McAuliffe asked me to write the afterword to this book.*

Many themes in the volume merit elaboration but, after reading it
through, what seems to me most worthy of separate commentary is the
repeated implication that good theater criticism is necessarily humanist
criticism. Tacit in the majority of essays (some of which extend its application to film criticism), explicit in Stanley Kauffmann's interview, this
shared opinion will be, for some, nothing more than evidence of a common political prejudice among the contributors. This prejudice is often
associated with Yale Drama School, and indeed a large number of the
contributors have intimate links there. Not all of them do, however,
which lends support to the idea that there is something else behind the
opinion as well, something more substantial that I could not have understood fully back at Yale: the voice of experience. Humanism, as
American theater critics understand the term, is as much a response to
the real-world conditions in which they must practice their craft as it is
an ideological preset. Theater critics function in a strikingly singular milieu, and if stressing that starts to sound like the professional snobbery
just referred to, then so be it. Here are some reflections on what turned
my nose gradually upward.

Humanism and humanists have been under siege for the past generation in a way that young intellectuals have been forced to face more
squarely than our teachers ever were. The old guard of American theater
critics, represented here by Robert Brustein, Richard Gilman and Kauffmann, made their reputations in the 1950s and 60s when it was still possible to make one's living as a literary journalist. *The New Republic,
Commentary, The Saturday Review, Commonweal, The Nation*: these
were only the most famous few of many possible outlets for well-
informed, timely commentary. Theater writers generally slouched into

---

* This essay is a slightly revised version of the Afterword to *Plays, Movies, and Critics*, ed. Jody McAuliffe (Duke Univ. Press, 1993).

academia, if they went at all, often to supplement the New York lifestyle necessary for anyone who wanted to follow the theater. Any child of the first generation weaned on television who is interested in serious theater writing—particularly the kind that appears while shows are still running—has radically different prospects. Most of the intellectually reputable weeklies have now disappeared. The few that still exist pay token fees and, in any case, show little interest in new critics other than the direct descendants of their own old guard. The would-be critic in my generation faces a Sophie's-Choice-of-the-mind: enter academia, thereby sacrificing the feeling of immediacy to a living art, or join the mass media, sacrificing the chance to probe seriously and the self-respect and satisfaction that come from it. Most of my former cronies chose academia, which placed us directly in the path of a machine programmed to annihilate us; the dominance of deconstruction-era politics, which continues to see our "impressionist" methods (the term is Kauffmann's) as irresponsible and naive, was all but absolute when we arrived.

A sampling of the other camp's arguments is in order, though I make no claim to objectivity. "Humanism" first got into academic trouble long before our teachers became its unwitting deputies. Marxist critics lumped the term together with "liberal humanism" and used it to describe a state of mind that could be summarily dismissed as representing the ambitions and world view of only a small, privileged socio-economic class. Here is typical swipe by Terry Eagleton; the topic is the Cambridge journal *Scrutiny*, whose presiding figure was F. R. Leavis:

> . . . it represented nothing less than the last-ditch stand of liberal humanism, concerned, as Eliot and Pound were not, with the unique value of the individual and the creative realm of the interpersonal. These values could be summarized as "Life," a word which *Scrutiny* made a virtue out of not being able to define. If you asked for some reasoned theoretical statement of their case, you had thereby demonstrated that you were in the outer darkness: either you felt Life or you did not. Great literature was a literature reverently open

to Life, and what Life was could be demonstrated by great literature. The case was circular, intuitive, and proof against all argument, reflecting the enclosed coterie of the Leavisites themselves.
(*Literary Theory*, p. 42)

One glaring problem in this passage is that Marxist critics, without
harping on the word, also habitually make assumptions about what
"Life" is and tend to be quite self-righteous about them, their assumptions presumably being "un-intuitive" and based on sounder sociopolitical analyses than "Leavisites" are capable of. More to the point,
though, in trying to ridicule away a term like "Life" simply because
some people use it vaguely, Eagleton shows that his ostensibly broad-
based ideological critique is really bounded by the borders of literature.
Like most specialists in printed art forms, he is oblivious to the slippery
circumstances that make live performance so fascinating to write and
think about. To comment on an art that involves living beings and takes
place over time, without ever resorting to words like "live," "liveness,"
and "lifelike"—to say nothing of "life" and the notion that it is universally shared—is to be hobbled indeed.

The subject gets stickier when use of such terms reflects a flirtation
with faith and religion, as is often the case with Gilman. An example is
this passage from his *Seagull* essay, which might also be seen as a sort of
humanist retort to Eagleton's point about circularity.

> ...the subjects of imaginative literature, in which I include plays as
> texts (and also in performance...) don't exist independently of the
> writing itself. They're not like prey waiting to be pounced upon by
> a verbally gifted hunter, or seedy rooms needing to be refurbished
> by a painter in words. In turn, writing isn't the expression or treat-
> ment of a preexisting reality but an act that discovers and gives life
> to a "subject" within itself.

There is more than a touch of elitism in this organicist assertion that
great artworks take on independent lives. The "life" inside Gilman's

"'subject' within" can't be perceived by all onlookers, and certainly not by those inured to such mysteries by, say, the mental habits of dialectical materialism. Gilman would remain unfazed by this criticism, however, as would most of the other critics in this book. If he uses without hesitation a phrase like "fundamental life," if Kauffmann quotes without historical apology a 19th-century passage about "the energy of life," if David Wyatt grounds his thoughts on Sam Shepard in a notion of "life as an unending and often unwilling competition for space and love," it is because none of them is afraid of generalization. The so-called arrogance of the humanist critic has nothing to do with imposing prescriptive patterns; it has to do with insisting on the value of seeing forests for trees. Some just happen to be more zealous than others about their forests, and they can sound like keepers of a faith. Faith: a bold drive to generalize, based on a commitment to the soundness of one's perceptions so strong that one is inclined to apply them to everyone and everything as a universal organizing principle.

This is my point in a nutshell: one cannot write *well* about the theater without making some provisional assumptions about the universality of one's responses. The theater is too public a forum, too much of its aesthetics is wrapped up in the responses of large groups of people, for a voice with no pretensions beyond its singularity ever to be very illuminating. A theater critic cannot afford to write in constant fear of being associated with Matthew Arnold and his assumption that all hypothetical audiences shared (or ought to share) his middle-class liberal values. No such assumption is necessarily implicit in critical speculation: say, a guess on why the audience laughs at a given point, or a judgement that a given line sounds trite. The theater critic is not in a reading chair, at ease and alone; the job involves observing not only a performance text but also a thousand other minuscule signals involving the mood, the receptive spirit, of other spectators. The theater critic describes an experience in a group partly as a surrogate for a group, and any pretension to hermetic, or wholly uncontingent, response is as much a lie as the old Arnoldian claim to speak for everyone. Furthermore, theater criticism deals with the "unreferrable." That is, you can't ask your reader to turn to page 256 of a published text, or to study a detail in a painting. Not only does each split second in a play speed by; it speeds by differently at every performance, so even repeated viewings can't provide unambiguous reference. Theater critics must choose and fix certain split seconds in order to deal with the subject at all, which means necessarily using themselves as examples of how the audience responds.

Critics who do not do this will sadly disappoint their readers. Which brings me back to the topic of forums for publication, another special circumstance for theater criticism. Theater, unlike classical literature, is not (yet) predominantly a university phenomenon. It still lives by its ability to attract large numbers of spectators from the general public—albeit within a narrow demographic range, but that is hardly the fault of the medium per se—and as long as that is so, the question of "appeal" will be a legitimate part of the critic's subject. For one thing, writing about appeal—what makes people go to, or stay away from, a cultural event—often means speculating about universals. For another, the theater critic, especially in a period when serious uses of the stage are waning, has many reasons beyond egotism for wanting to affect appeal, for wanting to make people see more in productions that bring dignity to the medium—and this must be done in journalistic forums such as *The Village Voice*, *The New York Times* and *The New Republic* if it is to reach a readership that bears some relation to the medium's spectatorship.

Today it is this sort of critic, not the poet, playwright or academic writer, to whom the classic Horatian directive to teach and delight applies. If the serious theater has any enduring role in our period of massive domination by electronic media, it is as a proudly elitist medium. Renting a video and watching it on a private box inside a private box is the first and easiest choice after prime-time pap. Unthinking "envelopment" by a film in the spirit of "hedonism" mentioned by Kauffmann is a close second. But something must serve those vestigial "obligations to culture" that Kauffmann speaks of, that part of the common man's conscience that always wants to know he could try harder if he wanted to, the part that feels superior to the glut of programming around him pitched at an eleven-year-old consciousness. That something is theater. In the age of TV and video, theater is a standing opportunity to reach out, a place you have to get dressed and go to, where (unlike the movie theater) something other than passivity will be asked of you. And critics who weather the disapprobation of their academic colleagues in order to write for these reachers are not condescending or making disingenuous nods to populism. Quite the opposite: if they have the humanist spirit about them, they are displaying the Horatian courage of their elitism, daring to guide while fully aware of the complexities of their action.

Of course, in the current American intellectual environment, any assertion of cultural leadership meets skepticism and hostility. The Enlightenment is out, pluralism and diversity are in, and anyone who questions the rectitude of that displacement is truly, to use Eagleton's phrase, "in the outer darkness," oblivious to the barbaric fundaments of all existent institutions, the theater among the worst. If addlepates like Jürgen Habermas defect from the program, that only proves their fundamental indifference to the world's horrible social inequities and dominant metanarratives, chiefly of interest to the white, upper middle-class graduate students who dominate American humanities departments. No values handed down "from above"—that is, from people not previously disenfranchised—are dependably acceptable during these culture wars. The poison spread by centuries of racism, sexism and classism was so ubiquitous and pernicious, says the theory, that the whole world must be remade ("invented," "written") before we may legitimately speak of meaning again, particularly meaning that aspires to universality. Having courage to generalize and judge informedly, however, recognizing and having the courage of one's unavoidable elitism even in the face of all this loudmouthed denigration, is not *only* arrogance; it is also a reflection of a risky commitment, an emotional investment in one's subject and one's unique perceptions, without which a strong writerly voice is impossible and a confident teaching manner unlikely.

For some readers, perhaps for many, much of what I have said will sound arrantly patriarchal. I cry no mercy but ask only that my argument

not be misconstrued. Nowhere in this essay do I contend that my opinions and perceptions, or those of critics with similar political prejudices to
mine, have any stronger claim to universal validity than other people's.
Nor do I think that feminist critics—or gay, African-American, Hispanic-
American, or any other voices previously excluded from theater discourse—should not be heard and actively welcomed. What I do mean is
that any feminist who does not generalize from her perceptions as a feminist spectator will write theater criticism with very little appeal, persuasive weight, and longevity, even among feminists. And that last sentence
itself is a giveaway. I include myself and feminists in the same human club
in order to claim to know something (*not* everything) about their reactions, leaving me vulnerable to the wrath of all who want to define the
club in order to exclude me. Intolerance of that wrath is an ideological
preset to which I plead guilty.

I am also aware that the United States has produced numerous embarrassing examples of critics who bring shame on the humanist tradition by abusing their authority—a problem that grows more severe
every day because of the compromises publications must make in order
to survive competition from film and broadcast media. Kauffmann is
understandably pleased with the "horizontal slice" of his *New Republic* audience, comprised of "the most intelligent nonspecialist[s] in
film"; that audience confers on him one of the country's rarest writerly
privileges. Most of the rest of us write in much more trying circumstances. Newspapers exert constant pressure on writers to betray their
ideas through brevity and oversimplification, and glossy magazines subject them to the irresistible seductions of American fame. Because saying clever and brutal things guarantees the domination of one's
opinions over other critics' in the popular imagination, sensationalism
is a path to hegemony. To say as many have, however, that *all* theater
critics offer a behavioral model based on power politics rather than values and standards, is to make against criticism the same charge Puritans
once leveled against the theater: that bad apples *do* spoil the whole
bunch. On the contrary: a few abusive parents do not make all parent-
ing pathological.

In the fall of 1992, I changed universities. After two years in the Performance Studies Department at New York University, a department peopled by rich white folks so afraid of ratifying a rich white folks' canon they could never adopt a curriculum, I left to teach at Hunter College—which was like moving from nyu to the real NYU. It would be hypocritical of me to make too much of my newly democratic surroundings, but I mention them because the move reinvigorated me in unforeseen ways about my humanist leanings. Like much of the City University system at the moment, Hunter is a physically dilapidated place whose demographics reflect those of New York City. My students there generally don't write with the panache of ivy leaguers; they lack experience and hence expertise in the written discourse by which academic achievement is usually measured. They have something, though, that my chic downtown students often lacked: a hunger to know. They burn with curiosity about what their parents and grandparents never read, a daily reminder that not every member of groups previously excluded from Western culture is intent on scrapping past values. My students don't come eager to dump Marlowe, Kleist and the Wakefield Master from the syllabi without reading them first; they want to know what the fuss about those figures was based on. Hunter students are a bit weak on Derrida, but they have the street smarts to know a hearty historical meal from nouvelle-theory cuisine.

After a decade and a half in the field, then, I have come to believe that the Yale Drama School—while hardly an indispensable fundament, as this collection shows—offered exemplary preparation for an American theater critic. Ostracized by the English Department for not being "real doctoral students," ostracized by the directors, actors and designers in our own school for being intrusive eggheads, we were treated to a shockingly accurate preview of the environment in which we would subsequently work. Americans—both spectators and practitioners—will follow a good theater critic, but only rarely will they admit it. The most influential among us is a shepherd with a reluctant flock. We interpret that reluctance as the glimmerings of consciousness, though, and push on with our missions, even though the silence around us is sometimes deafening. And we work every day with a basic truth we Yalies would quickly have forgotten had we scaled those high Gothic university walls: that is, people aren't interested in your ideas until they feel you have thought a bit about what their full, rightful measure of humanity is.

Something
the Dust Said

Stardust Melancholy

THIRTEEN YEARS AFTER HIS DEATH AND 50 YEARS AFTER THE premiere of *Waiting for Godot*—the play that made boredom (of a sort) respectable in the theater—Samuel Beckett is still something of an incalculable quantity. Among professors, aficionados, and major arts institutions, his stature could hardly be more secure. He is *the* indispensable playwright of the 20th century, standing perfectly, edgily, on the cusp of the print and media ages, the modern and the postmodern, the esoteric and the familiar.

At the same time, certain basic questions about this author's appeal and accessibility refuse to go away. His Nobel Prize and the ever-growing mountain of criticism about him aside, whom is Beckett really for? Is he, as his partisans have always argued, a dramatist who can please a wide general public if only audiences would drop their conventional expectations and steer clear of intellectual "analogymongering" (Beckett's word)? Or is he necessarily more rarefied than that, a sort of magical Maeterlinckian "blue bird" that instantly turns pink and mundane upon contact with the adulterated air of the entertainment industry, with its incessant trend- and fashionmongering? Obviously, Beckett has millions of devoted admirers, but do directors and producers serve his legacy when they reach out to the benighted masses, compromise with them, to try to win him millions more? No undertaking in recent memory has pressed these questions more than Michael Colgan and Alan Maloney's "Beckett on Film Project," one of the most ambitious investments to date of talent and cultural resources on Beckett's behalf.

Colgan conceived "Beckett on Film" as a media-friendly extension of the acclaimed Beckett Theater Festival he produced in 1991 as artistic director of Dublin's Gate Theatre—which visited Lincoln Center in 1996. In a June 2000 interview with the *New York Times*, he described himself as driven by "missionary zeal" to connect Beckett with a new, wider audience, introducing him to a generation brought up on electronic media by producing new film productions of nineteen of Beckett's twenty stage plays (excluding the never-produced *Eleuthéria*), many with internationally famous actors and directors such as David Mamet, Harold Pinter, John Gielgud, Jeremy Irons, and Julianne Moore.

The resulting films, released last winter in Ireland and the United Kingdom, have now arrived in the United States as videos. Seven of the shorter ones were broadcast by PBS in September, in a one-hour "Stage on Screen" program hosted by Irons, and on New Year's Day PBS will follow up with a broadcast of Michael Lindsay-Hogg's film version of *Waiting for Godot*, timed to coincide with the 50th anniversary of the play's world premiere at Théâtre de Babylone in Paris. PBS currently has no plans to broadcast any more. Americans who wish to see the remaining eleven works must purchase the whole project on DVD for $149.

Before I say anything else about these films, let me acknowledge that there is superb work in them, by both directors (always the most vulnerable target in Beckett) and actors. "Beckett on Film" is no cynical effort to stoke the star-maker machinery with a novel, sexily inscrutable fuel but clearly a product of loving and intelligent devotion that is often remarkably successful at subordinating star egos to the needs of Beckett's art. There is another side to the project, though—particularly pronounced in its American broadcast form featuring reductive wraparound commentary by Irons ("Beckett created chilling images of human entrapment"; "Beckett broke nearly every rule of drama")—that illustrates the cost of spreading the good word of Beckett via mass-marketing tools in the media age.

Beckett is no stranger to celebrity or publicity frenzies, of course. When Bert Lahr tussled over who was "top banana" in a Miami *Godot* ridiculously billed as "the laugh sensation of two continents," or when Steve Martin and Robin Williams carved out time from Hollywood careers to appear as Didi and Gogo at Lincoln Center, Beckett's drama and its intended performance context were more or less intact. Adapting the works to another medium and using celebrity clout to pry open doors of mass-media popularity and "Masterpiece Theatre" respectability that Beckett never knocked on are other matters entirely. Walter Lippmann once said that the real problem with evangelists is not that they are always bad but that they are "possessed with the sin of pride." These are works by a writer who once famously said that "to be an artist is to fail, as no other dare fail," and the presumption behind the very form they have ended up in, broadcast TV and video, is that pride and worldly success are fundamentally good.

Beckett, as is well known, disliked adaptation and would never have approved this project (he turned down dozens of similar requests). Adaptations nevertheless took place with remarkable frequency even during his lifetime, resulting in a variety of small scandals that made the question of authorization—who had permission and who didn't?—eclipse the much more interesting question of what was actually achieved and how it stacked up to what Beckett conceived. All of these artists, then, deserve a close look at what they produced.

The nineteen films were originally shot in 35 mm, on sets, without audiences. For me the gems among those broadcast in the U.S. (and I've seen only these eight so far) are Lindsay-Hogg's *Godot*, Mamet's *Catastrophe*, and John Crowley's *Come and Go*. The former two take shrewd advantage of film's particular affinity for realism to enhance important aspects of these plays. Andre Bazin once wrote that the difference between theater and cinema "is much less a question of actor and presence than of man and his relation to the decor." Theater can't meaningfully exist without actors, said Bazin, but "drama on the screen can...A banging door, a leaf in the wind...the mainspring of the action is not in man but nature." Beckett's theater is famous for stressing actorly presence more than any other, inviting audiences to brood on that presence within flagrantly symbolic, hermetically sealed worlds (Clov: "There's no more nature"). Still, *Godot* and *Catastrophe* at least accommodate the possibility of a real world, of "nature" outside the entrapping, metaphorical box the audience shares with the actors.

Only one other film record of *Godot* has circulated widely in America before this one, and interestingly enough it was made for television and then transferred to 16 mm film for rental-distribution in the days before VCRs. Directed in 1961 by Alan Schneider and starring Zero Mostel and Burgess Meredith, the film had a cartoonish setting with puff-pillow background hills that epitomized TV-studio artifice, and its cast took frequent liberties with Beckett's lines ("It's worse than TV," ad-libbed Meredith on the line "It's worse than the pantomime"). The actors in Lindsay-Hogg's film version, by contrast—now transferred to DVD—are letter-perfect in their lines, and their setting looks for all the world like a real, muddy dirt road with rocky berms on either side, the sort of desolate place whose utter nondescriptness might well seem artificial to a viewer with no memory of such forgettable roadsides all over Ireland.

The gain of this bleak setting is enhancement of the play's given circumstances. The unchanging, slate-grey sky makes Didi's complaint about the cold more plausible than it is in a climate-controlled theater, for instance, and the real dirt on the ground, shown in closeup, makes an action like Gogo's retrieval of the chicken bone seem much more desperate than it does onstage. The loss of the setting is that it nullifies the play's numerous "theater jokes," which deliberately confound the characters' given circumstances, calling their verity and consistency into question. Was Gogo really beaten before each act? Is Pozzo really blind? Lucky really dumb? The first-act gag when Pozzo enters with the rope and then exits out the opposite wing before Lucky is seen, for instance, is impossible without a proscenium, and Didi's second-act reference to the audience comes off as witless when addressed to the camera ("There! Not a soul in sight! Off you go! Quick! *[He pushes Estragon towards auditorium. Estragon recoils in horror.]* You won't? *[He contemplates auditorium.]* Well I can understand that").

The greatest value of this new *Godot* film is that it preserves the splendid performances of Barry McGovern and Johnny Murphy as Didi and Gogo for posterity. After a decade playing these roles together (in the Gate production, directed by Walter Asmus), these two are like an old married couple who have refined their patter and squabbling into a sublimely self-conscious art; even the hints of stale repetition between them seem germane to the play's "rehearsed" aspect and are therefore poignant. Their smooth Irish accents make many lines that previously sounded abstruse seem habitual and down-to-earth, and their admixture of naturalistic and artificial behaviors is consistently strange (look at their inscrutably smug faces, for instance, when they "accidentally" fall on the fallen Pozzo). It's true that all the action is pushed much more toward the naturalistic than it was in Asmus's stage production, which laid much greater stress on self-consciously repetitive gestures and movement patterns, but to me this adjustment was understandable, necessary, if the film was to satisfy as film.

Whatever one may think of the ground rules of "Beckett on Film"—no cuts, no text changes, no gender-bending, all reportedly key to securing the Beckett estate's permission—it seems clear that once launched on the road of film production, the producers' most pressing concern had to be how to make good films. The one means of guaranteeing bad ones was to avoid creative transposition entirely and simply mount stage productions recorded by cameras running on automatic at the back of the house.

Catastrophe is the most natural candidate for filming in the Beckett stage canon. As Beckett's only play with an unambiguous political thrust, it comes off as more realistic than the others and is thus (ironically) less dependent on the metaphorical resonance of actors' literal presence in a theater. Written in 1982 and dedicated to Vaclav Havel, this brief work takes place in a theater where a dictatorial director (played by Pinter) and his servile female assistant (Rebecca Pidgeon, sporting a good British accent) prepare a silent Protagonist (John Gielgud in his last acting performance, at age 96) for humiliating public display.

The material was perfect for Mamet, who knew instinctively how to maximize both its cruelty and its implicit subversion of authority, and who also understood that a theater interior, carefully filmed, could resonate deeply as a figure for a ruthless natural universe. Dimly lit close-ups of Gielgud's puffy, varicose skin stress the actor's actual frailty and ratchet up the emotion behind his character's climactic act of defiance: raising his head without directorial sanction. Mamet also sharpens the action by harrying it, as it were, cutting too quickly for comfort from shot to reaction shot and back as Pinter's abrasive voice jabs out degrading orders. The manic editing strongly suggests the presence of a tyrannical film director behind the absurdly pompous stage director, cleverly building on Beckett's basic conception of autocracy embarrassing itself. This five-minute *Catastrophe* was more powerful for me than the four ten-minute-plus stage productions I've seen.

John Crowley's *Come and Go*, by contrast, is a superb film made without significantly altering the dramatic terms of the stage play: the actors do just what they would do onstage with the camera centered in front and stationary except for occasional, unobtrusive zooms. This six-minute "dramaticule" from 1965—a quasi-conversational interlude for three impersonally behatted women seated on a bench, who rise and exit in sequence, leaving the remaining pair to whisper about the absent one—is an exquisitely unsettling bit of drollery (the whispers seem to be about terminal illness). *Come and Go* established the general features of all Beckett's later drama: the primacy of a meticulously delineated stage picture; the patterned movements of ghostly, depersonalized figures who speak in "colorless" voices and walk "without sound of feet"; the use of surrounding darkness as a sort of animate void that swallows and regurgitates figures at will. All this is beautifully realized by Crowley with a subtlety and technical perfection that recall nothing so much as Beckett's own television plays.

What's this now? Television plays by Beckett? Yes, as it happens, he wrote six plays for television (and directed them himself), as well as six others for radio and one film, all of which are as penetrating in their self-conscious uses of those media as his plays are of theater. You will not learn about them from Irons's wraparound commentary, however, and "Beckett on Film" doesn't include new productions of them. They are nevertheless unspoken yardsticks of achievement for any Beckett film. One reason Beckett opposed adaptation was that he devoted considerable time and attention to thinking through how his lifelong preoccupations of being and non-being, minimalization of means, "non-relation" in art, and much more, could be explored in recordable media. The figure called O (for object) in *Film* (originally played by Buster Keaton in 1964), for instance, isn't merely an aloof old man scurrying for sanctuary in a busy urban environment but also a soul in flight from "perceivedness." *Film* is about film, the diabolical pursuit of all inquiring and defining eyes (divine, artistic, or mechanical), and its emotional and philosophical heft issue from the fact that O is literally *not there*—he is an image made by light projected through celluloid. Similarly, Beckett's television-play characters are nominally people but more emphatically patterns of tiny, fluorescing dots whose ghostly comings and goings on box-like screens are typically viewed within isolated, box-like rooms.

The only one of this first group of "Beckett on Film" directors who apparently ignored Beckett's media works is Damien O'Donnell, and as it happens, his project, *What Where*, is one of the two stage plays that Beckett himself reimagined for television (the other was *Krapp's Last Tape*). *What Where* (1983) is Beckett's last stage work, about serial, seriocomic torture within a clan of nearly identical figures in long grey gowns and long grey hair. It was transformed by Beckett in 1986 into a still stranger television work in which oval-shaped faces pop in and out of a black background like sentient peas trapped in a diabolical shell game. O'Donnell had no obligation to follow this precedent, of course, but what he did do—set the action in a tomb-like library and dress the characters in identical, clean-cut, Mao-like jackets—is considerably less mysterious than either original. The specific setting picks up amusingly on the pun in Beckett's line "Give him the works"—immersion in the classics as torture—but it also discourages broader meditation on the nature and identity of the cruel power at hand.

Is Bam, the play's putative overseer, really a privileged dictator, and if so, why does he have the same decrepit (or understated) appearance as the others? Are "the works" all authored by Bam, and if so are the other characters (named Bem, Bim, and Bom) really his mental play-things, their torture a figure for his introspection? And what of Bam's preoccupation with "switching on" and "off"—are these references to the engagement of his imagination, or the author's, or ours? None of these questions seem apropos in O'Donnell's admittedly eerie library, an environment much more befitting an explicitly political work like Wallace Shawn's *The Designated Mourner*. At the end of this most deeply ambiguous of Beckett puzzlers, when Bam's voice says "Make sense who may. I switch off," the blackout ought to seem weightier than closing time in a crypt.

Breath, directed by the visual artist Damien Hirst, is a similar case. Hirst is best known for exhibiting sectional slices of real cows, sharks, and other dead animals in galleries and museums, and he brought his distinctive sensational touch to this wry, 35-second piece in which the curtain rises and lowers on a pile of trash as an inhale and then an exhale are heard. The film's trash pile, in typical Hirstian fashion, is mostly medical waste sitting atop a thin white sheet that twirls and flies through black space like a fugitive satellite. The breath is the play's only human presence (it's Beckett's most concise statement regarding the theater event as a birth and death), but as Bazin might have predicted, in the film the breathing sound reads as "nature," possibly wind, or the whoosh of the flying object. (Remember Bazin's point: that film viewers tend to look to nature as the mainspring of action.) Watching this fanciful caper, I wondered whether any play existed, anywhere, less amenable to filming than *Breath*. Only the juggernaut of a "Complete Plays of..." project like Colgan's could have planted the idea of adapting it seriously in anyone's head. That Hirst couldn't help trying to make the piece exciting when its very point is its dullness, however, reaches to the heart of that question about Beckett's supposedly dormant potential for mass appeal.

In 1998, I was invited to speak and lead a talk-back session at Classic Stage Company after a performance of Andrei Belgrader's production of *Waiting for Godot* (starring John Turturro and Tony Shalhoub), and two spectator comments from that evening have stuck in my mind ever since. One man said, "What Beckett wants to say in *Godot* is perfectly clear, but the pace of life is so hectic today that the work just seems rooted in another time." Another added: "I was bored in the wrong way. I see the courage in the work, but I'm just not sure that emptiness, or 'the void,' is the dominant metaphor in our life today." These were intelligent remarks, not at all in the typical philistine mold of Beckett skepticism from a generation ago, and a crusade like Colgan's "Beckett on Film" project challenges them directly. Colgan thinks the skeptics are wrong; Beckett is *not* antiquated, bleak, un-hip, or unsuited to the crammed consciousness of the information age. Perhaps the challenge is somewhat more threatening than that, though. Perhaps the really important question is: how far from Beckett should those who care about him ever travel to meet such intelligent people as those back-talkers on their own irremediably worldly turf?

At least two of the "Beckett on Film" directors have thoroughly thought-out ideas for adaptation: the Hollywood heavyweight Anthony Minghella (*The English Patient, The Talented Mr. Ripley, Iris*), who directed *Play*, and Enda Hughes, who did *Act Without Words II*. In both these cases the finished works are much more conventionally entertaining than the originals; they are also richly cinematic and tolerably sensitive to the sources of dramatic power in the original dramas. In *Play*, three heads, two female and one male, protrude from identical grey urns and take turns speaking at tongue-mangling speed (mostly about the details of their love triangle), "provoked" by an interrogative light that could be seen as a fourth character. Famously, this action repeats in its entirety after playing through once.

No filmic substitute is possible for the way *Play*'s purgatorial situation entraps the audience along with the plainly uncomfortable stage actors (who can neither fully stand up nor sit down), and Minghella didn't waste energy seeking one. Instead, he chose to illustrate the implied post-death environment, setting the work in a mistily gloomy landscape, replete with a *Godot*-like tree and dotted with hundreds of muttering heads in urns extending into the endless distance. A camera replaces the persecuting light, repeatedly "capturing" the three actors in urns in the foreground (Alan Rickman, Kristin Scott Thomas, and Juliet Stevenson) from various angles while calling frequent attention to itself through abrupt interruptions of leader footage, burned out footage, noisy power-zooms, and more. The overall effect is edgy, strange, and interesting: purgatory as an interminable film shoot, humanity as actors condemned to endless reiterations of a salacious and trivial love story. At the same time, the sacrifices are blatant to anyone who knows the original: realistic detail and special effects are now the main foci, rather than the desperate lines spat into the darkness ("Is anyone listening to me? Is anyone looking at me?") and the awful basic circumstance of rote repetition. No language, no matter how powerful, could compete with the attractively caked blue-grey clay on these actors' faces, or the marvelously particularized, Blakean background that practically promises spectacular magic.

Act Without Words II also features a mysterious offstage force that controls the characters' destinies, and Hughes's approach to it combines animation with film historical reference and a different sort of technical self-reflexiveness. The work is a lugubriously comic mime for two characters who represent opposing attitudes to life: initially concealed inside adjacent sacks with a single pile of clothes beside them, they are prodded awake, in turn, by a goad that enters from the stage-left wing, after which they proceed through dressing and other routine activities, one at a "slow, awkward" pace, the other "brisk, rapid, precise," after which they undress, reenter the sacks, and await the goad again. The filmed action takes place within three frames of an animated strip of film stretched horizontally across the screen, where the goad is a cartoon and the actors (Pat Kinevane and Marcello Magni) move with the halting, discontinuous flow of a silent-film. Loud clicking of a projector is heard during quiet transitions between the contrasting slow and fast music, and the halting movement occasionally accommodates modest magic tricks (the disappearance of a carrot, for instance). Otherwise, Hughes makes no effort to provide cinematic corollaries for the offstage force. Her emphasis is on maximizing the activity's comic melancholy in its new film context, which required careful and resourceful thinking outside her medium's usual box.

Neither of these works has the full enigmatic tenacity of Beckett's originals, but both are smart, earnest, and splendidly executed: they deserve to be called films, not just filmed plays. The only work I've seen so far that strikes me as a travesty of Beckett's play is *Ohio Impromptu*, directed by Charles Sturridge—reportedly a late replacement for Tom Stoppard, author of *Travesties*. *Ohio Impromptu* is a 1981 piece for two men, called Reader and Listener, dressed identically in long black coats and long white hair, who are seated at a table with their heads bowed and propped on their right hands with a single black hat between them. In the play, their faces are hidden or half-hidden as one reads aloud to the other about a presumably bereaved man who "moved from where they had been so long alone together to a single room on the far bank." The suggestion is that only one man is really present, the man in the story who moved "in a last attempt to obtain relief," and the reading is part of his imaginative mourning or healing process. Beckett, however, adds the extra enigma of an extraordinarily quiet and subtle conflict between the alter egos. Listener interrupts Reader six times by knocking on the table, cuing him to repeat the previous phrase. Only when Listener knocks again is Reader apparently allowed to continue, and only when the story ends do the two look at each other, as if for the first time.

In Sturridge's film, both men are played by Jeremy Irons, whose face is visible almost the entire time. As Reader he remains taciturn but as Listener he becomes a veritable fount of superfluous acting, providing innumerable realistic expressions such as nods, blinks, fidgets, and sighs. These choices render a pointedly enigmatic emotional encounter largely comprehensible, and they make the whole timeless episode seem rooted in a unique (i.e. non-cyclical) moment. Furthermore, Irons glances at himself so many times that he ruins the bombshell climax of the final shared look. Sturridge, it seems, was so eager to advertise his rather obvious perception that the two men may be one (Reader fades away at the end and the black and white, windowless room acquires a window and color) that he neglected the play's other ambiguities. When his camera isn't dwelling devotedly on Irons's deep, pained expressions, it's panning or circling to include both figures in gratuitous, "look no seams!" displays of technical prowess.

The silver lining in this story is that Sturridge and Irons help clarify an important issue. It isn't possible to be both a movie star and a great Beckett actor—not at the same time, at any rate. One has to choose, because the two paradigms are mutually exclusive. Saying this isn't to advocate any morbid new religion of failure and obscurity, or part of any sectarian attempt to preserve Beckett for an effete coterie of initiates. It's a recognition of how this artist's aesthetic of diminution, restraint, and humility has always challenged the ego-worshiping norms of the buzz-happy, sped-up modern world. Interestingly, less confusion reigns on this issue in other arts, where Beckett has long been a major influence and a favorite object of direct transformation by painters, sculptors, musicians, choreographers, and video artists. It's in the theater—with its perpetual, inexorable compromise between art and show biz—that Beckett's ardent supporters have most often found it hard to accept that he was genuinely indifferent to much of what they craved from this world.

> From a 1968 letter to Alan Schneider: "Olivier & Plowright came up with a hot offer for [the radio play] *All That Fall* at National. I said no but they came over and insisted. Larry kept saying: 'it'd make a GREAT SHOW'! However said no again. Impossible in the light…They were a bit fed up with me…"

The man is now gone, of course, so his work needn't be held hostage to this indifference. Nevertheless, the act of advocating or promoting him ("a GREAT SHOW!") is still and will always be paradoxical, because the most beneficent media apparatus inevitably molds everything it touches to its own shape, making the alien ordinary, foisting names on the unnamable. As Beckett's Unnamable says of the voices that persecute him: "I am walled round with their vociferations, none will ever know what I am, none will ever hear me say it, I won't say it, I can't say it, I have no language but theirs."

I think there is great value in the "Beckett on Film" productions, even the short-sighted ones, provided they aren't misconstrued as standard or definitive. Colgan began this project by saying that his dearest wish was to introduce Beckett to thousands for the first time, and he will no doubt have that satisfaction. These DVDs will find their way into private collections and school libraries far afield of the urban centers where Beckett is a household name and live productions of his works are usually seen. But this ease of access confers a major responsibility on the Beckett estate: having sanctioned Colgan, it must take care that the DVDs don't stand without competition for decades and *become* standard. A greater loosening of restrictions now seems inevitable, lest what began as a sincere attempt to refresh a reputation end up doing permanent harm to it.

(November, 2002)

Krap's First Tape

———

S O HERE IT IS AT LAST, FORTY-EIGHT YEARS AFTER IT WAS WRIT-
ten—the play Samuel Beckett wanted to keep forever from print.
It's difficult to say which would have sickened him more, the fact
of *Eleuthéria*'s publication or the tawdry public argument it has caused
between two of his oldest friends. One needn't take sides in this argument to feel that the appearance of the book is a welcome anticlimax.
Nine months of good- and bad-faith allegations, recriminations and
transatlantic legal threats, assiduously reported in feuilletons and monthlies, have left us hungry for literary substance. This is a play by Beckett.
More, it is the last, long mystery work among what he called his "trunk
manuscripts." The least respect we can pay him now is to read it and de-
cide for ourselves whether it really did belong in the drawer.

No one—including the partners of Foxrock, Inc., the publisher (Barney Rosset, John Oakes, and Dan Simon)—disputes that Beckett did not
want *Eleuthéria* published. Written in French before *Waiting for Godot*,
it was circulated unsuccessfully among Paris theaters in the late 1940s
and then suppressed as a failed experiment. (The directors Jean Vilar and
Roger Blin seriously considered but passed on it.) After submitting it for
publication at Editions des Minuit, the author withdrew it around 1953
and, over the next four and a half decades, consistently resisted appeals

to change his mind. Even after similar appeals brought the publication of other texts he also deemed failures, such as *Mercier and Camier* and *Texts for Nothing*, Beckett refused to release *Eleuthéria*—reiterating his refusal, according to Jérôme Lindon, head of Minuit, on his deathbed.

The play was never much of a secret, though. As S. E. Gontarski explains in his lucid, informative introduction, Beckett didn't destroy the typescripts or manuscript notebooks, and these became, with his approval, part of several university archives. For twenty years, scholars have been reading them, making bootleg copies, and publishing criticism about the play as if it were (or would soon become) generally available. Furthermore, about a third of the work *was* published with Beckett's permission in a special 1986 edition of *Revue d'Esthétique* dedicated to him. And that same year, he told Rosset, his American publisher for thirty-three years, who had recently been fired from Grove Press, that he would help him "start over" by "adapting" *Eleuthéria* for publication.

When Beckett went back to work on it, however, he "saw it was hopeless. Nothing to be done. I couldn't face publication," as he told me later that year. He gave Rosset the story *Stirrings Still* instead and returned to his old position of withholding the play. Today, Rosset insists that Beckett would have eventually allowed him to publish *Eleuthéria*; "I mean, it took us nearly twenty-four years to convince him to publish *Mercier and Camier*," he explained in a December phone interview. For him and his Foxrock partners, the situation parallels that of Kafka, whose writings Max Brod judged too important to destroy after his death, as the author had requested. In January, Lindon reluctantly granted permission for the English edition and shortly afterward published the original along with a foreword explaining his bitter feelings about the affair.

As it turns out, the play bears out neither extreme argument about it. It was not, after all, a hidden masterpiece like *The Trial* or *The Castle* whose suppression would have impoverished us beyond forgiveness. Nor is it, as Lindon writes in his foreword, simply a catastrophe, an embarrassing "*pièce ratée*" ("failed play") that will damage Beckett's reputation and keep "newcomers" from dipping further into his oeuvre. *Eleuthéria* is a fascinating, rare instance of Beckettian excess, 191 pages of casting about for dramatic forms and techniques to accommodate his incipient aesthetic of diminution and renunciation. At times windy, redundant, even confusing, it will certainly take its proper place as a minor, formative work that is buoyed by eloquent and hilarious passages and the tantalizing seeds of great themes, devices and characters to come.

The basic situation involves a young man named Victor Krap—formerly a writer, like his future namesake Krapp—who has withdrawn from his bourgeois family to live alone in a sparsely furnished room. To his chagrin, no one will leave him in peace there. His family and others (a quasi-supernatural glazier, a doctor who offers him a suicide pill, and an Audience Member who climbs down from a box, for instance) try physically to remove him and then, worse, understand him, reduce his retreat "from life" to a philosophical position they can file away in neat mental drawers. Victor's retreat is, among other things, a metaphor for Beckett's repudiation of traditionally entertaining dramatic conventions, the constant invasions of Victor's privacy functioning as figures for (and sometimes literal discussions of) the various pressures the author feels to adapt to received forms (and hence give up his *eleuthéria*, Greek for freedom).

The first act communicates all this by way of a standing visual joke: two simultaneous actions take place on a split stage, one called "main," one "marginal," and the marginal is clearly of primary interest. Victor moves in a silent, vaguely rhythmic pattern around his room, which takes up three-quarters of the stage, while up to eight annoyingly arch characters borrowed from French farce cram into the remaining space and discuss him. Interestingly enough, the discussion, with its absurd physical circumstance, self-consciously employed clichés, and barely concealed violence beneath exaggerated social conventions, strongly recalls Ionesco, although *Eleuthéria* predates *The Bald Soprano* by two years.

The similarity is revealing, since this attempt to write an "anti-play" lands Beckett in the same cul-de-sac that trapped Ionesco his entire career: settling for the half-measure of enlarged or satirized conventions rather than investing in a deeper search for a *via negativa* truly purged of tendency and teleology. To read *Eleuthéria*—particularly its dated parody of manners comedy—in light of *Godot*, *Happy Days*, and Beckett's other dramas is to crave those singular essentialized images that accomplish at a glance what this split, revolving stage (it turns between acts so that the Krap morning room at one point "fall[s] into the pit") cannot in three acts.

As he obviously realized himself, Beckett peppered the play with "gimmicks" (one of his most caustic epithets during the 1980s) because he hadn't yet made the profoundly simple discovery from which the rest of his drama grew: that the theater event itself, with its rising and lowering curtain, is a birth and death, an exquisitely metaphorical vessel that may be filled with essentialized tensions and agons without elaborate explanation or adornment. He goes out of his way in Act I, for instance, to convey that the bourgeois characters are unimportant, then provides unwanted details about them for two more acts—Mrs. Krap's "broken heart," hanky-panky between the doctor and Victor's fiancée, etc.—failing even to invest those details with the sort of ambiguities that make his subsequent characters and plots so richly inscrutable and iconic.

One longs for the stage to clear out, for Victor to achieve, if not his preferred aloneness, then at least a state of persecution by only one other person, such as the Glazier or Dr. Piouk—the tête-à-tête as essential life compromise, the next best thing to solitude. And the worst is that Beckett plainly knows this, but instead of turning these characters into worthy foils for Victor, he makes them detached connoisseurs or editors (already an avant-garde cliché in 1947) who offer running dramaturgical commentary and try half-heartedly to foist changes on the play. "Have to keep the rubbernecks well entertained," says the Glazier. There is a pervasive sense of derivativeness, particularly regarding the 1928 surrealist classic *Victor* by Roger Vitrac, also a highly self-referential satire about the misfit son of a respectable bourgeois family.

Beckett isn't exactly a novice writer at this point and could have easily made even this cliché reflexivity work as Pirandellian comedy, had he focused on the battle between Victor and the would-be audience advocates (or on the effort to repair his "window"—read "life"—against his will). As it is, the would-be advocates become preoccupied with murky power struggles among themselves, and the pressure on him to "take on some shape" builds and dissipates again and again. It's as if Beckett deliberately abandoned focus in the final acts out of sheer disappointment with the meager fruit his dramatic strategies were yielding, leaving sixteen of his characters floundering around in search of an author and one in desperate flight from him.

His own patience with such an impulsive, histrionic gesture understandably lessened as his self-scrutiny and criteria for economy grew more and more severe after the 1940s. On the other hand, he may have been too hard on himself to see that *Eleuthéria* is also intensely and enduringly funny at many points—replete with that morbid Irish jocularity, unpretentious punning, and lidless stare at the unfathomable for which he is cherished. The Glazier alone is a trove of memorable aphorisms: "Nothing bores like boredom"; "Nothing like medical men for dancing on graves"; "I don't know any more what I wanted, but I wouldn't be surprised if I had it." And Dr. Piouk is scarcely less quotable: "Everything aspires to be either black or white. Color is the missing of a beat."

It's a testimony to the considerable translating talents of Michael Brodsky that his English version gives an accurate taste of the original's peculiar tone and humor. Brodsky has an unusually good ear for Beckett's idiosyncratic accents in French and is marvelously resourceful in finding English equivalents for the text's numerous neologisms and archaisms. "Flim-flam," for instance, the term for Victor's rhythmic movement, carries just the right double meaning of nonsense and humbug that Beckett meant to convey with his odd "*manège.*" Similarly, "Words? He has been wording?" ("*Paroles? Il a parolé?*"), "one of his brogues" ("*sa godasse*"), and a hundred other passages offer deceptively simple solutions to problems that require fluency in both French and the little known tongue of early Beckettese.

Occasional points of unwarranted stiffness remain, but these could easily be fixed in rehearsal, where all good play translations are truly finished. As matters stand, however, neither Brodsky nor anyone else may ever be able to make such adjustments because, according to Oakes, the Beckett Estate "currently has no plans to grant performance rights." In

December, remembering Barney Rosset's attempt to stop performances of a 1984 *Endgame* that departed from the published stage directions, I asked Rosset hypothetically whether he would object if directors of *Eleuthéria* wanted to alter the text for production. "Let them do what they want," was his answer.

(June, 1995)

The Last Biography?

"I CAN'T GO ON, I'LL GO ON," SAMUEL BECKETT MIGHT BE quipping from his grave as 1500 more pages on his life appear in print. He is an author who achieved his stature largely by focusing on his *inner* experience, stripping away the integuments of recognizable reality in an increasingly rigorous aesthetic of diminution, concentration, and withholding. Beckett himself insisted that his life was "devoid of interest," discouraging all would-be biographers until 1989, the year he died. And scores of critics took him at his word during his lifetime, writing studies that treated his texts primarily as formal objects, modern artifacts or relics whose geographical and cultural-historical references functioned best in a sort of ideal space beyond specific biographical ground.

This attitude, right or wrong, never had a hope of satisfying Beckett's international public, whose thirst for information and gossip about the Nobel-prizewinner was bound to be slaked sooner and later. The race for sooner was won by Deirdre Bair, whose *Samuel Beckett: A Biography* appeared in 1978 and stood without competition for nearly two decades despite its plenitude of factual errors and facile applications of the life to the work. Discouragingly, admirers were never in short supply for such revelations as: "*Waiting for Godot* is a metaphor for the long walk into

Roussillon, when Beckett and Suzanne [who were running from the Nazis in unoccupied France] slept in haystacks...during the day and walked by night."

Anthony Cronin defends Bair in the preface to his *Samuel Beckett: The Last Modernist*, writing that her book "has come in for a good deal of criticism in professional Beckett circles, much of it unwarranted and some of it unjust." His sense that he is her spiritual comrade is astute, for his biography is as intrinsically salacious and persistently inaccurate as hers, perhaps more so. Cronin apparently conceived his book as a non-scholarly competitor to James Knowlson's *Damned to Fame: The Life of Samuel Beckett* (1996), which preceded *Samuel Beckett: The Last Modernist* by about a month in Britain and was written in a straightforward, factual style that deliberately avoided the kind of novelistic plotting that imposes meanings that the facts don't justify. If Knowlson's 800-page study is an anti-page-turner, though, it has the unique virtue among Beckett biographies of thoroughgoing accuracy—a virtue that was lost on reviewers in the *New York Times*, the *Wall Street Journal*, and several British newspapers, who praised Cronin's breezy, talk-show style at Knowlson's expense.

In fact, Cronin, an Irish comic novelist, is not a patient enough researcher to do without a real biographer's help. His book is so sloppy that, by the end, it struck me as something of a testament to the lamentable disappearance of fact-checking in our time. Moreover, he does not seem to have asked himself why the story of Beckett's life needed to be told. Hearsay, rumor, and anything else that served the needs of his preconceived novelistic scheme take precedence over truths that might have emerged from open-minded investigation and assessment.

Early on, I suspected that Cronin's trouble with facts might be familiar and forgivable—something simple, like an inability to read Beckett's cramped handwriting. In one important letter to Beckett's intimate friend Thomas MacGreevy, for instance, he confuses "positive" with "possible," "comments" with "torments," and "indicative of" with "denoting." Similar errors appear in other transcriptions. Soon enough, though, these errors slip into a more generalized pattern of carelessness that includes indifference to the correct quotation of notorious remarks (the American premiere of *Godot*, in Miami, was billed as "the laugh sensation of two continents," not, as Cronin has it, "the last sensation") and the proper citation of important collaborators (the great Beckett actor was David Warrilow, not Warilow, and the translator of the play *Eleuthéria* is Michael Brodsky, not Nobel Prize-winning Joseph).

Writing with the smug disdain of an anti-intellectual snob, Cronin often simply does not bother with the fussy business of proper attribution or the clear distinction between fictional characters and Beckett himself. Since so many of Cronin's attributed and unattributed facts and quotations turn out to be wrong one soon loses trust in his very motivation for taking on a writer so fundamentally different from himself. Here he is smirking at his own cleverness, for instance, after supposedly catching Beckett at filching:

> According to Brian Coffey, a Dublin contemporary who came to know Beckett a little later, [Beckett] did not share the Aldington-MacGreevy admiration for Eliot, remarking on his borrowings and calling him a "jewel thief." Yet *Dream of Fair to Middling Women* fully recognizes Eliot's existence by overt, if unacknowledged, quotation, or borrowing—one of Eliot's own borrowings from Julian of Norwich being borrowed again by Beckett.

How inconvenient that Eliot's "Little Gidding," the poem in which the reference to Julian of Norwich appears, was written in 1942, ten years after *Dream of Fair to Middling Women* was completed. One senses here a desire to trump the author, catch him in white lies, force clay feet upon him.

The book's overall narrative is, alas, approximately as sound as its facts. The plot that Cronin imposes on Beckett's life is a trite morality tale building on myths first purveyed by Bair. Cronin clearly does not like the young Sam Beckett at all, much less his writing, and Bair's portrait is consequently useful to him: that of a hypochondriacal layabout who tends to booze and whore it up when he isn't too inert even for that. To this Cronin adds such vices as homoeroticism, class-driven apoliticism, and obsession with masturbation—all of which are miraculously redeemed on page 373 (of 621), when the tone instantaneously switches from condescension to elation. Cronin uses his discussion of the trilogy, the first writing he really respects, to begin a wholly new portrait of a transfigured Beckett possessed of abundant, unforeseen literary and personal virtues. The loathsome and iniquitous youth with clay feet is forgotten for good.

Had Cronin waited just a month or two to check his manuscript against the book by Knowlson (who footnotes nearly every sentence), he would have saved himself untold embarrassment, learning much to revise his plot. To wit, his subject was, according to the verifiable evidence, a teetotaler through the end of his university years. Beckett also took active political positions at every point in his life, from a schoolboy debate defending women's emancipation to a 1929 article attacking Irish censorship to his Resistance activity to a ban on productions of his plays in apartheid South Africa to an appeal against martial law in Poland. As to masturbation, Cronin's repeated and unfootnoted remarks leave him looking immeasurably more concerned with the matter than Beckett was.

The book's subtitle, "The Last Modernist," promises a coherent argument about historical context. True to form, Cronin offers nothing of the sort, barely defining what he means by modernism, much less why Beckett should be seen as its last avatar. The term, as it turns out, is merely his preferred tool of reductivity, the byproduct of his need to entomb the works safely in preexisting categories, repatriate them in a static country wholly discovered by himself. Tellingly, his interest in Beckett flags after *Play* (1962-63) and dies after the Nobel Prize is awarded (1969). The last twenty years of Beckett's life are dispensed with in collapsed and sketchy fashion. It seems that the late plays and the works for film and television produced during that period do not fit any modernism thesis, concerned as they are with such still current issues as the ascendance of visual over spoken language, the benevolence and malevolence of the camera eye, and the interpenetration of real and technologically mediated presences in performance.

Cronin does have a modest contribition to make: he describes the Irish milieu in which Beckett grew up with first-hand familiarity, and he tells a handful of amusing anecdotes for the first time. The disrespect inherent in his carelessness, however, as well as the intellectual compromise inherent in his overpowering impulse to novelize, place his book squarely on the bottom of Beckett's biographical heap.

(1998)

Suffering Fools

THE MOST INFLUENTIAL PLAY OF THE 20TH CENTURY TURNED 50 years old this year—a dangerous age for any work of art in the land of eternal youth. The operators of our hype machines tend to grow resentful when any influence sticks around for too long, as if culture were a sort of warehouse in which inventory becomes burdensome if it disappears too slowly. *Waiting for Godot*, however, isn't merely another dramatic commodity—like, say, *Death of a Salesman*, which returns once again to Broadway this winter, for its 50th anniversary, in a production the author assures us is "really new." Written in 1948 by a very different sort of author (Beckett: "Success and failure on the public level never mattered much to me, in fact I feel much more at home with the latter, having breathed deep of its vivifying air all my writing life"), *Godot* has yet to exhaust the newness it was born with.

There is a tendency to believe that plays anointed "classic" are produced more often than they really are, and that's one reason why directors who ought to know better sometimes convince themselves of a need to modernize Beckett's world—adding, say, an airport runway locale to *Godot* (George Coates), or a mental-ward setting to *Endgame* (Alfred Kirchner), or a mound of car windshields to *Happy Days* (Robert Woodruff). The truth is, though, even *Godot*, Beckett's best known work, is still read much more than seen, and skimmed or intuited much more than read, so superimposed modernizations invariably end up as dull spectacles of bootless competition, unhappy efforts to make a director's ingenuity shine over Beckettian effects that were unfamiliar and poorly understood in the first place. Directors courageous enough to ignore the inner voice that says "advertise!" and devote themselves to searching for the enduring strangeness and provocativeness in the action were never common and grow rarer every year.

At least one good one is still around, it seems. Andrei Belgrader's mostly stunning *Godot* at Classic Stage Company actually takes numerous liberties with Beckett's text—inserting a swipe at the Public Theater, for instance, and a waltz by Didi and Gogo to the hummed tune of "The Merry Widow"—but all of these blend in seamlessly because they stem from intense and intelligent investment in the moment-to-moment action. The show is fresh because it doesn't try to outdo any competitor, funny and original because it doesn't start from the premise that the material needs rescue, repair or improvement. Its hugely talented cast—featuring John Turturro, Tony Shalhoub and Christopher Lloyd—is as interested in opening up virgin territory in the play-as-written as in reinvigorating it with their famous personalities. Stars have seldom been in better alignment.

The action takes place on a rectangle of thick grey foam rubber that muffles the actors' footsteps and thus gives palpable reality to Didi and Gogo's doubts about whether they really exist. This rectangle is backed only by a row of striplights and the theater's black brick rear wall, with a diminutive rock and a ridiculously thin tree completing the impression of a space that is self-consciously theatrical even before the actors enter it (set by Andrei Both). When Turturro-as-Gogo is discovered struggling with his boot at the opening, he soon turns the episode into a bout of strenuous physical clowning—falling over backwards, bending into silly contortions and splits—the first of numerous shticks that would be perfectly at home in *Fool Moon*, the Broadway show Bill Irwin and David Shiner built around their physical clowning in 1993 and recently brought back for a limited run.

It was a stroke of luck that *Fool Moon* opened the same week as this *Godot*, not only because such virtuosic buffoonery is always delicious in its own right, but also because Shiner and Irwin are terrific reminders of the low comic basis of Beckett's supposedly philosophical humor. Their cheerfully wordless show contains none of the Irishman's melancholy or ruminativeness, but when Irwin struggles with a microphone cord that eventually defeats him and is then dragged upward by the act curtain, it's impossible not to think of Beckett's *Acts without Words*, which hark back to the same tragicomic *commedia dell'arte* tradition: mischievous offstage agents used as metaphors for capricious gods. And when Shiner rudely and gymnastically climbs over spectators or enlists them as volunteers and then mocks their clothes and demeanors in disdainful silent asides, he assumes the same vaudevillian posture of haughty separateness from character that Didi and Gogo do when they stop cowering momentarily to give Pozzo acting advice, or commiserate with the audience on lines like "Nothing happens, nobody comes, nobody goes, it's awful!"

At the same time, the differences between the clowning in *Fool Moon* and the clowning in *Godot* are also crucial. Shiner and Irwin have more or less stable roles to play whereas Turturro and Shalhoub don't. In *Godot*, as Robbe-Grillet once wrote, "everything happens as if the two tramps were on stage *without having a role*." Shiner and Irwin play absurd characters whose firm contours allow us to judge certain behaviors as inappropriate and laugh at them. Didi and Gogo's contours are, even on close examination, as flimsy as the prop tree. One character seems to stand for the intellect but nevertheless has prostate problems; the other seems to represent the belly but speaks French and quotes classical authors. All information about their backgrounds seems unreliable (was either one ever really in "the Macon country"?), and their speech is an extremely odd blend of academic jargon, music-hall banter and idiomatic Beckettese.

It's this built-in uncertainty about who these characters are, the strange transparency of their deliberately artificial natures, that has made them so appealing over the years to star comedians like Bert Lahr, Zero Mostel and Steve Martin. Stars invariably sign up for such a project assuming their familiar personalities will provide the character contours that the play doesn't, but those who truly end up refreshing this work are the ones who come to understand that Beckett is actually stronger than their narcissism. In other words, they too ultimately have to surrender to the hell of the circumstance, and turn on the spit, or the play will embarrass them without mercy. Turturro and Shalhoub, to their credit, seem never to have doubted this.

What a fascinating Gogo Turturro makes. His eyes twinkle with childlike joy during the character's many moments of reflection and memory, and his famous exaggerated sibilants and Brooklyn drawl have a soothing effect that alternates, schizoid fashion, with occasional aggressive outbursts accompanied by mad eyes and a phony foreign accent. Shalhoub's Didi ought to be intimidated by these outbursts, but in keeping with the clownish logic that governs their relationship, he never is. Droopy-eyed and physically stiffer than Turturro, Shalhoub moves his arms and shoulders as little as possible and often wears a pure-hearted grin that gives him an air of still paternal calm. This is always temporary, however, because each time the void descends on the scene, the calm clears out like Godot's skittish messenger boy.

Turturro and Shalhoub listen closely to one another the entire time, registering and relishing each other's every message and signal, spoken and unspoken, and investing all their exchanges with clear intention. The communication between them is so intimate and efficient it's a source of the production's surprising beauty, making the many lags and disconnects in the dialogue all the more toughly poignant. Almost any sequence could serve as an example: the sustained glance that draws a big laugh from the tossed-off suggestion that Didi is "eleven," for instance, or Shalhoub's astonishingly focused delivery of the "Was I sleeping" speech, the first I've heard that makes the remark "habit is a great deadener" seem inevitable rather than anticlimactic.

Belgrader has also sprinkled the action with posed or "mugged" moments, which turn out to be oddly orienting rather than annoying or cloying because they seem to match the coy unpredictability of the cosmic forces watching over this play. Turturro strikes a heroic pose, for instance, after Shalhoub says "All mankind is us," and the four principal characters all lie on their backs flailing like overturned beetles after they fall to the ground in Act Two. Lloyd's Pozzo is the anchor of this strategy because, as a bald, stentorian, whip-cracking ringmaster, he generates his own histrionic aura that cuts two different ways. On the one hand, he's arrogant, boorish and repellent, on the other gregarious and vulnerable, unusually coherent, and unusually intent on pursuing genuine social intercourse with Didi and Gogo. Interestingly enough, they claim the emotional upper hand with him whenever they choose, exploiting the weakness implicit in his silly poses.

Deep as my admiration is for this production, however, I have two objections, neither trivial. One has to do with Richard Spore's sluggish delivery of Lucky's long speech, which ruins its humor. This seemingly nonsensical torrent of words actually makes some sense if one carefully parses the long sentence, but the joke that it makes sense despite itself is lost if one eliminates the torrent. The other objection has to do with the child actor playing the Boy (let him remain nameless), who swallows his lines, has little control over his body and thus has the same mood-destroying effect on the end of each act that opening a window onto the street would have. These problems wouldn't seem nearly so egregious in a lesser production, but in a first-class one like this (which moreover may have a chance to move beyond its initial venue), they cry out to be noticed and fixed.

(1998)

David Shiner and Bill Irwin in the third Broadway run of Fool Moon *at the Brooks Atkinson Theatre, 1998.* CREDIT: JOAN MARCUS.

Bill Irwin in his own adaptation of Samuel Beckett's Texts for Nothing *at Classic Stage Company in New York, 2000.* CREDIT: DIXIE SHERIDAN.

Send in the Clown

SAMUEL BECKETT'S LATER PROSE IS A REMARKABLE SUBSTANCE. It reminds me of one of those unstable heavy elements that, under "normal" atmospheric conditions, can exist for only a brief time before breaking down into more "normal" constituents. To read it closely is to feel simultaneously tickled by ordinary impishness and bewildered by quicksilver slips in consciousness and a sinuous, filmic shifting of self-contradictory imagery that refuses to resolve into singular scenes. One does acquire vivid impressions—say, of a verbally hiccuping, free-floating, black-humored, hyper-articulate describer of uncertain location or form—but these don't stay in the mind for long. By the time the book is back on the shelf, they have transmuted, alas, into much simpler, more mentally "tangible" memories.

The so-called difficulty of Beckett's writing up through the novel-trilogy, *Molloy*, *Malone Dies* and *The Unnamable*, written between 1947 and 1950, has been exaggerated. The narrators in those works do play around with truth and occasionally leave their locations and physical forms uncertain, but they are always grounded in a central story-telling consciousness that obviously controls the mental games, playfully switches the multiple identities on and off and ultimately reassures itself of its continuing existence and purpose through exquisitely logical logorrhea ("I can't go on, I'll go on"). The shorter prose after *The Unnamable* is a different animal.

In 1951, Beckett found himself in a creative impasse and a profound depression. He felt his towering achievements were behind him—*Waiting for Godot*, completed in 1948-49, sat ignored and unproduced until 1953—and the nature of those achievements left him frozen. In a now famous 1949 text on painting called "Three Dialogues," he identified his self-created cul-de-sac: art is "the expression that there is nothing to express, nothing with which to express, nothing from which to express, no power to express, no desire to express, together with the obligation to express." Trouble is, this obligation to express the ineffable "nothing" leaves the artist in danger of becoming a negative hero. "All that is required now," Beckett continued, "is to make of this . . . admission, this fidelity to failure, a new occasion, a new term of relation."

You could call his impasse at this time a "crisis of relation" or "relatedness." It had to do with figuring out how to "go on" without making a fetish or conceit of "going on. The thirteen *Texts for Nothing* are the residue of this struggle, fragmentary transitional pieces from a period of tremendous frustration when he worked out the methods and insights that would carry him through his next great period of creativity. His severe elisions, reductions, and concentrations during this period could never be confused with any pretentious pose or prepackaged philosophy.

The wonderful clown Bill Irwin deserves hosannas just for attempting to enter the *Texts* imaginatively. There are shattering beauties in these pieces, but discovering them takes unusual patience and perseverence— even, I imagine, for the new vaudeville performer sometimes called "the thinking man's clown." Like *Fizzles*, the *Texts* weren't conceived as a single story, only occasionally refer explicitly to one another, and are of widely differing quality. Thus, the usual difficulties of staging Beckett's nondramatic prose—illustration is almost always disappointing and reductive compared with what a reader's imagination can provide—are compounded by the unusual difficulty of the prose chosen.

I happen to think what Irwin has done here is brilliant. It's one of the most confident and intelligent prose adaptations I've seen. (By the 1980s,

Beckett was such an avant-garde icon that, even before his death in 1989, every one of his nondramatic works had been adapted for the stage, with or without his permission.) I can also see, though, that the 70-minute show at Classic Stage Company—consisting of *Texts 1, 9, 11* and *13*—might be hard going for those unfamiliar with the material.

The creature spat out of the orifice at the top of the terrifically steep, 20-foot-tall, rust-colored mud chute designed by Douglas Stein doesn't even come across as fully human at first. He breaks his fall with a split that would cripple most of us, brushes off his faded but immaculate, ill-fitting tramp-with-bowler outfit (which will be filthy by the end) and tries to return up the impossible slope—to undo his "birth," as it were. Various slapstick impediments intervene—sliding back down, stepping in holes, puddles, tripping over rocks—which ought to humanize him, except that his exceedingly strange, stiff-rubbery movements and cadaverous white face with intense, eagle-blue eyes keep him suspended in a puppet-like aura.

He can't get comfortable anywhere on the hill, not only because it's too lumpy but also because his own body is foreign to him. When he tumbles, for instance, he doesn't break his fall with his arms, as one might expect, but rather folds them under him, dropping like a sack. And when he walks, he doesn't so much step from place to place as rock, pedal, prance or float in a tantalizing, flat-footed tiptoe. It's as if his head and each of his limbs were controlled by a separate, offstage, infernal jokester. Even scratching his balls comes off as inadvertent choreography.

This is the sort of meditative physical comedy on which Irwin built his reputation. It has sustained him marvelously in several productions of *Waiting for Godot*, and it's perfect for the relatively conventional "scene" of *Text 1*. This is the only one of the *Texts* grounded in a more or less stable image of place ("The top, very flat, of a mountain, no, a hill, but so wild...quag, heath up to the knees, faint sheep-tracks, troughs scooped deep by the rains") and the effort of a coherent, embodied consciousness to thrust itself reluctantly into life by telling itself stories. The narrator may be dead—"They are up above, all round me, as in a graveyard"—but that suggestion is purely in the spirit of morbid farce that infuses the dramatic works from *Godot* and *Endgame* to *Play* and *Film*. Great clowns have always worked wonderfully in these works—that is, when they're willing to subordinate their personal shtick somewhat and play second banana to Beckett.

The greater challenge is really in the later *Texts*, which are increasingly cryptic and preoccupied with tortuous, picayune, and self-canceling deliberations. The astonishing disembodied consciousness of *Text 13*, for instance, is no longer even interested in locating an essence of "self," or in projecting coherence on anyone or anything through the telling of stories. It's like a mind-spirit roaming the ether, and can be just as hard for readers to grasp.

Irwin does "domesticate" this and the other disembodied voices to some extent—as any individual actor would—by resolving them into a singular personality whose private jokes, sillinesses and poetic inclinations we can grasp psychologically. Beyond this, though, his project here involves thwarting the essential "relatedness" of the clown, who, regardless of any ambience of melancholy or misadventure he might possess, always exists for the purpose of entertainment in the audience's mind. The clown is the negative hero par excellence. For my part, though, I was stunned at how Irwin was able to complicate this too tidy picture with both his body and his voice.

He never clowns in this performance in the sense of begging for love, and he always speaks in odd, unexpected phrasings, elongating certain words and swallowing others, sometimes using those strange deliveries to set up arbitrary little adventures for his arms and legs. At one point, for instance, the act of warding off an imaginary blow ("what if finally they had plucked up heart and slightly stressed their blows, just enough to confer death") transforms into a bizarre looping motion for his arm, which then pulls his whole body so badly off balance that he falls. This sort of "play" may not exactly be a mind in the ether, but it's a long way from the cogently broken wholeness of the characters in *Godot* or *Fool Moon*.

There are points—frequent ones—when Irwin's swallowed words and other verbal-musical strategies simply prevent one from hearing or comprehending his lines, and this is when one remembers why Beckett loathed adaptation. There are good reasons why he called some of his later pieces "plays" and others "stories" or "texts." Although his later plays are themselves sometimes dismissed as difficult, they actually contain many effective aids to apprehension, such as repetition and richly ambiguous, nearly still tableaus on which the audience can meditate as it ponders the words. Some adapters have made changes in the nondramatic prose to duplicate these dramatic circumstances—a freedom the Beckett estate would never allow today.

For better or worse, Irwin speaks his four chosen *Texts* as published. His staging (if not always his delivery) is shrewd, fun and uncompromising. At its best it also produces flashes of the uncanny experience of reading these strange journeys into the turbulent void of perception and imagination.

(2000)

American Dreams

Documentary Solo Performance

The Politics of the Mirrored Self

———

I N MID-1995, SHORTLY AFTER THE FINAL DISINTEGRATION OF the five-member, post-Wall directorate of the Berlin Ensemble that left Heiner Müller sole leader, I asked him whether Brecht would continue to be central to that theater's repertory. "Absolutely," he said. The German critics who were then loudly insisting (along with some former members of the directorate) that Brecht was an outdated paradigm were "idiots," and Müller had half a dozen exciting Brecht projects in mind that he hoped to begin in the near future (pending approval by the recalcitrant Brecht heirs) to maintain his theater's provocative political profile. I felt compelled to justify my question, explaining that, in my country, Brecht was not only currently out of fashion but had never been properly *in* fashion, even during his lifetime, not even among the theatrical intelligentsia. Puffing on his cigar, Müller said quietly, "That's because Americans are all innocents." The most difficult audiences in the world, and "the most dangerous people," are "those who feel innocent of everything."

The whiff of intellectual bigotry in these remarks aside, they contain a

truth that reaches beyond Brecht to the general challenges of political theater in the United States. It has been thirty-three years since Guy Debord
coined the term "society of the spectacle" for the conditions of sweeping,
media-driven trivialization and perpetual public distraction that began to
emanate from America to the rest of the consumerist world after the Second World War. By now these conditions are familiar on every continent,
making the primary preoccupations of political theater in many countries
the restitution of elided memory and history, and the canny yet tentative
re-introduction of critical thinking as a species of fun. Müller pinpoints
one of the biggest enduring hurdles in America: for much of its history,
our culture's congratulatory self-image as the world's benefactor, as well
as its deeply ingrained myths of optimism, possibility, and self-reliance,
have made it doggedly resistant to any theater based on guilt.

   This essay is an appreciation of a particular group of contemporary
American solo performers—some of whom do and some of whom don't
acknowledge their ties to the idea of documentary—as a powerful response to this and other challenges. These artists seem to me to fuse a
psychological and political appeal, linking compassion and identification
with objective scrutiny in a way that, though Brecht might not have approved of it, amounts to a new, peculiarly American form of individual-
istic *Verfremdung*.

   The primary artists I have in mind are Anna Deavere Smith, Marc
Wolf, Danny Hoch, and Sarah Jones: not an immediately harmonious
grouping, perhaps, for those who know their work. My linkage of these
artists depends on being able to steer the discussion of solo performance
away from its usual emphasis on identity politics and toward a more elementary debate about the public's receptivity to politics and critical
thinking per se. It also depends on loosening the definition of "documentary" to a point where it could apply as well to John Leguizamo,
Eric Bogosian, Eve Ensler, David Cale, Lisa Kron, Pamela Gien, Spalding
Gray, Dael Orlandersmith, Whoopi Goldberg and dozens of other
soloists whose work may not be a product of field research but is unthinkable apart from the performers' experiences in some degree of first-
hand witnessing.

Guilt and Cunning

Solo performance is, of course, a field rife with self-indulgence and incipient monumental egotism, and I have sat through as many shows demonstrating this as anyone—typically performed by frustrated and mediocre New York actors trying to jump-start their me-machines with sitcom-shallow autobiographical monologues. Over the years, though (as Jo Bonney has marvelously documented in her recent collection *Extreme Exposure: An Anthology of Solo Performance Texts from the Twentieth Century*), a critical mass of serious work has appeared that amounts to much more than a passing trend. Cheap, convenient and seemingly diminutive as it may be, the best solo performance has arrived at a unique political opportunity, a subversive moment of clarity concerning what Debord called the spectacle society's "sham battles between competing versions of alienated power."[1] This refers to the discouraging vagueness and confusion in our age about the exact location and identity of those responsible for material conditions, as well as the public apathy and passivity that follow. Inflated as this claim for soloists may sound, it is justified, and the achievement is all the more impressive in that the art generally contains little direct analysis of power structures or political institutions. Solo shows are built on individual stories, and the choice and handling of those stories determine the art's political strength.

Like everything else, this genre didn't arise in a vacuum. Its individual origins aside (and I'll come back to this topic), it is partly a reaction to what has not worked in larger-scale theater, the past quarter century or so having been a conspicuously dismal period for political theater in America. Happily, we have now emerged from the era of "splinter theater," when many of the country's most politically vital groups voluntarily ghettoized their creative and political energies by playing only to select communities defined by ethnicity, party, gender or geography. But in fact, the basic complacency and unreflectiveness of the commodity-obsessed public have remained largely unaffected by the gradual "mainstreaming" of race- and gender-bending practices, as is also true of the continued use of dated and impotent agit-prop techniques by expressly

"Brechtian" companies such as The San Francisco Mime Troupe and Irondale Ensemble.

The Mime Troupe's play about urban development and gentrification, *City for Sale* (2000), co-written by Joan Holden and Kate Chumley and directed by Keiko Shimosato, was a perfect example of an application of the fifties and sixties "nuts-and-bolts" approach to *Verfremdung* that seems irredeemably naive today. Holden and Chumley were actually very good at clarifying the complexity of the housing issues they raised, but precisely because of that clarity, the cartoonish characterizations and broad clowning in the piece were irritating. The technique seemed to apologize for the material's complexity, like a set of children's theater blatancies arbitrarily imposed on a subtle, adult tale.

If today's general theatergoing public thinks of political theater at all, it most likely thinks of innocuous, media-friendly sketch comedy in the vein of Capitol Steps (a Washington group founded by former Congressional staff members, which prides itself on "giving equally to both sides," inadvertently reflecting the classically cynical corporate attitude toward political donations) or of moralistic parables like *City for Sale* or the plays of Clifford Odets, Lillian Hellman, and Arthur Miller. (The sixties and seventies "social protest drama" of such authors as Imamu Amiri Baraka and Miguel Piñero has dropped off the popular radar.) The sentimental parable tradition of Odets, Hellman and Miller, also sometimes known as American social protest drama, has long been popular and is likely to remain so because, as Brecht pointed out, it allows spectators to congratulate themselves on their sympathetic feelings without seriously questioning their behavior or beliefs. But the sad truth is that the ostensibly anti-sentimental tradition of Brecht is scarcely more effective in our savvy and self-satisfied era. His parables come off much more as didactic exercises in oversimplification than as fervent efforts to make the world appear changeable (the theoretical basis of *Verfremdung*). *City for Sale* is all too typical. Almost every new play written in this tradition leaves me broken-hearted; they invariably start out as passionately told stories about specific people, then end up as underwhelming clichés about, say, the fact that Chicanos exist (as in the California group Culture Clash's 1998 *Culture Clash in Border Town*) or the fact that a powerless woman grasping for sexual independence will be exploited (as in Suzan-Lori Parks' 1999 *In the Blood*).

These are the outlines of the general impasse out of which a few clever forms of guerilla theater, documentary theater, and solo performance have shown possible paths in the information age. "The question is," as the guerilla preacher Reverend Billy put it succinctly when I interviewed him last winter, "how do you tell an 'original' story in 2000?" That is, how do you tell a truly personal tale "that will not be immediately folded into some big meta-story that politicians or the media manufacture?" How can the artist "be heard, and heard politically" by people who do not tolerate being compared with any fictionally drawn category of exploiters and who prefer not to think politically in any case? Effective political art in boom-time America must be cunning—much more so than in previous ages when institutional targets had less complex cosmetics and were less proficient at seeming nebulous—and the documentary impulse is a form of cunning even if its practitioners don't always see it that way. Nearly half a century of media saturation has made us stupider in many ways, but one way it has made us smarter is in our unprecedented familiarity with stories. Among its many other motives, documentary solo performance is a search for a freshness and unpredictability that carries the force of gossip, for powerful topical narratives that are not easily dismissed or second-guessed, and for performance circumstances in which *Verfremdung* becomes a living concept again because the reality of the performer-researcher has been made an active part of the art.

It is crucial to remember, in considering this work, that no previous society has ever placed the sort of burden of self-invention on its citizens that ours does: that of constructing a fully satisfying self from scratch with little more than the trivializing idiocies of consumer and pop culture as guidance. As the social philosopher Zygmunt Bauman recently wrote: "The way individual people define individually their individual problems and try to tackle them deploying individual skills and resources is the sole remaining 'public issue' and the sole object of 'public interest.'"[2] However little we may really be interested in anyone else, we do seem willing to listen to people's individual stories as possible keys to our own individual development—and that is the narrow political opportunity the solo performers exploit. The fact of their authentic individuality (or that of their stories) seems to me far more important in explaining their popularity than any ostensible authenticity in their research, if they even do real research.

Smith and Wolf: Road Pictures

More has been written about Anna Deavere Smith than about any of the other artists under discussion, largely because of the immense public interest in and anxiety over the topics of her pieces *Fires in the Mirror* (directed by Emily Mann in 1992, about the 1991 riots in Crown Heights, Brooklyn, sparked by the accidental killing of a black boy by a rabbi's motorcade and the retaliatory killing of a Jewish student) and *Twilight Los Angeles, 1992* (directed by Christopher Ashley in 1993, about the 1992 riots in Los Angeles, sparked by the acquittal of four police officers for their beating of the unarmed motorist Rodney King). As is well known, both these works were based on the same technique: interviewing large numbers of people about the selected tumultuous events and then impersonating some of them onstage, using their exact words and mannerisms. Smith developed this technique for several years, touring colleges and other forums with commissioned shows based on local hot-button issues (such as feminism and racism at the University of Pennsylvania and the Five Colleges at Amherst), before she became widely known. She also ultimately applied the same method in *House Arrest*, her recent solo piece about the American presidency, although in earlier phases that show employed up to fourteen actors.

Smith's overall title for these linked projects is *On the Road: A Search for American Character*, whose echo of Jack Kerouac's prototypical Beat romance *On the Road* (1957) deserves a moment's pause. As she writes in the introduction to the published text of *Fires in the Mirror*, Smith's goal, like Kerouac's, has as much to do with the act of travel ("The spirit of acting is the *travel* from the self to the other") as with arrival at a destination (such as a preconceived, tendentious political position). Smith says she sets out in her interviews to "find the individuality of the other and experience that individuality viscerally,"[3] implying that her faith in the existence of "authentic speech" and "true character" (phrases she uses elsewhere) is an endorsement of the myth of unfettered individualism—the picaresque vision-quest in search of it—that Kerouac preeminently represents in the postwar era. I consider this implication to be the essence of her political cunning: wittingly or unwittingly, she appeals to a prevailing ideology, seems to flatter it, and then deconstructs it gently and thoroughly in performance. Her strategy is to enshrine the principle of the inviolate, holy Self in order to question and challenge it.

As anyone who saw these works can testify, it was the specificity and savvy with which she, a black woman, inhabited the personas of so many different parties to the conflicts—people of both sexes and various races and classes—that engrossed audiences. Her process of impersonation was at all times more compelling than her facts and information. Her impressions weren't entirely convincing by the standards of fourth-wall realism, and they weren't meant to be. She built the characterizations around penetrating enlargements of isolated traits and mannerisms, but the fact that she was always visible beneath the intensely studied character surfaces was what gave the pieces their strangely persuasive texture. The ever-changing split in her persona assured spectators of the constant presence of a discerning editorial eye and selective, framing hand.

In several interviews Smith has spoken of her process of inhabiting characters who are plainly repellent or guilty of disgraceful deeds, and she unfashionably explains that "love," not "judgement," must be the essence of her task if she is to make such behavior real enough to be submitted to fair criticism. "We're in a weird moment," she told the radio host Lenny Lopate on WNYC in October 2000, "where we think the search for a lie is the same as the search for the truth." But actors must always employ lies in one sense, must "create a fiction to illuminate a truth." Thus (again quoting from *Fires in the Mirror*), she considers her residual "unlikeness" to her characters a "bridge" that encourages openness to metaphor. The conventional, naturalistic, "self-centered" American acting technique, she says, "has taken the metaphor out of acting. It has made the heart smaller, the spirit less gregarious, and the mind less apt to be able to hold on to contradictions or opposition."[4] In the end, what was most moving for me in her performances was the risky and provocatively metaphorical spectacle of an artist imposing form on the agents of a shapeless crisis, of her boldly self-conscious artistic sensibility giving cogent shape to a painfully raw and chaotic reality.

Appropriately enough for a cunning cultural critic, Smith's technique turns out to be transferable. In 1999, a relatively unknown New York actor named Marc Wolf, who gratefully acknowledges his debt to her, applied her method to another selected topic—the U.S. military's "Don't ask, don't tell" policy on homosexuality, which divides millions of Americans as bitterly as issues of race and class. The resulting show, *Another American: Asking & Telling*, which played at the Theater at St. Clement's in New York and then traveled to numerous venues around the country, drew its power from many of the same sources as Smith's pieces. Wolf, who is gay and has no military experience himself, spent three years gathering documentary material and conducting over 200 interviews with people on all sides of this controversy, and he clearly understood as well as Smith did the value of *not* blending completely into his eighteen onstage impersonations.

Just as the immediacy of Smith's performances depended on her physical presence (one reason why her recent film of *Twilight Los Angeles* was unfortunately much less powerful than her stage show), so too did Wolf's. With Smith, for instance, one thought: this woman actually sat with both Reginald Denny and the unapologetic brother of the man who beat him almost to death, and then steeled herself to switch back and forth, within seconds, between their radically opposed points of view. Similarly, with Wolf, one thought: this is the man who tracked down dozens of victims and bigots, activists and establishmentarians, convinced them to open up to him, and then imitated them all with apparently equal enthusiasm. He also promised anonymity to many of them, making the audience aware that careers, and perhaps lives, depended on his secrecy. Neither Smith nor Wolf was a mere actor in any received sense; they were conduits for testimony that might otherwise never be heard and thus possessed a certain secondary "authenticity" as witnesses of witnesses.

Furthermore—and this is a key point—both artists were remarkably good at keeping their performances from feeling tendentious even though their sympathy with certain people and positions was obvious. Wolf was clearly searching for common ground in the fact that gays and military people are both frequent objects of stereotyping, and this sense of "biased fairness" was evident both in the nuanced content of each vignette and in his selection and arrangement of scenes. His play's stories (or pieces of story) seemed to comment on one another like a sequential argument that left each side complexly human. The spookily calm reminiscence of Edward Modesto, for instance, an ex-Army Colonel who served a prison term for dressing in women's clothes, was followed by the smug explanation of the official rationale for "Don't ask, don't tell" by Charles Moskos, the Northwestern University sociologist who helped develop it. Then an unnamed colonel's startlingly honest and persuasive explanation of the danger of tampering with soldiers' macho "warrior ethic" was followed by the recollections of an unabashedly effeminate Vietnam veteran, nicknamed "Mary Alice," whose humor and eccentricity had been crucial in keeping his unit alive.

On a more practical level, both Smith and Wolf also achieved the rare feat of attracting truly integrated audiences. Smith wrote in *Fires in the Mirror* that some of her main goals were to "1) bring people together into the same room (the theater) who would normally not be together, and 2) attract people to the theater who don't usually come to the theater."[5] The same is true of Danny Hoch, whom I'll discuss in a moment, and of John Leguizamo, whose 1998 solo show *Freak: A Semi-Demi-Quasi-Pseudo Autobiography* (about growing up Hispanic in Jackson Heights, Queens) attracted the most racially and generationally diverse Broadway audiences that I've seen since *Twilight Los Angeles, 1992,* partly because of his insistence that thirteen-dollar tickets be available for every performance. A May 2000 *Washington Post* feature article about *Another American* quoted a retired navy Captain who attended Wolf's show in uniform at the Studio Theater in Washington: "You try to change attitudes. You don't do it by giving statistics, you do it by telling stories like these." Wolf added, "They're stories that military people are not supposed to tell, so by inference the American community is not supposed to know them."[6]

Wolf's remark touches on the root idea that binds together all this work: violating public secrets. Solo artists foil invisibility and stigmatization, and though the reasons their subjects are invisible and stigmatized differ in each case, the basic strategy is always the same. By speaking the unspeakable, making the seemingly unremarkable remarkable, or simply by leaving the impression of having been "on location" (the defining notion of documentary), these artists destroy the simplistic scaffolding that prevents fuller truths from being recognized.

The Documentary Idea: Alone Again, Naturally

Let me digress briefly in order to clarify how the documentary concept does and doesn't seem to me valuable in describing these performers' work. In recent decades, there has been a great deal of hand-wringing among critics and journalists over deliberate misrepresentation and indifference to truth in the mass media, which has made it difficult to speak on anything but the crudest level about factual representation and its inherent quandaries. Because we are lied to regularly and shamelessly in other media (in the form of spin, staged news, docudrama, infomercials and more), it has sometimes been suggested by prominent theater practitioners that theater should be preserved as a pillar of integrity regarding the reliability of documentation and of fact presented as such (a bizarre thought when you consider the historical mistrust of theater and theater people).

This idea harks back to Peter Weiss's effort in the 1960s to distinguish his work from that of Rolf Hochhuth and others who blended fact and fiction more obviously than he did in an effort to keep audiences and readers interested. Weiss wrote that, ideally, "documentary theater shuns all invention . . . in opposition to the incoherent mass of information which constantly assails us from every side."[7] More recently, Eric Bentley (author of the 1972 documentary drama *Are You Now or Have You Ever Been?*, about the House Un-American Activities Committee [HUAC] investigation of the entertainment industry) inveighed against docudrama by complaining that it was a way for an author-director to "have it both ways and, while strongly suggesting one version of the facts, also [avoid] affirming anything for sure." The only way to avoid this "boomerang," which leaves viewers "free to think that the fictions are facts . . . [and] equally free to think that the facts are fictions," is to "abide by a clear set of rules that the audience will understand, whereby no fiction will be foisted on them as fact."[8]

Deliberate misrepresentation is obviously reprehensible. And there is no question that plays and films in which the reliability of fact is paramount have been very valuable over the years, both educationally and historically. For the purposes of this essay, however, I set aside such material as "historical drama and film," distinguishing it from "documentary drama and film" by pointing out that the purpose of the former is principally to inform and entertain, not to change the audience's perceptions of its own world. These definitions are difficult to keep separate, of course. The strength of the latter form, however, radiates from the fact that it never pretends to a detached objectivity that isn't really possible.

Elsewhere in the essays just quoted, both Weiss and Bentley suggest that they, too, understand the impossibility—indeed the undesirability—of keeping fact innocent of fiction. All arranged presentations of facts are inevitably editorialized. As the playwright and poet Sergei Tretyakov said as early as 1927 about Soviet documentary film, the question is always one of "gradation in the falsification," and an artist's priority is necessarily "on the attraction, on the effect."[9] Weiss provides a good illustration, since he prided himself on composing *The Investigation* entirely out of minimally altered excerpts from the Frankfurt trial transcripts of the Auschwitz murderers. One of the most unforgettably immediate experiences I've had in the theater was a staged reading of that work in Germany

1. *Anna Deavere Smith in* Twilight: Los Angeles, *1992, 1993.* CREDIT: JAY THOMPSON.

2. *Marc Wolf in* Another American: Asking & Telling, *1999.* CREDIT: CAROL ROSEGG.

3. *Danny Hoch in* Jails, Hospitals and Hip-Hop, *1998.* CREDIT: PAULA COURT.

4. *Sarah Jones in* Surface Transit, *2000.*

in 1988 (memorializing the fiftieth anniversary of *Kristallnacht*) that was cast exclusively with actors in their seventies and eighties—that is, with actors who had literally been witnesses. Several days afterward, however, it occurred to me that neither I nor most of the other spectators really had any idea whether those actors had been in Germany during the Holocaust or whether they'd been Nazis or not, any more than we knew with certainty that Weiss had accurately transcribed the trial transcripts. The play, in other words, had had its effect, and like all documentary audiences we had trusted in others (professional experts in competition with the documentarian at hand, presumably) to verify questions of verity.

Documentary is perforce a loose concept. It is nothing more than a tacit agreement by artist and audience to meet on a chosen field of presumably factual reference; to make the rules tighter than that would drain it of dramatic impact. A common truism in the field of film and television documentary is that the secret is to follow people around until they say what you want them to say. Cynicism aside, however, a similar editorial imperative pertains to the arrangement of materials in documentary theater.

As many commentators have pointed out, the "theater of fact" (Kenneth Tynan's term), or "theater of testimony" (Emily Mann's), tends to be woefully perishable in any case, its appeal closely linked with the media age's craven appetites for the "purely" voyeuristic and confessional. Writing recently in *The New York Times*, Charles Marowitz stated and then overstated this case, declaring that all "manufactured authenticity" and "neo-naturalism" on the stage—such as Brian Johnstone's *Lifegame*, Rob Berger and company's *Charlie Victor Romeo*, and David Mamet's dialogue—represented a "drought of imagination": "By appropriating real-life people in real-life circumstances, artists have turned themselves into poachers and the public into voyeurs."[10] Just as there is no point in condemning all fact-based material en masse this way, there is also no point in aspiring to a factual purity that contravenes the theater's gloriously slippery nature. The best documentary theater ingests the medium's inherent duplicity and also recognizes (as mentioned earlier) the public's sophistication regarding stories and its resistance to guilt.

In 1998, the visual artists Jochen and Esther Gerz organized another public reading of Weiss's *The Investigation* in Germany. The Gerzes had the text read aloud by 300 volunteer non-actors—subscribers of the Hebbel Theater, the Berliner Ensemble, and the Volksbühne—and the result was an insufferable spectacle of armchairish psycho-purgation penetratingly described by one critic as "political karaoke."[11] The situation was uncomfortably similar at the May 2000 New York premiere of *The Laramie Project*, a work by Moises Kaufman and the Tectonic Theater Project based on some 200 interviews with the people of Laramie, Wyoming, about the homophobic murder of Matthew Shepard. This unquestionably loving and earnest piece claimed to be about the self-exploration of the Tectonic company members as much as their reportage about the Laramie townspeople, but (partly because there were eight actors) this self-exploration was dilute and superficial, giving the whole affair an air of self-congratulation and implying that it would have worked equally well, or better, on video. At the time I wondered: was this really just a weak text that good actors simply couldn't make compelling? Or did the very presence of more than one actor actually make the text seem weaker than it was by defocusing—continually interrupting and restarting—the audience's imaginary engagement and identification with the many different characters?

My general experience over the past two decades has been that group documentary plays are almost always disposable, their full power dependent on the ephemeral newsworthiness of their topics. This danger is much less with solo pieces. (Again, let me stress that I'm not speaking of commonplace historical drama, which can also take the form of solo works, such as William Luce's *Barrymore*, Pam Gems' *Marlene*, and Martin Sherman's *Rose*.) Consider, for instance, the four "plays of testimony" in Emily Mann's 1997 volume *Testimonies*. The public issues at the center of the later works, *Execution of Justice* (1984) and *Greensboro: A Requiem* (1996), had enormous news value in their time, and the private ones that dominate *Still Life* (1980) and *Annulla* (1977, revised 1985) had none, yet the earlier two works (particularly *Annulla*, essentially a solo piece) read as fresher and more stageworthy today than the others. The main reason seems to me that both are basically portrait studies constructed as self-analytical monologues.

The self-analytical monologue is no guarantee of profundity, of course, as David Hare's pseudo-questing travelogue *Via Dolorosa* demonstrated on Broadway in 1999. Describing his experiences during a 1997 trip to Israel, Hare elucidated, through many quotes and reported conversations, not only the Israeli-Palestinian conflict but also various political issues relating to the factionalizing of Israelis and Arabs. In his stage debut at age fifty-one, however, he was utterly inept at illuminating the relationship of the teller to this wide-ranging tale. He spoke frequently of "faith" and "homeland," for instance, but his revelations about those matters were few, shallow, and detached. Moreover, his embarrassingly wooden gestures, badly strained voice, and inability to characterize the people he quoted homogenized the emotional tenor of the show and made one wonder whether he was aware that he occasionally came off as, say, a colonialist snob (mocking a settler's ignorance of Trevor Nunn, for instance), an egotist (scoffing at a woman's ignorance that he wrote *Plenty*), and a phrasemaker ("Myself, I would like Jerusalem more if it weren't so important").[12]

In 1968, the television producer Arthur Barron wrote a provocative essay distinguishing between two divergent traditions in documentary that is applicable to the media-age bias I'm describing. On the one hand, Barron wrote, is the historical paradigm, an emphasis on "film as knowledge" leading to the belief that "documentary's chief function is in energizing, motivating, and informing the masses by rendering the complex issues of the day understandable and meaningful"—the tradition of Louis and Auguste Lumière, John Grierson and the British School, V.I. Pudovkin, Sergey Eisenstein, the Office of War Information, "CBS Reports," "NET Journal" and much more. On the other hand is the personal paradigm, an emphasis on film as emotion and drama whose seminal documentary figure was Robert Flaherty and whose other exponents include D.A. Pennebaker, Richard Leacock, Albert and David Maysles, William Jersey, and Ed Pincus. This "personal documentary" tradition focuses not on "great issues" but on "human events in human scale..."

not topicality, but timelessness . . . not expertise and authority, but ordinary, real, human beings swept up in the currents of life,"[13] and our preference for it defines an important aspect of taste in our age.

We lean toward the personal paradigm perhaps partly out of journalistic laziness (it requires less homework) and in part out of a deeper-seated postmodern preference for micro- over macro- and metanarratives. But more significantly, I think, we choose the personal because of our culture's more and more overpowering ethic of self-actualization. The more we fetishize independence and nurture the narcissism that supports and girds it, the more self-conscious we begin to be about mirrors. Solo artists turn the mirror into a political tool (recall Smith's *Fires in the Mirror*). They provide the audience with opportunities to identify with the other through a transformed single individual and thus bring the power of the mirror to the representation of otherness.

Hoch and Jones: I am a Camera

Thirty-year-old Danny Hoch says he grew up in a forsaken neighborhood in Queens called Lefrak City, though his mother, who raised him alone, insists they really lived in Forest Hills. In any case, his formative experiences didn't revolve around the expected skin privileges of a white kid from a "nominally Jewish household," as he calls it. No culture was dominant on the streets where he spent his time, and he describes hip-hop as the "common language" among his diverse friends. The two solo pieces for which he has become nationally known, *Some People* (1993) and *Jails, Hospitals & Hip-Hop* (1998), both directed by Jo Bonney, are collections of fictional character sketches in which he mimics a remarkable variety of New York voices and attitudes with astonishing precision, familiarity and insight. His people range from a Caribbean radio host taking poignant calls from listeners in the dead hours of early morning, to a Polish handyman with execrable English who nevertheless manages to insinuate an array of complex feelings for his absent wife and the woman he's helping around the house, to a teenage "homeboy" practicing his hip-hop routine while banging on a box and talking more revealingly than he knows about his ex-girlfriend, to a Cuban father reluctantly visiting a therapist after the police killed his son, to a Puerto Rican guy "accidentally" crippled in a police shootout who tries to chat up a girl in a hospital waiting room, to a white, teenage wannabe gangsta-rapper from Montana who imagines himself interviewed by Jay Leno but keeps getting interrupted by his mother.

Hoch stresses in the introduction to the published texts of his shows that he doesn't consider himself a documentarian: "A few people think I am some anthropological/theatrical case-study guy. But I don't tape-record or interview people to then play them on stage. This is my world! These are my inner monologues, layered composites of stories and voices from me, my family, my neighborhood, my people." Nevertheless, as he himself admits a few lines later, the exoticism and foreignness (and I would add, the specificity and realism) of his characters are key factors in the notoriety he has gained in middle-class theatrical venues where people like his characters rarely go. "I think all the hoopla about my work comes from people simply not being accustomed to seeing traditionally peripheral characters placed center stage. Well, these characters are center stage in *my* world."[14]

Still later he muses candidly on skin privilege and its vocal equivalent: "I often wonder if my skin were darker, or if I couldn't flip my linguistics during meetings to sound 'businesslike and un-threatening' (I swear somebody said that to me), if I would have had the success I've had with these two shows. Was I a 'safe in' to the 'disenfranchised voices of America' for the rich and middle class? Maybe."[15] His honesty recalls the scholar Sandra Richards's remark that "a viewer's sense of the ease with which [Anna Deavere] Smith [switches] racial identities is aided by the fact that she is a light-skinned African-American woman."[16] Unlike Smith, though, Hoch has had the effect of his art questioned in public by at least one critic, who complains he "never decides what view to take of his subjects" (Jessica Winter, writing about the 1999 film *Whiteboyz*, co-written by and starring Hoch as a lead character modeled on the Montana kid "Flip" from *Jails*).[17] The solo performer Dael Orlandersmith

has similarly questioned whether Hoch's work is an inadvertent adver-
tisement for "gangsta-chic"—the trend perpetuated by corporations like
Tommy Hilfiger that encourages white suburban fantasies about the
coolness of being inner-city-black.[18]

My own view is that Hoch isn't peddling any particular fantasies.
Fantasy is his dominant theme, complemented by the complex denial
mechanisms that so often buttress fantasy. The political provocation in
his art begins with his willingness to travel this territory without tiptoe-
ing around questions of race and class. Furthermore, rappers make up
only a small portion of his hugely varied dramatis personae (although
admittedly they provide high points in both his solo shows). The most
startling aspect of these shows is the detail and perceptions of the figures. If all solo performers are cameras to an extent (another twist on the
documentary idea), then Hoch is a remarkably acute and sensitive instrument. He simply sees more in the models that become his figures
than most people expect of any actor-author—especially of one dealing
with such a bitterly polarized (and hence usually reductive) arena—and
thus anyone who needs to know too quickly or categorically what he is
"representing" is bound to be confused and disappointed.

Hoch's purpose isn't just to "keep it real" as a white rapper. He is interested in the myth of "keeping it real," in the profusion of open questions about what the "real" is in a society saturated with "simulations"
(Jean Baudrillard) and "prefabricated 'pseudo-events'" (Guy Debord)
that affect the aspirations of the disenfranchised and enfranchised alike.
He sees that "thug life" is a veneer used to manufacture moral superiority ("It's just cooler to be the oppressed than the oppressor. Who wants
to be the oppressor? Shit, not me").[19] Moreover, television, the watching
of television, and resentment at television's distortions of reality are mentioned in almost every one of his vignettes (a repetition that makes the
theater seem like his preferred means of illuminating and apprehending
the world, as well as the best means of forcing such reality-rumination
on a spectacle-benumbed audience). His people swagger and bluster
about their goals, principles, pride and (in the case of the rappers) media-
dreams while betraying the most intimate feelings of shame, ignorance,

powerlessness and self-hatred, and this layering creates an impression of doubling that is as Brechtian (as effectively *verfremdet*) as any performance of Smith's.

When Hoch quickly clips on a pair of earrings to play a young Puerto Rican woman named Blanca who ridicules her bisexual boyfriend's suggestion that they use a condom, for instance, he changes his accent but not his comfortable baritone vocal register, inviting us to think as much about the performance of Blanca's character as about her life circumstances. And when he rolls up his pant leg to play a motormouthed, angrily intelligent prison inmate walking to get a toothbrush with a newcomer, telling him to "just plead guilty" and explaining how he was arrested when a cop flew into a rage at his indeterminate race, Hoch also steers attention toward the dangerously blind social game of self-representation. (The advice to "just plead guilty" comes from the inmate's presumptions about the judge's presumptions about the character who is not seen, who is also of indeterminate race). Every sketch in Hoch's shows is as preoccupied with the business of looking shrewdly at the process looking as it is with the enacted pictures and behaviors themselves.

Sarah Jones is another soloist who works these same fields of perception, and is as keen an observer of character as Hoch, but because she is female and dark skinned (she's actually the product of a mixed marriage), she necessarily reaps a different crop. Jones is a twenty-five-year-old actor and hip-hop poet who won the 1997 Nuyorican Poets Cafe Grand Slam Championship and developed a solo piece called *Surface Transit* about eight fictional New Yorkers, which Hoch produced at P.S. 122 in 2000. Directed by Gloria Feliciano, her piece, like Hoch's work, is a tour de force of transformation with an astonishing variety of characters, and several situations in it are analogous to situations in his shows. *Surface Transit* spins a significant variation, though, by establishing links, some distant and some intimate, between the characters in its vignettes.

Pasha, for instance, is a Russian immigrant and the widow of a black American who speaks with brittle courage to her daughter while making cornrows in the child's blond hair. The figure presented after her is Lorraine Levine, the elderly, narrow-minded and bigoted Jewish woman

Pasha cares for, who is capriciously thinking of firing her and who fills her time by making mischief with various lies and half-truths over the phone. And later, Joey, a deactivated Italian-American cop, turns out to be the former best friend of Levine's son—a fact we learn only near the end of his long, crude harangue to his psychiatrist about his rage at losing this friend to the "illness" of homosexuality. So it goes in grim and violent but also sometimes incongruously bright and humane circularity—a richly varied world in which everyone is, poignantly, estranged by only one degree of separation. The circle of submerged connectedness is like a round dance reminiscent of Arthur Schnitzler's *Reigen* (*La Ronde*), with the universal denominator of sex in *La Ronde* replaced by the quintessentially American denominator of self-invention.

Here, as with Hoch, Smith, and Wolf, it is the precision of the portrayals that supervenes—the meticulousness of the accents and the exactitude of the coughing, cackling, sitting, handling the phone—as well as the jarring contrasts between performer and characters, which stun the audience into a political receptiveness that the stories alone probably wouldn't generate. Jones's own self-confidence and severe, statuesque beauty, for instance, provide an extremely strange and unsettling foil for Pasha's heartsick determination and fragile humility. The three characters closest to Jones herself establish these contrasts most powerfully, however, because they are written with the greatest originality and acted with the most affection and sympathy.

Sugar Jones (note the name) is a black, British, unemployed actress who becomes imprudently emotional while narrating a past sexual assault (by Joey, it turns out) during an audition for a reality-TV show called *SICK* (*Seven Immigrants, a Campsite, and Kayak*). Rashid is a young recovering rapper who relapses into marvelous hip-hop rhymes while leading a meeting of "the reformed MC wannabe-Junior Mafia revolutionary new Black Panther society of Hunter College." And Keisha Ray is Rashid's strong-willed and confident girlfriend who, tired of fending off predatory males while waiting for a bus, launches into a magnificent feminist response to Gil Scott-Heron's "The revolution will not be televised": "your revolution will not happen between these thighs/

the real revolution/ain't about booty size/the Versaces you buys/or the Lexus you drives."[20] These three sketches lift the production beyond the sententiousness and stereotyping that sometimes seeped into the earlier scenes, steering it toward a broader commonsensical feminism built on compassion and sophisticated fairness. In the end, the two seemingly antagonistic hip-hop poems, male and female, proudly complement and strengthen each other. Rashid's anti-commodity machismo is held up against Keisha Ray's patriarchy-popping hubris. There is no question of parochialism, naiveté, or tendentiousness because the human "camera" in front of us is far too trustworthy in its own right.

The greatest political strength of Hoch, Jones, Smith, and Wolf is that they are themselves caught in the social maelstroms they invite us to probe and understand. They are meticulous mimics but also courageous explorers of both the flattering and the unflattering sides of the others they choose as alter egos. Like the creators of all political theater in America, solo performers must negotiate the terrain of guilt, mined though it is, but they have an important edge in accomplishing that: the transparency of their self-reference. That is why I call their risky project of self-characterization by opposition and contrast an all-American version of *Verfremdung*. This notion is paradoxical in basic ways. Brecht's very reason for proposing "estrangement" was to show that supposedly "natural" and "inevitable" events and behaviors were part of human-controlled historical processes and were thus changeable through volitional action; he avoided Naturalism because its positivist ethos seemed inconsistent with that aim. The idea that being swept up in any sociopolitical maelstrom might be politically useful to an artist would have been entirely foreign to him.

Nearly half a century after his death, however, in the land whose HUAC investigations sped his return to Europe, Americans sympathetic to his goals necessarily pursue them based on a more particularized view of American society than he ever applied. The grip of psychological realism on the American imagination, for instance, has outlasted decades of avant-gardist efforts to dislodge it, and the style is now divorced from its positivist heritage and available to the Left, the Right, and the apolitical alike.

Today, a generation after feminists insisted that "the personal is political," the personal dominates politics as much as it does drama in theater, film, and television. (Furthermore, according to a recent article by Sue-Ellen Case, the detached attitude of the smoker that Brecht proposed is now a figure for patriarchal remoteness.)[21] For politically minded, information-age Americans, estrangement lives primarily as a means of seeing ourselves voyeuristically seeing ourselves, as a non-mediated form of self-actualization based on critiques of self-actualization. Ours is an era obsessed with witnessing, and an effective *Verfremdung* is nothing less than a reason to consider one sort of witnessing more persuasive than another.

NOTES

1. Guy Debord, *The Society of the Spectacle*, trans. Donald Nicholson-Smith (NY: Zone, 1995), 36.

2. Zygmunt Bauman, *Liquid Modernity* (Cambridge: Polity, 2000), 72.

3. Anna Deavere Smith, *Fires in the Mirror* (NY: Anchor, 1993), xxvi-xxvii.

4. Ibid., xxix.

5. Ibid., xxviii.

6. Steve Vogel, "A Telling Theatrical Experience," *The Washington Post*, May 17, 2000, A25.

7. Peter Weiss, "Fourteen Propositions for a Documentary Theatre," *World Theatre*, V. 17, N. 5-6, 1968, 375-77.

8. Eric Bentley, *Thinking About the Playwright: Comments from Four Decades* (Evanston, IL: Northwestern Univ. Press, 1987), 189-90.

9. Sergey Tretyakov, Victor Shklovsky, Esther Shub and Osip Brik, "Symposium on Soviet Documentary," in *The Documentary Tradition: From Nanook to Woodstock*, ed. Lewis Jacobs (NY: Hopkinson and Blake, 1971), 30.

10. Charles Marowitz, "Let's Not Forgo Imagination for Voyeurism," *New York Times*, Oct. 29, 2000, 5, 22.

11. Harald Martenstein, "Karaoke für den Kopf," *Der Tagespiegel*, May 27, 1998.

12. David Hare, *Via Dolorosa and When Shall We Live* (London: Faber & Faber, 1999), 37.

13. Arthur Barron, "Toward New Goals in Documentary," in *The Documentary Tradition: From Nanook to Woodstock*, ed. Lewis Jacobs (NY: Hopkinson and Blake, 1971), 476-77.

14. Danny Hoch, *Jails, Hospitals & Hip-Hop and Some People* (NY: Villard, 1998), xiv.

15. Ibid., xv.

16. Sandra Richards, "Caught in the Act of Social Definition: *On the Road* with Anna Deavere Smith," in *Acting Out: Feminist Performances*, ed. Lynda Hart and Peggy Phelan (Ann Arbor: Univ. of Michigan Press, 1993), 52.

17. Jessica Winter, "Corn Doggy Dogg," *Village Voice*, Oct. 6-12, 1999. Smith's art has been publicly questioned at times, but not (to my knowledge) for the same reasons. When she performed *Twilight: Los Angeles, 1992* in Los Angeles, for instance, local performers complained that she was an outsider opportunistically appropriating their stories and seizing a limelight that properly should have been theirs.

18. Somini Sengupta, "A Multicultural Chameleon: Actor's Experience Spawns Polyglot Cast of Characters," *New York Times*, Oct. 9, 1999, B1, 7.

19. Hoch, xvii.

20. Quoted from Sarah Jones, "Surface Transit," unpublished ms.

21. Sue-Ellen Case, "'Wer raucht, sieht kaltblütig aus': Brecht, Müller, and Cigars," *drive b: brecht 100 (Theater der Zeit Arbeitsbuch/The Brecht Yearbook* 23), 1998, 163-9.

The Gospel According to Billy

HIS PULPIT, WHEN HE PERFORMS IN THEATERS, IS A RED *Village Voice* distribution box stolen from a street corner, with his own picture displayed in the window. He wears a clerical collar over a black shirt and a white dinner jacket, the bleached-blond tips of his Roy Orbison hairdo adding just the right touch to his uncannily accurate Jimmy Swaggart imitation. He rushes in, flashes a politician's smile, and begins preaching to his typically hip, downtown congregation of faithful non-believers: "We believe in the God that people who don't believe in God believe in. Hallelujah!"

This is Reverend Billy, a.k.a. Bill Talen, minister of the Church of Stop Shopping, and over the last few years, his brand of mock-evangelism poised on the border of real belief has risen to lucent prominence in the depressed landscape of radical theater in New York. Talen is a self-sacrificial political gadfly, a theatrical species generally given up for dead in the United States—Alisa Solomon calls him "the Al Sharpton of the ultra-ironic yet politically committed Downtown set"—and like his spiritual predecessors in the 1960s, he doesn't confine himself to the controlled environments of auditoriums and playhouses. With startling information-age savvy, he also dreams up pointed and often hilarious guerilla theater for (in his words) "the tight proscenium arches that are in the subways, in the lobbies of buildings, and in parks."

In 1997 Talen began preaching on the sidewalk outside the Times Square Disney Store, eventually conducting numerous "preach ins" and political actions inside the store, which led to several arrests. During the same period, he also preached ninety-second sermons as Reverend Billy on National Public Radio's "Morning Edition" and performed the character in solo plays at various venues around New York City. By the end of 1999, no less to his surprise than to anyone else's, he had become a lightning rod for the creative and political aspirations of an extraordinary range of other theater artists and community groups.

The week-long festival he organized and co-hosted in December of that year at Judson Memorial Church, called "Millennium's Neighborhood (Not a Celebration of the Malling of New York)," drew more than 1200 spectators on its first night, despite no pre-opening coverage in the city's major newspapers. Conceived as an alternative to the Disney-led millennium celebrations in Times Square, it was devoted to the causes of resisting consumerism, battling the encroachment of corporate monoculture in New York, and (in Talen's words) reclaiming "contested and surveilled public spaces." It began with a "permitless parade" from Charas Community Center (a former public school that New York City is trying to sell for luxury development) to Judson Church, led by two men bearing aluminum crucifixes with large Mickey and Minnie dolls ducttaped to them. Performances and exhibitions by some eighty artists, pranksters, and activists followed, among them, the Surveillance Camera Players, who led group addresses to the cameras attached to street lamps in Washington Square Park, and the labor advocate Charles Kernaghan, who arrived directly from the World Trade Organization protests in Seattle and delivered a fiery lecture on Central American sweatshops.

Talen now enjoys a unique seriocomic celebrity. He not only has a growing following as a performer but is also frequently sought out by local groups just as an actual spiritual leader might be. During 2000, he was at the center of protests against the efforts of New York University to tear down a 19-century building in which Edgar Allan Poe once lived and replace it with a tower for the law school, and he was arrested again several times for that. His main work, however, is on his own quasi-sacred stage: he conducts comic church services featuring clownish deacons, obscene exorcisms, propagandistic canonizations, and a gender-bent gospel choir, usually leading his audience out of the theater afterward to commit a political action on the theme of the evening. These actions have included defacing a dot-com billboard in Silicon Alley, applying orange stickers to Starbucks logos to replace the mermaid's missing nipples, and hiding a cassette player behind the toys in the Disney Store in order to disturb the utopian environment with "anti-shopping speech." (One example of such speech: an interview with the Middle Eastern food sellers who were evicted from the lobby of the old Selwyn Theater—now the American Airlines Theater—in the preparatory purge for the new Times Square).

Born in Minnesota in 1950, Talen was brought up in a Dutch Calvinist tradition, which he rejected at sixteen. After graduating from Franconia College in New Hampshire and occasionally taking part in anti-war and civil rights protests, he moved to San Francisco and became a performer, honing various storytelling routines incorporating music and poetry. His transformation into a staunchly political artist occurred while he was co-artistic director of Life on the Water, a theater in Fort Mason that hosted radical and marginalized groups from around the world, as well as prominent author-actors from New York such as Spalding Gray, Reno, Holly Hughes and John Kelly. Watching these artists perform convinced Talen that he had to concentrate on his own art.

He moved to New York in 1994 and became an artist-in-residence at St. Clement's Church, where he began developing the Reverend Billy character under the guidance of Sidney Lanier. Lanier—the former vicar of St. Clement's, Tennessee Williams' cousin, and the model ("only the noble parts," he says) for the character T. Lawrence Shannon in *Night of the Iguana*—helped Talen through what had become a serious spiritual crisis by giving him religious readings by the pre-Christian Gnostics, scholars Elaine Pagels and John Dominic Crossen, and others. Talen related these to the tactics and values of his own comedian-heroes—chiefly

Lenny Bruce and Andy Kaufman—began studying the demeanors of preachers in New York's Pentecostal churches, and found himself with an act whose power no one could have anticipated.

One has to see Reverend Billy in action to truly understand his allure. At first glance, he is easily confused with a simple parody preacher in the vein of Don Novello's Father Guido Sarducci from *Saturday Night Live*, but to watch him through an evening's performance is to realize he is engaged in a much more complex (and benevolent) deception that harks back to P. T. Barnum and Herman Melville's *Confidence Man*. Talen co-opts the persona of a right-wing televangelist and uses it to awaken actual spiritual hungers in his ostensibly impious audiences. Faced with what the philosopher Ernst Bloch once called the "swindle of fulfillment" in rampant consumerism, Talen nullifies it temporarily with his own counter-swindle, which is all the more effective for being obviously phony and live.

Flooding the halls he performs in with an astonishing torrent of righteous words about the spell of consumer narcosis, he ends up offering hundreds of hard-core artsy skeptics (often in their twenties) their first chance ever to shout "Hallelujah!" and engage in Pentecostal call-and-response. In so doing, they find themselves possessed of a precious community not accessed via flickering screens, as well as a delightful channel for various inchoate angers he has done them the service of naming. Just as a placebo is sometimes more effective than medicine, a phony preacher is sometimes more comforting and inspiring than a real one. Talen's subjects range from the encroachment of deadly suburban blight on the city's neighborhoods (proliferating Gaps, Banana Republics, Starbuckses, and the like), to the outsized role a media giant like Disney plays in shaping American values and determining who is seen as an American, to the general debasement of a democracy that now defines freedom as consumer choice.

Talent and charisma aside, much of his effectiveness has to do with his lucidity about the differences between making radical theater today and doing it in the 1960s—an era when religious trappings and rituals were embraced by groups such as The Living Theater, The Bread and Puppet

Theater, and Jerzy Grotowski's Polish Theater Laboratory with an earnestness that would now seem naive. Talen taps the lode of emotion behind religious expression in a much more sophisticated and ironic fashion. He doesn't rely on the hollow superiority of irony, though, but rather uses sophistication as an enticement into a no-pressure self-searching process that his audiences are prepared to accept. It's a delicate operation, as he explained in an interview in February 2000, "because the whole 'spiritual' thing has been completely hijacked. All the language has been hijacked by people we're in mortal combat against: if it's not the right-wing fundamentalists, then it's the New Agers, who are just as fundamentalist. But if you start by simply saying 'stop shopping!', and stop right there, then suddenly we're all at the edge of this abyss together and it's the beginning of an invitation back into your own individual chaos."

Communities are solidified by adversity, the partisan bonds formed and strengthened by action against a common problem or enemy, and Talen's key perception is that the lived reality of consumerism, murky though its contours are, can serve this purpose if described with appropriate humor and intelligence. He is a penetrating observer of what Nigel Thrift has famously called "soft capitalism," referring to the late 20th-century shift from a "hard," factory-based, locally rooted economy whose power-brokers cultivated images of control, leadership and steady management to a global, extraterritorial, more loosely organized one in which young executives style themselves as rebels and corporations purvey metaphors of deracination and unaccountability such as "dancing" and "surfing." Those who run today's international economy are so dispersed, hard to identify, and responsible to different interests that any totalizing picture is prima facie too complicated to fan any flames of protest. Thus, like all good preachers, Talen zeroes in on selected issues, such as the use of public space and de facto media censorship, and artfully fits them into a larger picture while telling and enacting engaging stories.

Public space is a perfect subject for his sort of theatrical intervention because the tool of protest—theater—is itself an example of the sort of non-commodity-centered interactive human engagement that malls, airports, corporate plazas and the like are deliberately designed to discourage.

Reverend Billy preaching on the sidewalk outside the Times Square Disney Store, 1999. CREDIT: MICHAEL RUBOTTOM.

Similarly, the commercially circumscribed content of mass media is a natural target for any brand of live performance designed to operate subversively beneath the mediated radar of mass culture. Talen says: "It is my feeling that in the Age of Information most statements can't carry progressive values. Such words disappear in thin air, become instantly nostalgic or stylistic. We seem to lack a critical culture right now. Why? Information carries meaning hypnotically but not powerfully. Stories, in contrast, create meaning when we observe the experience of a changing individual." By "stories" he means the kind Walter Benjamin described in "The Storyteller" that pass down "counsel" or individual wisdom, which are increasingly melted down and remolded to serve the culture's corporate super-narrative, or else ignored by the media.

Reverend Billy is hardly the first to take aim at these targets, of course. What sets him apart from other theatrical prophets of capitalist excess, however, is his understanding that effective critique must point inward and outward at the same time. As Daniel Harris concedes at the beginning of his excellent recent book on the aesthetics of consumerism, *Cute, Quaint, Hungry and Romantic*, it is ridiculous to "single out corporations as the source of all that is crude, manipulative, and mercenary in our society, while...whitewash[ing] the consumer as a helpless victim....If there *is* a conspiracy, we ourselves are its tacticians, as well as its beneficiaries. The aesthetics of consumerism are not foisted upon us; they emerge out of a rich and imaginative collaboration between the forces of capitalism and our own fears and desires. If there is kitsch in our daily lives, it is because there is kitsch in our minds." One has only to visit Reverend Billy's amusing and informative Web site (www.revbilly.com), with its sincere invitation to "confess your shopping sins" via e-mail, to appreciate his grasp of this complicity.

Talen's array of corporate targets over the years has also shown an awareness of the need to adjust his tactics to subtler moral questions and more complex attachments by his young audience. He has progressed from Disney (the classic, arrogantly despotic multinational trying to impose its regimented and sentimentally sanitized world-view on idiosyncratic New York City), to Starbucks (a young, fast-rising multinational giving lip service to social consciousness as it rapaciously expands), to NYU, one of the largest landowners in Manhattan, which Talen calls "the quintessential abusive non-profit" because of its architectural depredations in Greenwich Village. (In January 2001, after weeks of well-publicized protests and street theater around the Poe House, NYU agreed to a settlement in which the design of its law school tower was altered to incorporate the Poe House facade and restore it to its original 1845 appearance. Several interior elements will also be preserved and a room will be dedicated to Poe and made available for readings and lectures.) An important precedent for Reverend Billy's wilier actions in the Disney Store is the subversive form called "invisible theater" invented by Augusto Boal for use during the period of military rule in Brazil—and this connection makes sense in that different ideological tyrannies nevertheless invite similar responses. The greater challenge for Talen, though, has been in adapting such techniques to his other campaigns.

My favorite example of this is the "Starbucks Invasion Kit" sent out by e-mail to followers in New York and made available on his Web site in the summer of 2000, whose main feature is a script intended to be spoken loudly (and improvised on) by two people seated at a cafe table.

THE NEO LIBERAL AND THE HAPPY FETUS

NL: The music at Starbucks is just perfect.

HF: I don't care about perfect—the music could be Barry Manilow.

NL: Understated. A selection from early Miles, old Cuban music, world music...

HF: I'm just happy to have Starbucks wrapped around me like a prophylactic. I don't have to deal with New York craziness.

NL: It's a script for me, Starbucks. They've given me a soundtrack and a drug to make my heart race and now I'm the romantic lead in some kind of movie... some vague movie... don't you feel that? I'm just waiting to start the scene of a movie, sitting here. It's a nice wait. A nice moment, just before the moment where I stand up and enter the action.

HF: But we don't have to start. I'm not starting any action in my life right now. I don't want to be born. IT'S LIKE I'M A HAPPY FETUS INSIDE MY MOMMA MERMAID!! I'M FLOATING IN MY PLACENTA!!

The dialogue continues in this vein for five minutes or so, until the Happy Fetus is thrust into life after the Mermaid's water breaks ("I'M SLIDING INTO PUBLIC SPACE . . . STARBUCKS IS CLOSING AND I'M BECOMING A CITIZEN AGAIN"). This event then terrifies the Neo Liberal with the prospect of new responsibilities ("OH NO—IS THIS THE REAL MOVIE?"). People as far away as Utah and Hawaii have e-mailed Talen to let him know they have used his script to hilarious effect in local Starbuckses. The common thread in the reports has been that the scenario leaves many of the amused "eavesdroppers" feeling flattered—after all, they've been intelligent enough to follow the heady scenario—which then disposes them to congratulate the performers and fall into political discussions with them.

The immediate future looks brightly contentious for Reverend Billy. He recently became the subject of a full-length documentary film, *Reverend Billy and the Church of Stop Shopping*, directed by the German Dietmar Post and produced by Lucia Palacios, and he is featured in several other new or forthcoming films: among them, *A Day in the Hype of America* by the Seattle group Global Griot, and *culturejam* by the Canadian Jill Sharpe. He tours and teaches at various colleges around the country and raised international eyebrows when his peace marches and church services held in the wake of September 11, 2001 (under the banner "The Church of Stop Bombing") received media coverage in seven European countries. He is producing a CD of "gospel songs and refracted vespers" and writing a book called *What Should I Do If Reverend Billy Is In My Store?*—the title taken from a memo sent to New York Starbucks managers from executives in Seattle. He also has a new solo play in development, entitled *What is Peace?*, featuring a street encounter between Reverend Billy and a business executive, doctored tales from Talen's childhood, and meditations on "Otis," the wild coyote that made headlines in 1999 by making its way to Central Park.

Still, Talen's is essentially a lonely and dangerous art involving frequent police harassment that he suffers by himself. There are times (especially during smaller gatherings) when one feels that his followers are as fascinated by the spectacle of a man throwing his body in front of a train as they are moved by the content of his sermons. In theater, as in all art pitched to even the most curious and engaged in our brave new culture of information glut, virtual values and twenty-four-hour cyber-shopping, the toughest political task is to maintain the notion that critical thinking truly matters.

(2001)

Robert Wilson's
21st-Century Academy

J UST PAST THE BUSY SHOPPING TRAFFIC OF TONY SOUTHHAMP-
ton, on an obscure road beside the first fields where the Montauk
Highway seems briefly friendly again, stands a pugnacious little
windmill straight out of a cartoon *Don Quixote*. Beside it is a gravel drive-
way leading up a hill, where a squad of giant water jars from Java preside
like fat sentinels, flanked by a twenty-foot-tall chair, bright white and
skinny as a reed, and a fishing-line sculpture resembling the prow of a ship.

At the top of that hill, on almost any day in July or August, you can
find Robert Wilson, the theater's sultan of slow (his stage-crossings can
take twenty to thirty minutes), presiding over an astonishingly animated
beehive. Here, dancers and musicians practice sequences and phrases in
the shade beside weatherbeaten sheds. Artists sketch and assemble stage
models under a tent housing a giddy variety of chairs, all different from
one another, while art photographers obsessively document them.
Groups of young people rake, mow, prune, and set tables for enormous
meals—until they are called to rehearsal by Wilson, that is, and instantly
drop everything.

"An institution is the lengthened shadow of one man," said Ralph

Waldo Emerson. But what of a man who never stands still, and is as famous for the variety and international distinction of his many collaborators as for his own monumental creations? Perhaps such a bobbing, quaking, many-headed shadow is an apt paradigm for the "institution of the future" in a shrinking and sped-up world.

Wilson is probably the most prolific theater artist in the world. An astonishingly tireless man who premieres eight to twelve new projects each year in an array of far-flung countries, he directs, designs the sets, co-designs the lighting, and usually choreographs them all. He also organizes an army of loyal acolytes in the presentation of twice as many touring productions of older shows throughout the world. He estimates that he spends ten days a year at his apartment in New York.

For many years, critics have compared Wilson's majestically conceived, punctiliously crafted theater of slow-moving, dreamlike images with Richard Wagner's. Friends and detractors generally agree that this tall, soft-spoken man from Waco, Texas, did more than anyone else in the late 20th century to broaden public notions about the vocabulary of theater, and to keep alive Wagner's avant-gardist dream of a *Gesamtkunstwerk* that would demolish the borders between the discrete arts. Now the fifty-eight-year-old Wilson is building his own Bayreuth—minus the nationalism and the exclusive dedication to the founder's work.

The Watermill Center in Water Mill, New York, is a six-acre property that Wilson bought for $410,000 in the late 1980s and donated to his non-profit organization, the Byrd Hoffman Foundation. It currently operates only in the summer, and for several years it has been the birthplace of all his theater projects, including *Time Rocker, Orlando, HAMLET: a monologue,* and *The Lady from the Sea.* It is intended purely for early development, not for final performance of his shows, and it will not contain a fully equipped theater even when the $7 million reconstruction of its main building is complete. The finished Center will operate year-round, housing Wilson's archives and extraordinary collection of art and furniture, and hosting international conferences, exhibitions and creative projects by Wilson and other artists. He hopes it will also preserve his legacy after his death.

In the meantime, the life of Watermill is a bustle of intense creative activity, driven in no small measure by the obvious delight of his collaborators at having rare sustained time with him. He spends at least six weeks a year here, consecutive if not restful ones. His longstanding habit—extremely unusual in the theater—is to work on many different projects at once, jumping from one to another to another, sometimes in the course of a single day, and taking two to three years to bring each to final fruition.

Among those on the schedule for the summer of 2000 (in various stages of development) are: a work on "sustainable life in the 21st century," commissioned by the Aventis Foundation; an adaptation of *The Cabinet of Dr. Caligari* for the Deutsches Theater in Berlin; an adaptation of Gogol's *The Diary of a Madman*, starring the prominent Russian actress Alla Demidova; the Janacek opera *Osud/Fate* for the National Theater in Prague; a production of Chekhov's *Three Sisters* for the Stockholm Stadsteater; and a musical called *WillmS* about the life, loves and death of Shakespeare, written by the veteran Broadway producer Edward Padula (*Bye Bye Birdie, A Joyful Noise*) and Robert Mansell.

There is a certain droll solemnity in the atmosphere at the Watermill Center, beginning with the profusion of iconic objects scattered about the grounds. The most conspicuous of these are his chairs, hundreds of them, of every imaginable size, vintage and style, some obviously rare or unique: from Africa, Asia, Indonesia, early America. And some designed by him. They are arranged in precisely parallel rows beneath large white tents set up like a cloister, with two areas of empty flooring separating them, a square patch of bright grass in the middle, and neatly groomed flower beds and walkways on the sides. This is Wilson's temporary rehearsal arena during construction—a sort of immaculate Chinese scholar's garden reconceived by a minimalist connoisseur.

The center's three-story main building is a former telecommunications laboratory for Western Union, built in 1926 and once the workplace of some 250 people. This massive structure, too—Bauhaus-boxy on the wings and, in the center, still brick-fronted with a dilapidated, concentration-camp-like watchtower on top—is already something of an artifact. Currently a half-reconstructed shell (about $2.5 million must still be raised to finish it), its spacious, high-ceilinged halls are filled with methodical arrangements of wildly varied rare furniture and artworks.

An exquisitely peeling and rough-hewn chicken-coop door Wilson found on the street in Barcelona (think Ed Kienholz) hangs near a Zulu hat made of bright-red human hair. A Noguchi rocker from Martha Graham's 1944 *Appalachian Spring* sits beside ancient African fertility poles and a table Wilson designed for *Einstein on the Beach*. His own works blend in seamlessly with the priceless antiques. The place is like a fanciful "please touch" museum for grownups, where one may freely handle Bauhaus pottery by Hedwig Bollhagen from the 1920s, or a 4000-year-old neolithic wooden figure from China, but the shoes of Nureyev, Balanchine and Jerome Robbins are enshrined under glass.

Wilson redesigned the building with the eminent architect Richard Gluckman (best known for his expansion of the Whitney Museum in New York and his renovations of the Andy Warhol Museum in Pittsburgh and the Georgia O'Keefe Museum in Santa Fe). They have preserved the basic shape and square classical plan of the original but, to judge from the prominently displayed model, the new tone will be much more severe and monolithic, with a tall doorless opening planned for the central axis, looking across the entire grounds to a circular outdoor arrangement of Stonehenge-like standing stones from the Indonesian island of Sumba. This marriage of the ancient and the austerely modern is obviously key to Wilson's preferred working atmosphere, as is the presence of all the cherished pieces by his modernist design heroes, like Frank Lloyd Wright, Buckminster Fuller, and Gerrit Thomas Rietveld.

Wilson's theater work has been frequently admired, particularly outside the United States, for its intrinsic internationalism. Primarily an idiom of powerful pictures set to music, to which spoken texts (of greater or lesser power) are added at the last minute, it incorporates material from widely disparate cultures and reaches across borders much more easily than most text-centered theater. The Watermill Center thus boasts a certain polyglot aplomb.

At the communal meals consumed under another large tent—deliciously prepared on two hot-plates and a propane grill (for 60 people!) by the Mexican cook Jose Luis Barreras and his Argentinian assistant, Laura Bejarano—one hears a babel of languages: English, German, French, Spanish, Japanese, Portuguese and more. The scene in many ways recalls the retreats for communal creation founded over the past few decades by several other prominent international theater figures: Peter Brook (in France), Tadashi Suzuki (in Japan) and Eugenio Barba (in Denmark). What's unusual is to come across such a cosmopolitan enterprise on the East End of Long Island.

Wilson explains his vision for Watermill by telling a story from his days as an architecture student at Pratt Institute. Challenged by one of his teachers (Sibyl Moholy-Nagy, the widow and biographer of the Constructivist leader Laszlo Moholy-Nagy) to design a city in three minutes, the young Wilson drew an apple with a crystal cube inside it. The apple, he said, symbolized the organically formed "medieval village" and the crystal cube "its cathedral," a central place of public congregation and learning. Watermill, he said, ought to be a "village center" and "place of enlightenment" in this sense, except that the "village" around it must be seen as global.

He continued: "André Malraux said after the war in France that he hoped, as a cultural policy, that they could maintain the following: a balance of interest in protecting the art of the past with an interest in protecting the art of our time; and on the other side of the coin, a balance of interest in protecting the art of the nation, the homeland, the community, with an interest in protecting the art of all nations." Wilson raised his arms, as if to indicate these are first principles. "It's so simple." To his frustration, however, such simplicity can be hard to explain to American arts foundations.

Wilson is still bitter sixteen years after the failure to raise all the money to bring together the many parts of his huge international project *the CIVIL WarS* for performance at the Los Angeles Olympics. ("They were afraid I was taking money away from the local arts organizations.") *Einstein on the Beach*, he recalled, was commissioned by the

French government in the mid-1970s and created by himself and Philip Glass in Wilson's loft in New York (although it had its premiere in France). "It would be not impossible but unlikely that the United States would commission two Frenchmen to make an opera in Paris...But we have to support art wherever it's happening. We never know where it's going to happen."

So far, most of the Watermill Center's funding has come from outside the United States. Each summer culminates in a fundraising benefit on the grounds, featuring an art auction and outdoor theater events staged by Wilson. This year, the party will include an appearance by Paul Simon.

The summer population of the Watermill Center fluctuates between fifty and sixty—a mixture of administrators, established theater professionals invited to collaborate on specific projects, and interns. Most of the interns are accomplished students and emerging artists themselves, who hope to work with Wilson professionally or simply learn more about his unusual working methods. Fifteen to twenty are hand-picked by him out of about 100 annual applicants, and some 200 have participated since the program began in 1992.

These young people are essential to the organization's smooth operation, living communally in rented houses, arriving before Wilson each year to prepare the grounds and buildings, and continuing to do housekeeping and maintenance chores throughout the summer. According to the center's Web site—robertwilson.com—this reflects "the idea that an artist works differently in an environment that he/she has helped to create and maintain."

One does hear a bit of whining and grumbling about this arrangement, but much less than might be expected. All the interns seem to feel individually respected by Wilson and grateful for the bonds they are forming with him and one another. The working atmosphere in rehearsals is also curiously unhierarchical, with intern photographers, painters, and art historians put to precisely the same uses as experienced actors and dancers. Inés Somellera, an actress from Mexico who has been invited to the center three times, still volunteers to do chores and insists that the place "would never continue if it exploited people."

The Center charges a tuition of $5000, but Linda Jackson, the executive director of the Byrd Hoffman Foundation, estimates that the Foundation finds scholarships for ninety percent of those who attend. Marianna Kavallieratos, a dancer from Greece, has been to Watermill nine times. She arrived this year with her nineteen-month-old son Nikitas, confident that he would have dozens of loving companions. "For me, this is like a second home," she said.

Wilson clearly enjoys working with these ambitious young people in ways that challenge their declared talents and expertise. His early pieces incorporated non-actors, and he is still intent on teaching others about the theatrical value of unexpectedly simple modes of being and doing. He chose a French photographer, Carole Fékété, for instance, to act in a scene from the Aventis Project workshop and then corrected her as if her metier were performing: "be careful when you sit. You're moving in your mind before you move in the body. You can't do that. The mind is a muscle."

The professional performers, of course, hope to impress him and be cast in the roles they rehearse in the workshops, and with them his corrections can be more severe: "Please be careful not to express! If you try to express yourself, it's unbearable [pause] to me. First, just the movement. Then you'll feel it." "The movement is already there. You can't start any movement, ever. The movement can only continue."

At one point, Wilson improvised a dance more than four minutes long (rehearsals almost never involve text at this stage, even when a script is available). Then, after a single demonstration, he asked the American actor Kameron Steele to reproduce it. Steele did so, quite accurately but necessarily with variations, and Wilson liked some of them, made a note to compare them with the videotape of his own version. The professionals are crucial to his work, not only because of such shared creation but also because he regularly leaves sequences in their hands to teach to the rest of the company, rehearse, and show him again days later.

A typical day finds Wilson arriving in the morning to make a rehearsal tape for the Aventis Project with Michael Galasso, his musical collaborator for nearly three decades, after which he spends about thirty minutes with A. J. Weissbard, a longtime lighting collaborator, discussing final details of his design for the upcoming Giorgio Armani exhibition at the Guggenheim Museum in New York. (He is carpeting the entire museum.)

Next he returns to the rehearsal tent to stage the prologue to *WllmS*— a tableau in which the dying Shakespeare lies on a ramp, covered with an enormous rug, while his wife, daughters and lawyer hover nearby. Padulla, the co-author, is visiting for the day and remarks that the scene is already so clear he could probably cut some of the dialogue. No one tells him what they all must be thinking: that all the dialogue may ultimately be unnecessary.

Meanwhile, Wilson interrupts his work to chide the company for leaving shoes, bags, food and water bottles around the audience area— "Please, I just work better in a room that has an order"—after which his stage manager reminds him that he has to call Russia. The call lasts over an hour (Alla Demidova will be delayed, it seems, and hence so will the entire Gogol project), after which he is pulled into a meeting on the photo-spread he agreed to do for the Christmas issue of French *Vogue*. It will consist of scenes from his Paris Opera production of Mozart's *Die Zauberflöte*, done with babies.

No time to return to rehearsal, which continues without him in any case. He has agreed to conduct a performance workshop for children at a local television studio—part of a serious community outreach effort he and others at the center have made in surrounding towns.

Why does Wilson take on so many projects at once? "I don't know," he says. "I think it's just my nature. I can't work on one thing. I have to work on many things. Everyone asks me the same question."

Is there a cost to it? "Maybe. But it's just the way I am."

His critics have certainly thought so over the years, frequently accusing him of falling into mannerism, facile repetition, and factory-production, and also questioning his basic assumptions about language (that it can be treated as merely one item among many in a composite stage vocabulary).

For his part, Wilson finds the discussion of quality versus quantity tedious. "I work on things over a long period of time. I start one thing, then I leave it, start another one, leave it, start another one, leave it, then I come back to one and I see it from a different perspective because I've been thinking about other things. But I've lived with it. It's been in the back of my head."

He pauses a moment to reflect on the Aventis Triangle Forum, a recent conference at the Watermill Center for business people and scientists. The forum dealt with the same subject as Wilson's new piece: sustainable life in the 21st century. "Last week I had fifty-five professionals here from all over the world, from Hong Kong, Japan, Latin America, North America, Europe. There were scientists, people in fields outside the arts, and these people usually meet in a rented room at a Hilton hotel. Here they are with all these kids running around, and they're eating with them, talking with them, in a room with blue geese flying over their heads. It's mixing the arts with scientists." That's the creative environment of the future, he insists, quoting the anthropologist Edmund Carpenter, who had visited the previous summer: "It's like the academy of the 21st century."

(2000)

Dayzed

———

I NCLUDING *The Days Before: death, destruction & detroit III*, I'VE
now seen a dozen Robert Wilson productions over fifteen years in
Germany and the United States, and my reactions to them have
ranged from wonder to dispassionate appreciation to frustrated boredom to a sort of elated boredom arising mysteriously after many hours
of the frustrated kind. *The Days Before*, part of The Lincoln Center Festival, is an intermissionless 105-minute piece that is extremely short by
Wilson's standards and is his first U.S. premiere since 1986. The reports
that it was based on Umberto Eco's 513-page novel *The Island of the
Day Before* (1994) lessened rather than increased my expectations, for
reasons I'll explain, but I nevertheless still hoped for at least a reprise of
that mysterious delayed elation. In the end, the work produced almost
entirely frustration.

I belong (I might as well confess right away) to that benighted party
of avant-gardist infidels that has never accepted one of the main premises
of Wilson's "theater of images"—that language can be effectively de-
moted to the status of a choral player in a monumental latter-day
Gesamtkunstwerk, made to behave as one docile cooperative partner
among many in a totalizing stage poetry. This has always seemed to me
a naive Artaudian dream that young theater students might fantasize

about but people with a modicum of practical experience properly give up as absurd.

Certainly, Wilson's famously slow-moving, otherworldly pictures are gorgeous and powerful; they're also responsible for broadening our era's vision of stage action. They don't work in the way he believes when he couples them with substantial texts, though. In countless interviews, he has claimed that as long as he doesn't set out consciously to interpret or illustrate texts, they can simply hover and shimmer on his complicated stage like lighting effects or abstract designs, in gloriously "boundless" ambiguity (his word). As all the symbolists and even the founder of sur-realism acknowledged long ago, however, language just will not put up with being sidelined or neutered in this manner; for words have mean-ings that raise a juggernaut of expectations. It's not a question of deny-ing the existence of valid and valuable experience prior to language but rather of recognizing that language, when present, takes over as the very tool of our understanding, the filter through which our brains apprehend the world, including dreams and Wilson's dreamlike pictures. Andre Bre-ton: "Quietly. I want to pass where no one yet has passed, quietly!— After you, dearest language."

Let me be very clear. I don't think there's anything wrong with a the-ater in which visual images are dominant; on the contrary, I think it's obvious that we'd all be poorer without Wilson's unique, provocative and often magnificent painterly sensibility. My point is only that it's counterproductive to make such theater on the pretense that language such as Eco's (or Wagner's, or Shakespeare's, or Heiner Müller's, or the *Gilgamesh* authors') is weaker or less demanding than it is.

For me, the best Wilson productions have been those, such as *Hamlet-machine* (1986) and *When We Dead Awaken* (1991), in which his sub-rational understanding of great plays (aided by chance and some dramaturgical assistance) resulted in brilliant interpretations, despite his disavowal of that word. Less satisfying but still extraordinary have been those, such as *The Golden Windows* (1992 and 1985) and *Einstein on the Beach* (1976 and 1984), in which the texts used were mostly insub-stantial and forgettable, which allowed Wilson's moving tableau (along with often strong accompanying music) to sear in memory as the crux of the event. The truly tedious productions have been those, such as *The Forest* (1988), *Death, destruction & detroit II* (1987) and now *The Days Before*, that have tried to use fragmentary literary morsels by Poe, Kafka, Darwin and many others as verbal background music. Nothing makes Wilson's pictures seem more quickly or irredeemably oversimplistic than those moments when the verbal aromas from those morsels waft through all the distorting screens and awaken the spectator's desire for their full meal of meaning.

The Days Before begins with a seriocomic prologue in which a woman in an owl mask and a man in a rooster mask engage in a silent dispute or altercation, entirely in gestures, after which a loud thunderclap booms and the strange geometric scrim projection that greeted spectators upon entering (of concentric hemispheres separated from their flat sides and spread out to form a double-funnel shape) disappears. The Tibetan singer Dadon Dawadolma then steps onto a platform over the orchestra pit and begins a long, slow, entrancing chant as an old rabbi opens an empty book and walks among Wilson's trademark angular furniture. Meanwhile, another man slowly crosses upstage clapping wood blocks, and yet another, dressed entirely in blue, sits stiffly to one side with fingers splayed, announcing: "And Solomon said, 'cut the baby in two.'" To some, this sequence may seem hopelessly vague and abstruse, but it is eerily beautiful and as endowed with ambiguous significance as hundreds of similar scenes in Wilson's other pieces over the decades.

To my mind, the show's problems start after the Solomon remark, when Fiona Shaw's vibrant voice is introduced reading a section of *The Island of the Day Before*, replete with grisly descriptions of flaying, impalement and other tortures, while eight or ten headless figures—black, birdlike specters consisting only of torsos and sleeves—rise from the floor and meander blindly about the stage. How much symbolic energy and surreal magic evaporates instantly in the bright defining light of just this first quoted passage! An interestingly vague, comically diminutive apocalypse (the thunderclap on the rooster's exit) is literalized and stamped permanently on the spectator's mind as a pseudo-Dantesque collection of lurid visions, and almost every selection from Eco in the rest of the evening is in the same overwrought apocalyptic vein, accompanied by similar, obscurely ominous live action and miscellaneously nervous music by Ryuichi Sakamoto.

Anyone who didn't already know *The Island of the Day Before* would likely come away from this show thinking of it as a feeble imitation of *Inferno*. If only its problems were so simple. The rigorous yet overwritten and often engaging story is about a 17th century Italian who is ship-

Robert Wilson's The Days Before: Death, Destruction & Detroit III *in Modena, Italy, 1999.* CREDIT: TILDE DE TULLIO.

wrecked in the south Pacific not on an island but on a deserted ship. As he explores his surroundings, this man reflects at length on his actual and imagined past and future, as his history is reconstructed by a pseudo-Borgesian, pedantically erudite modern scholar in possession of his letters. Wilson seems to have been attracted not to Eco's story per se but to his concept of vertical or parallel time—a notion dating back at least to Proust and Joyce that continues in elegant contemporary novels such as Anne Michaels's *Fugitive Pieces*, which holds that the meaning of events is often apparent only in the light of other events long before or afterward. Eco's handling of this parallelism may have reminded Wilson of his late collaborator Müller and the ideas they shared about layered historical memory and non-contingence of text and stage action. Unfortunately, Wilson found few ways this time of effectively communicating his interest.

The compressed *The Days Before* is like a series of his brief and unfunny "knee plays," usually used as segues, blown up and knitted together to fill an entire production. A woman shuffles about, puttering and nattering in German before slicing her head open with an oversized knife; roll paper is pulled by the rooster from the belly of a large, hovering blue angel, torn off, and then crumpled by smaller, walking black angels; grainy films of lapping waves, empty train depots and Stalin laughing, as well as stills of the Romanov family and others, appear on hanging screens as groups of actors pose as if for photographs; a mischievous red female angel (Lucifer?) starts trouble in her class of grey schoolchild-angels by barking; a white-suited Christopher Knowles sits on the apron amid a gathering of slavish, card-waving figures and half-sings, half-deconstructs the pop tune "Mandy."

Also, although most of the Eco passages are read by Shaw, who sometimes appears onstage, book in hand, some are read by Jeremy Geidt, Tony Randall and Isabella Rossellini seated in chairs, who seem to have had next to no rehearsal and bring no color or power to the words. Perhaps their dullness was deliberate, another of Wilson's attempts to disrupt the dominion of *logos*. Why bother to recruit stars, then? And why allow Shaw to embellish her lines so vividly?

If I hadn't seen the other disappointing Wilson pieces mentioned before, I would conclude from this show that he'd recently had a sudden attack of destructive ambivalence about his methods, perhaps out of anxiety about this rare American premiere. *The Days Before* not only forgoes his usual habit of enjoining us busy spectators to pass substantial time with his dreamscapes (and hopefully relax into gradual meditative reassessment of our initial boredom); it also dispenses with his longstanding principle of fortuitous conjunction, substituting lackadaisical illustration for chance affinity. The result is a joyless and discouraging spectacle of compromise from a famously uncompromising artist.

(1999)

Susan and Bob in Bed

ERLIN—SUSAN SONTAG'S EXCURSION INTO THE THEATER first met with skepticism in my mind in 1985, when I made a trip to Cambridge, MA, to see whether her production of Milan Kundera's *Jacques and His Master* at ART might reveal depths I had overlooked in that hopelessly facile play. Since then she has dabbled here and there as a director but—judging from her headline-jerking *Waiting for Godot* in Sarajevo—the strain of theatrical obscurity has lately become too much for her. Written in 1990, *Alice in Bed*, her first play, predates the Sarajevo affair, but I remember the old skepticism peaking again when I learned through the grapevine that the play featured an appearance by Henry James, America's foremost foundered theater traveler. The biggest surprise of Robert Wilson's recent Berlin Schaubühne production of *Alice in Bed* was that that convenient paradigm was wrong. The play, as it turns out, is good.

Not that we mortals had any way of knowing that until the fall publication of the text, which I read on the plane. Manuscripts of *Alice in Bed* have been circulating for three years at American theaters, most of which (a reliable source tells me) failed to respond to the submission, but those theaters kept the text on a tight leash, perhaps with the idea of preventing others from knowing they had ultimately passed on it. That is, or

Libgart Schwartz as Alice (left) and Joanne Gläsel as the Nurse in the world premiere of Susan Sontag's Alice in Bed, *direction and stage design by Robert Wilson, a production of the Schaubühne am Lehniner Platz, Berlin, Germany, 1993.* CREDIT: WILFRIED BÖING.

ought to be, the cause of some embarrassment now that the Alley Theater, having decided to produce the work, has been rewarded with a $100,000 grant for its production from the W. Alton Jones Foundation. Houston audiences may never see it done by Wilson, however, the director for whom it was reportedly written—Houston being the only place in Wilson's native land saturated with his work—and that is a shame, because the problems of the Berlin production, while severe, are the sort American collaborators might just solve.

Sontag says that her titular Alice is a conflation of Alice James, the brilliant and depressive sister of Henry and William, and Lewis Carroll's Alice, but her comments about that conflation also evoke a more recent, feminist reference, Teresa de Lauretis's 1984 *Alice Doesn't*. Sontag: "The all too common reality of a woman who does not know what to do with her genius, her originality, her aggressiveness, and therefore becomes a career invalid merged in my mind with the fictional figure of the Victorian girl-child who discovers the world of adult arbitrariness in the form of a dream."

As in de Lauretis's book, the play's men are act-ers, people with wills, standing in sadomasochistic opposition to a central female who is defeated from the outset. Sontag's Alice even has a sadistic female nurse who is essentially male in this sense, but to the author's credit the play never degenerates into Manichaean finger-pointing.

Most of its eight scenes depict Alice in, well, you know where, failing to get up, failing to want to get up, failing to challenge brother Henry's (Harry, to her) arrogant habit of narrating her life as if it were one of his stories, failing to meet minds, or bodies, with a shamelessly Shavian burglar. At the center, however, is not a male-female showdown but rather an all-female tea party—also indebted to an unacknowledged source, Caryl Churchill's *Top Girls*—in which Alice confronts various admired personages from history and literature. Alice seems to think that contact with Emily Dickinson, Margaret Fuller, Kundry from *Parsifal*, and Myrtha, Queen of the Wilis, from *Giselle*, will help her find her will, but neither she nor the others will even agree to be hostess (i.e. agree to accept responsibility for the gathering) and she ends up disappointed.

What is left? Most impactfully, a long monologue on a child's chair in a magnified bedroom describing an imaginary trip to Rome—"where Margaret lived," "where Harry descended"—in which Alice proves what a good production ought to have made obvious by then: the tragic sufficiency of her mental experience. It's as if the extraordinary specificity of her thoughts had offered an escape from the pressure of men's success surrounding her, and she had taken refuge in that diminutive plenitude. Only a director who also paints diminutively, yet specifically enough to leave a sense of plenitude, could construct her world without judging it, without glorifying or condemning its self-imposed boundaries. These are precisely Wilson's talents.

His elegant, unpainted wood-slat furniture constructions against a sand floor and changing cyc convey just the right neutrally priveleged, oriental air. And the occasional "designer jokes" that disturb the dominant stillness are appropriately wry—the nurse in wire-frame cothurni, Fuller's left arm a bird's head, arrows lazily falling and a beanstalk unobtrusively growing as Alice molders. The problem is, Sontag didn't write an exclusively still or wry play. She wrote a quasi-Beckettian mélange that plays morbidity off slapstick, and the production's clown bits are consistently inept. Not only is the comic timing botched in the vignettes involving M1 and M2, clownish gofers who perform technical tasks such as depositing mattresses on top of Alice whenever she gets too excited; those sequences are accompanied by insipid music (by Hans Peter Kuhn) that wants to imitate a silent-film score but ends up caught in its own eddy of ponderousness.

For a while I thought the production had another problem, ambivalence about whether the acting should be marionettish or naturalistic, but I was ultimately convinced that that was, in a roundabout way, a symptom of the lame comedy. Perhaps sensing the actorly void in the vignettes, the rest of the cast decided to act too much, uniformly asserting themselves as personalities, which Wilson is known to abhor but cannot always prevent in rehearsal. Contrary to cliché, there are American performers interested enough in him (or intimidated enough by the idea of him) to do what he wants, which is what this play needs; Lucinda

Childs in his Cambridge *Quartet* was a fine example. It goes without saying that we have musicians and clowns who understand silliness a bit better than these Germans. The frame of this *Alice in Bed*, its basic visual decisions, are sound, and it deserves to be mounted again in the land of Keaton and Chaplin—coincidentally also the native country of its author and director.

(1994)

German Questions

Marathon Mensch

IT WOULD BE HARD TO EXAGGERATE THE TENACITY OF FAUST IN the modern imagination. In the centuries since the appearance of Johann Spiess's *Faustbuch* in 1587 and Christopher Marlowe's *The Tragical History of Doctor Faustus* shortly thereafter, the adjective "Faustian" has become common coin around the globe, an astonishingly malleable trope for overreaching of every stamp. Faust himself, moreover, or someone very like him with a different name—an esoterically learned man, typically a secluded loner, who makes some sort of pact with crafty powers to realize his visions and desires and then confronts awful consequences—has been the subject of more spinoffs, remakes, and adaptations than any other classical figure except possibly Hamlet: tragedies, comedies, novels, stories, operas, puppet plays, films, dances, paintings, sculptures, comic strips, biographies, social studies, political tracts, and more, from dozens of different cultures, with dozens of different ideological slants. Faust clearly touches our quintessentially modern suspicion that the way we live has been purchased with a part of our humanity, and by common agreement, he belongs to the world, not just to Germany.

Strangely enough, though, the work generally acknowledged as the most morally capacious, psychologically insightful, and politically intelligent conception in the Faust literature is an exception. Johann Wolfgang von Goethe's monumental life-work—the two part *Faust*, written over six of modernity's most tumultuously definitive decades and completed in 1831 shortly before his death—is a masterpiece that happens also to be a national chestnut. Pushkin once called it "an Iliad of modern life," but Richard Wagner, who wanted to build a theater and found an ensemble for it, said Germans should read it like a national Bible. Georg Lukács spoke of it as "the simultaneous affirmation and negation of the tragic," a consummate "drama of the human species," yet the far less ideological Thomas Mann stressed its "folk character" and linked Goethe's genius to that of Luther, Nietzsche and the tradition of specifically German idealism. In the 20th century, German theaters produced *Faust* practically every decade in lavish, widely attended productions, with audiences converging on it as a sort of communal confessional inviting them to brood on the shifting state of their souls. (Gustaf Gründgens dominated this history with his three productions, over twenty-five years, presenting Mephistopheles as the most interesting character.) Elsewhere, the work has been much more revered than played, particularly in the Anglophone world, where directors tend to find it wordy, rhetorical, and old-fashioned.

I've seen a handful of *Faust*s in the United States. All were competent, about three or four hours long, and based only on *Faust I*, a powerful but conventional work driven by a story of love, betrayal, and heartbreak whose outlines were as familiar when it was published in 1808 as they are today. Before 2000, I had never seen *Faust II*—a much less perishable, extraordinarily free-form product of Goethe's middle and old age, replete with arcane allegorical references and involute interior action. For anyone who speaks German and enjoys watching the German theater throw itself extravagantly into absurdly monstrous and cerebral projects, as I do, *Faust II* is Mount Everest. The Germans perform it occasionally, always vastly shortened, and several high-profile directors (Klaus Michael Grüber, Claus Peymann, and Wolfgang Engel) have combined it with *Faust I* over the past few decades in productions that ran six to nine hours. For whatever reasons, I never got there, but Peter Stein's twenty-one-hour production of the entirety of both parts in Hanover in July, 2000, by contrast, had me itching to hop a plane.

The main attraction this time was Stein himself, a legendary figure who hadn't directed in Germany since 1991 and, at sixty-three, was fulfilling a thirty-year-old dream. Stein was a co-founder of the Berlin Schaubühne and its chief creative force during its glory days in the 1970s and early 80s. He had proposed *Faust* for the theater's initial season in 1969-70, then became distracted by other big projects (such as *Peer Gynt* in 1971 and *The Oresteia* in 1980), and had just begun planning *Faust* again when the Schaubühne fired him in 1985. His declared ambition from that point on, which frightened nearly everyone he approached as a potential collaborator, was to produce the whole work for the first time, without cutting any of its 12,111 lines or imposing any stage action not specifically mentioned by Goethe. (Actually, an uncut *Faust* has been presented every few years since 1938 by a partly non-professional cast at the anthroposophical center called Goetheanum in Dornach, Switzerland, but Stein dismissed this effort as "cult worship" rather than theater art, saying his production was the real "world premiere" because it was the first by a wholly professional company.)

He worked assiduously to realize his titanic plan even while employed as director of non-musical theater at the Salzburg Festival from 1991 to 1997, giving public readings in various European cities and recording all of *Faust II*, solo, on a commercially released, eight-hour, seven-CD set. Only when the Hanover world's fair Expo 2000 offered its sponsorship, which led to other large corporate and government grants, did the financing for the 30-million Mark ($20 million) production come together. It opened as part of the fair, ran there for four months, and then fulfilled a planned two-year run in Berlin and Vienna, consistently selling out its 398-Mark ($265) tickets a month ahead of each performance.

I was extremely curious about it even after reading the German reviews, which unanimously trashed the production for what the critics saw as its deadly literalism. Stein's *Oresteia* had long been a pinnacle of my theatergoing, and these were many of the same critics who had detested the painstaking realism in his 1984 production of *The Three Sisters*, which I also found breathtaking. I distrusted their motives, suspecting pet theories about both Stein and Goethe. Meanwhile, Stein was belligerent. "You take this text especially seriously," said an interviewer to him during his Hanover rehearsals. "What else?" answered the now respectable elder statesman who a few years ago was an upstart-evangelist of director's theater. "Should I take myself seriously? No! These illustrious people who pursue director's theater regard themselves as excessively important and aren't exactly bursting with inspirations because of it."

As it turned out, I was myself taken aback by the flatfootedness of the show's literalism. I also found a great deal to admire, though, as did the 460-odd Germans in the audience with me, apparently, since they all stayed to the end and carried on animated, appreciative conversations during the ten intermissions over two days. (In Hanover, one saw the production either in six evenings or over a marathon weekend, thereafter only in two-day marathons.) There is a venerable truism that all great artworks are mirrors that send people away with a version of what they came looking for. In Stein's *Faust*, I seem to have been looking for some capacious statement about the essence and promise of theater at the end of print culture. Stein didn't work from this premise, I presume, and I wasn't aware it was so pronounced in my mind until afterward. The show spoke eloquently to it, though—not only through the play itself, but also in its overtly commercial venue, in the light the production cast on the limitations of its hero-director, and in the light he did and didn't manage to cast on the totality of Goethe's conception.

Stein's *Faust* was presented by its publicists as an unintimidating, popular event—one that happened to have literary respectability but could be as much fun to attend as a circus or carnival. Its television commercials featured high-tech montages with lots of fire and acrobatic exertion, and its posters shamelessly packaged Goethe as tourist kitsch, immodestly featuring the names STEIN and FAUST (both peremptory German nouns, meaning "stone" and "fist") adjoined in mirror image. Inevitably, Expo 2000 was also part of the attraction—a preposterously large fair stretching over hundreds of acres, with more than 150 futuristic national pavilions reflecting its theme of the bright promise of technology. *Faust* functioned as the *de facto* German cultural pavilion, assuring visitors that the brave new world of unimpeded corporate boosterism—evident everywhere in the park's sea of logos—would never leave theater or the classics behind.

The performance took place in a huge, characterless, hangar-like hall divided with black curtains into two performance areas with a corridor in between. (In Berlin, the venue was an old bus depot.) The audience moved back and forth between these spaces every twenty to sixty minutes, watching action on one side while the other side was rearranged for the following scene. This system was more democratic than most people able to pay 398 DM for a theater ticket were probably comfortable with, but the constant to-ing and fro-ing soon became routine and was often amusing—as when the crowd arrived to find it had to stand, or when it rushed for the front rows in anticipation of scenes with nudity. The compulsory movement also created a peculiar social environment, fostering innumerable impromptu exchanges among strangers. In the "Rittersaal" scene (about two-thirds through), for instance, the audience was seated at long tables and left for ten minutes or so to chat with neighbors over individual plates of real wine and cheese.

This environment, more than anything else, colored my thoughts and impressions over the two days. I had read several intelligent articles beforehand about the meaning of *Faust* for Germans at the present cultural moment. One, by Peter Kümmel in *Die Zeit*, suggested that, although Stein was no doubt indifferent to Wagner's dream of "the spiritual unity of the *Volk*," he had nevertheless shrewdly exploited the economic boom of the late 1990s to realize Wagner's more practical project of founding an ensemble and building a temple for "the Bible of the Germans." (The production was registered as a for-profit corporation, with eighty employees contracted for three years.) Another essay, by Richard Herzinger

The ascension of Faust (Christian Nickel) to heaven at the end of Peter Stein's 21-hour production of Goethe's Faust, Parts I *and* II, *Hanover, Germany, 2000.* CREDIT: RUTH WALZ.

in *Theater heute*, focused on "the harmonizing ending" of *Faust II*, in which the "striving" Faust is redeemed by heaven despite his sins and the fact that Mephistopheles has technically won their wager. Herzinger wrote that this redemption did have "something arbitrarily forced about it," but it nevertheless gave the work power today as "a parable of the German happy ending": "The unified Germany of 1989-90 was founded on the bankruptcy of delusory projects, not only nationalist but also utopian-socialist in nature. The price for the redemption of the constantly striving, endeavoring Germans is the abandonment of their high-flying fantasies of world-reclamation."

There is truth in both these theories. I wouldn't argue specifically with either of them. I would question their immediacy for the average spectator, however—certainly for a foreigner like me but also for ordinary Germans. *Faust* in the theater (as distinct from the classroom or the scholar's study) is too engaging as a narrative to be primarily a forum for worship, and its story doesn't revolve around, or issue from, its ending in any significant sense. One is pulled in, for instance, by the love story, by pure titillation in scenes such as the Witches' Kitchen and the Walpurgisnacht, by Faust's various forms of overreaching (or "striving," if you prefer), and by the fact that he and Mephistopheles seem more and more like opposing aspects of a single, quintessentially human nature as the play goes on. Among the snatches of conversation I overheard during the many pauses between scenes were: an argument about whether Faust's blood-signature irrevocably bound him to his devil's bargain, a discussion of whether the Earth Spirit (a filmed closeup of a face surrounded by flames) was sufficiently "horrible," and whether Helen of Troy was sufficiently "glamorous." During the first day's long dinner break, two Hanoverians I'd never met before (an elderly woman and her granddaughter) fell into a remarkably sophisticated conversation with me about Mephistopheles's "scoffing" nature and its connection to the degrading trivializations of television.

For my part, I was reminded more than ever that *Faust* is basically a story about a lonely, isolated professor who yearns for a more active and erotic relationship with the outside world. He feels imprisoned in his own inwardness, having brought his knowledge, feeling and intuition to the pinnacle of refinement at the cost of his connections to everything and everyone outside them. Thus Goethe allegorizes the painful transition from the torpid, closed, and medieval "little world" (Goethe's phrase) of Margarete (Gretchen) to the more brightly dynamic, intellectually open but treacherous world of modernity. Stein's most significant achievement was to apply this modernity effectively to our time, dramatizing the transition to the age of shrinking attention spans, disappearing language faculties, and mass isolation behind flickering screens. For much of the marathon audience, the production's social immersion—twenty-one hours of jostling actual, unpredictable, sensually engaged comrades in an intellectually aroused crowd—was probably as novel and disorienting as Faust's.

Any fair-minded observer would concede that the German critics were justified in many of their practical, scene-by-scene objections. The settings (designed by Ferdinand Wögerbauer for Part I and by Stefan Mayer for Part II) were restrained and cautious to a fault. Most scenes were played in unremarkably conventional or generic environments, and several were inexplicably stuffed into bizarrely cramped compartments or spread out in open areas dully and sparsely adorned. The occasional touches of modernism—a varicolored, climbable cliff-face during the Walpurgisnacht, for instance, and a truncated pyramid with magnetic trees, human figures and other shapes moved around by actors during the Classical Walpurgisnacht—seemed passive and merely decorative. Heinrich Brunke's dynamic lighting often felt like a compensation for visual inertness. Now and then, one could perceive a plan to chart an expansive journey outward from Faust's claustrophic, Kafkaesque study, with its tall, dusty shelves crammed full of old tomes, reams and scrolls of paper, to arenas of greater and greater airiness and light, but this wasn't consistently followed. Moidele Bickel's costumes were inert, unimaginative: standard Goethe-era garb supplemented by fantasy-outfits straight out of commonplace storybooks, with only rare blips of assertive originality (such as a rolling-metal-cart hind-quarter for the centaur Chiron).

A few scenes were exceptionally designed. At the end of Part I, for instance, Gretchen was incarcerated in a cubic metal cage too small for her to stand or fully stretch out in. In Act II of Part II, actors on a conveyor belt used roller blades to create the impression of swimming. And at the end of Part II, Faust's heavenly redemption was depicted with droll magnificence as a sort of sacred abduction by aliens: a giant metallic spiral walkway descended from the ceiling and angels dressed in clinical white helped Faust remove his actor's makeup and clothes and then escorted him slowly upward, flanked by nearly naked boys of decreasing age. Fundamentally, however, Stein clearly made a decision to abandon interpretively active and challenging modern stage design—used so stunningly in all his previous productions—as if anything less than pure literalism would have smudged the figurative vitrine he thought to construct around his tome of beloved old words.

His choices were sometimes plainly ridiculous and amateurish: having Mephistopheles step out from behind two fifteen-foot-tall, bright red boots when the text says that he alights from "seven-league boots," for instance, or bringing a real black poodle onstage when Mephistopheles is said to enter as one. Furthermore—and this is a weightier matter—he didn't prove his main premise: that the entirety of *Faust* possesses a deep momentum and grand aesthetic arc in performance that benighted theater people have overlooked for nearly two centuries. Major sections of *Faust II* (his main reason for doing the production, he said) appeared superfluous in theatrical terms, just as previous directors said they were. The hour-long carnival that Mephisto stages at the Emperor's palace, for example—staged here by Stein as a tumultuous parade of monotonous, sparkling kitsch—came off as an obscure, tedious, and dated satire. Similarly, the fourth act of Part II—with its stereotypical thugs and its battle on a mountain spur that takes place entirely offstage while the principals chat and watch—was left to wallow in its own dramatic torpor.

This flagrant failure of imagination aside, however (and notwithstanding Stein's crass publicity blitz), there is also a sense in which the production benefited from low expectations—especially in Hanover. Bruno Ganz, the fifty-nine-year-old actor around whom the role of Faust was built, could not perform in Hanover because he had seriously injured himself in rehearsal. In his place appeared Christian Nickel, a thirty-one-year-old actor who was supposed to share the role (playing the rejuvenated lover of Gretchen, for instance) but who instead performed the entire show. One had to sympathize with Nickel, thrust as he was into an impossible mission. Neither vocally engaging nor physically spectacular, he was competent, flexible and sometimes genuinely moving.

The surprise was that he became considerably more than that in the end, simply by being a more or less neutral and efficient conduit to Goethe.

Six months later, I saw Ganz's performance when it was broadcast on German television (he had returned to the role in Berlin). As might be expected, he added heft, gravity, realism, variety, and maturity to Faust. Furthermore, Nickel blossomed under his lighter burden, and the alternations and combinations of the two actors were interesting and illuminating. Because of Ganz's ability to add virtuosic "star turns," however—his desperate exasperation and self-loathing leading up to Faust's suicide attempt, for instance, and his leering, gummy grins while gazing on the Walpurgisnacht orgy—he also sometimes stood in competition with the words. He was never gratuitously self-indulgent, but he did assert a specific and forceful presence. With Nickel alone, by contrast, one had no thoughts of either fireworks or incompetence and thus sat back to relax into wave upon wave of rhymed eloquence about human appetite, fulfillment, disappointment, and despair.

Interestingly enough, the portrayal of Mephistopheles added to this impression. This role was also shared by two fine actors, Johann Adam Oest and Robert Hunger-Bühler, who seemed clearly and significantly differentiated at first: one was droopy-eyed, languorous, and seductive, the other worried, weary, and weatherbeaten. As the production went on, though, they grew less and less distinguishable, and by the end their contrast hardly seemed important. For that matter, only two other actors stood out amidst the production's 600-plus roles played by the thirty-three-member company: Dorothee Hartinger as the superbly restless Gretchen, and Corinna Kirchhoff as the wonderfully vain Helen of Troy. Everyone else blended so effectively and anonymously into the choral background that I wondered afterward how Stein convinced them to devote three years of their careers to this project.

All the German critics complained about the show's long boring sections, and on one level they were right, but on another I think they missed the point. A certain quotient of boredom was necessary to abate the appetite for spectacle. As often happens in Beckett, the boredom drew one into an expansive *listening* posture whereby the literalism became a cradle for the deceptively "artless" art of the poetry (that famous verse in which, as Thomas Mann said, "every sort of high-flownness, every poetic extravagance, is foreign... [yet it] keeps on the middle path with a quiet masterly boldness").

A particularly chilling moment, for instance, was Mephistopheles's mocking lament for life's transitoriness late in Part II.

> *Was soll uns denn das ew'ge Schaffen!*
> *Geschaffenes zu nichts hinwegzurafffen!*
> *"Da ist's vorbei!" Was ist daran zu lesen?*
> *Es ist so gut, als wär' es nicht gewesen...*
>
> (Then what's the use of eternally striving,
> When all that's created is swept away to nothing!
> "There, it's over!" What's to be learned from that?
> It's just as good as if it never were...)

I have no memory whatever of which actor delivered these lines, or which expressions and intonations he used. I do remember perfectly, however, how after twenty hours or so, my mind had settled into a state of intense concentration on ideas and their formulation, on the wit, elegance, fluidity, and curiously timeless life of Goethe's words. During a passage like this, Beckett—with his lifelong theme of futile striving married to not-quite-final renunciation—seemed as much a precedent for Goethe as an heir to him. The hierarchy of real chronology was irrelevant. Especially with the magnificent metal spiral descending from the flies, I felt transported to one of those circular timespaces of Borges's where Kafka influences Hawthorne, where Racine and Mallarmé count as "the same writer," and the very notion of confident orientation is a hallucinatory dream.

Stein's key perception in *Faust* was the need to preserve this atmosphere of the greatest possible openness to wide-roaming reverie, even at the risk of seeming to abdicate his directorial duties. No one could ever accuse this director of excessive humility, but he does seem to have understood that, with this play, at this time, he couldn't present himself as an omniscient hero bearing definitive answers. For all his bravado and self-promotion, he grasped that monumentalism itself is now suspect, even though millions are still drawn to it, and that the public today prefers its idols to have clay feet. Hence the anomalous triumph of a director, and a Faust, in whom megalomania dances with caution and humility: neither Übermensch, nor even Übermensch-wannabe, but rather a striving, bungling, overcommitted man of the earth.

(2001)

To B.E. or not to B.E.

———

BERLIN—DURING THE TWO YEARS I LIVED IN BERLIN IN THE mid 1980s, nothing in the theater landscape was more surprising than the moribund condition of the Berliner Ensemble. In the absence of English-language articles to the contrary, the average American tourist—which I was, at the beginning—assumed the best about the theater Brecht founded. We went expecting to learn once and for all, for instance, how alienation effects *really* worked, how politically savvy actors and directors functioned as quarterbacks and cheerleaders in that Great Social Debate cum Sports Event described theoretically in our college readings. Few tourists suspected that their presence had become the bread and water of a theater that had lost its spiritual center and the respect of the working German theater world, East and West.

During the 80s, the BE coasted on the international reputation it earned while touring during the 1960s and 70s. Defenders said its problems were too various for any typical pathology to emerge, but certain generalizations were possible if you saw enough productions. I remember a deadly version of *Baal*, directed by the Chilean Alejandro Quintana, that tried to contrast slick and urbanely modern designs with the rough, no-nonsense acting style of Ekkehard Schall but couldn't compensate for Schall's incomprehensible mumbling and apparent lack of interest in the

role. There was a soporific *Threepenny Opera* directed by Manfred Wekwerth and Jürgen Kern, in which no one could sing and everyone tried to
imitate the voice of Lotte Lenya, which played occasionally on loudspeakers. Also acridly memorable is a tawdry, interminable staging by
Fritz Marquardt of Carl Sternheim's *Bürger Schippel*, in which derivative
and sledgehammerish conceptual ideas annihilated any subtlety the
seventy-nine-year-old bourgeois satire might have retained.

Various, yes. But these and other fiascos clearly shared a common failing: they all stemmed from a superficial, hackneyed, and uncritical view
of Brecht, the theater's putative guiding spirit, which grew more and
more visible in technical lassitude, gimmickry, and programmatic socialist politics in productions. As Heiner Müller once quipped, with the BE
in mind, "to use Brecht without criticizing him is betrayal."

By the time the Berlin Wall fell, the BE, which had always been state-
supported, was nothing less than the unofficial national theater of East
Germany, touted frequently by apparatchiks as a cultural treasure and
controlled by leaders with close ties to the government (Wekwerth as Intendant, Brecht's daughter Barbara and son-in-law Schall as backseat
drivers). Aesthetic judgements aside, the institution had generated so
much political enmity it was difficult to see who or what would support
it in a capitalist environment. Many thought, and some hoped, that it
would close. How conspicuous, then, how curiously heartening it was to
find, during a recent trip to Berlin, that the theater, now privatized, is
not only seriously struggling for artistic credibility but has reorganized
its leadership to avoid the cronyism, authoritarianism, and calcification
that plagued it before.

In the venerable bureaucratic tradition of addressing urgent problems
by assigning a committee to study them, several years ago the senate of
newly reunified Berlin asked for and received a lengthy "expert opinion"
on how to handle the sudden superfluity of theaters in the city. This 1991
report, assembled by a team of critics and professors, came under immediate attack for generally recommending the adaptation of Eastern
theaters to Western structures that had never proved all that worthwhile
in the West. The report nevertheless became the basis for a decision by

Cultural Senator Roloff-Momin that the BE no longer be led by a single Intendant but rather by a "directorate" of five artists who would generate projects on a rotating basis. This idea was subsequently refined by an inspired and passionate 5000-word letter that director Matthias Langhoff wrote to Roloff-Momin laying out his ideas about the theater and his possible future association with it.

Some of his suggestions were: that Müller, Brecht's "only successor," assume the role of new central playwright. That the BE eliminate repertory scheduling and perform one play at a time, avoiding even the possibility of museum-theater: "Blocks have the advantage of bringing out the transitoriness and ephemerality of productions; the theater is thus more prepared for risk, gambling, experiment." That long-term employment

The five-member directorate in charge of the Berliner Ensemble in 1993: (l. to r.) Fritz Marquardt, Heiner Müller, Peter Palitzsch, Peter Zadek, Matthias Langhoff. By 1995, all had resigned but Müller, who was left as sole leader. CREDIT: BERND UHLIG.

contracts be sharply restricted: "A good proportion is one-third permanent, two-thirds temporary personnel." And that the whole institution be "refounded": the aim is the "resuscitation of the idea of a theater which, through a different working method, calls into question the familiar course of theater life." A directorate was established, consisting of Langhoff, Müller, Marquardt, Peter Palitzsch, and Peter Zadek, and Langhoff's suggestions were largely accepted for trial.

So far, nothing in Langhoff's list has been touchier than the question of permanent contracts. Under GDR law, an actor attached to a theater for fifteen years or more could not be fired, and, in some cases, was guaranteed a minimum number of "central roles" per season—and court cases since reunification have established that this law remains binding. What to do, then, with old performers who were carried along for years out of favoritism or other political considerations but whom no one wants to work with now? According to an administrator who requested anonymity, the BE has a dozen such actors on payroll. "Twenty four and half million marks sounds like a lot of money," said Müller in a chat outside the BE canteen, referring to the part of the "private" theater's budget covered by the state ($14.8 million); "but when you consider that 18 million of it is fixed expenses, it's not that much at all."

And the directorate-era productions? I saw two of the three that have occurred. Palitzsch's production of Shakespeare's *Pericles* was so weak it was depressing, its resemblance to the Wekwerth-era milquetoast provocations so strong I thought I'd fallen into a time warp. Every scene was built on some shopworn A-effect, dusty out of the gate: specific locales indicated by one or two ostentatiously inexpensive objects; ridiculous armor-clanking by the knights gathered at Pentapolis to indicate the cumbersome nature of their warrior identities; Pericles a (normal) Caucasian, Thaisa in blackface, and their daughter Marina made up in robin's-egg blue to emphasize the multicultural significance of the prince's travels. Palitzsch apparently thought he was breaking new ground by removing the BE's orchestra seats and putting spectators on floor cushions, but that only added to the general motley, the sense that he was pulling out arbitrary directorial rabbits, each clumsier than the last. *Pericles* seen as a play that can't get started seemed like an inadvertent metaphor for a theater that couldn't get restarted.

That harsh judgement didn't survive my viewing of *Wessies in Weimar*, however, a three-and-a-half-hour hammer-blow of a production unlike anything seen at the BE before. This play by Rolf Hochhuth about the assassination of D.K. Rohwedder, head of Treuhand, the firm empowered to sell off all the GDR's "people's property," has received wide publicity since Chancellor Kohl spoke out publicly against its attempted "justification" of a political murder. Hochhuth, who said he wasn't trying to justify but rather "to understand" the crime, compiled what is really a 261-page essay in dramatic form, its realistic dialogue interspersed with press clippings and other archival material relating to the feelings unleashed when West Germany "occupied" East Germany.

No director could stage *Wessies in Weimar* satisfactorily without ruthless cutting and reshaping, if only for the sake of coherence, but what Einar Schleef did with it at the BE was more than the author had bargained for—his fierce objections generating even more free publicity. The truth is that this was less a premiere production of the play than a dance-theater piece conceived by Schleef using ten to twelve percent of Hochhuth's dialogue—as well as snippets from *Faust, Maria Stuart, Kabale und Liebe*, Brecht poems, and Free German Youth songs—as material for choral chanting. The obliteration of the author's realism notwithstanding, the essential subject for both Hochhuth and Schleef was the same: the seething, inchoate fury tearing at an erstwhile "officially happy" land.

The action, played in a desolate, empty, brick-backed space with a heavy metal curtain that descends between sections, consists of a narratively discontinuous series of loaded, moving images. In dim light, a double line of actors wearing military coats marches silently in a circle for twenty minutes, unfazed by the audience's increasingly bad-tempered catcalls: "Another hour and you'll be in Weimar!" "That'll do it!" "Knock it off!" The cast splits into male and female choruses that shout most of the play's lines rhythmically in unison, their rhythms conducted by chorus leaders. Volume is primary, clarity secondary, and the men's

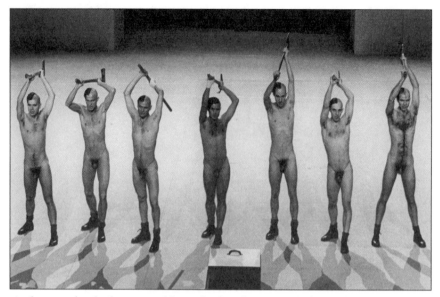

A chorus of naked, axe-wielding skinheads menaces the audience in Einar Schleef's production of Rolf Hochhuth's Wessies in Weimar, *Berliner Ensemble, 1993.* CREDIT: UTE SCHEDEL.

voices dominate the women's. A naked actor masturbates while speaking a monologue Hochhuth intended for a bureaucrat on the phone with his mistress, a scene some have cited as evidence that the production does question the patriarchal. Much more omnipresent and memorable, however, are the brazen images of aggression, such as lines of skinheads, naked above their military boots, running repeatedly at the audience with axes raised over their heads—images which smack as much of homage as of critique.

One admiring critic began his review: "That's a German evening!" Indeed. The excess, the obdurate resistance to compromise, the reverence for mass response, the idea of attack as a form of therapy, of pain as a substitute for healing: the music of this performance was that of a German shepherd barking incessantly outside one's window. Understanding the cathartic intentions, I must admit to a faintly jingoistic pride that Schleef and I hear different drummers.

Personal reactions aside, however, if the BE is to revitalize its reputation, it will have to turn *Wessies in Weimar* into a watershed event. Controversial as the production was, not even Schleef's enemies could sensibly level the old accusation of curatorial pedantry; if Brecht was present at all it was as the spirit of direct political confrontation. The directorate—now a foursome (Langhoff recently resigned, unable to adjust to life in Germany after a decade in France)—has abundant future plans: *Fatzer/Germania*, Müller's assemblage of fragments by himself and Brecht; a Palitzsch production of *Baal*; Zadek productions of *Antony and Cleopatra*, *He Who Says Yes*, and *He Who Says No*. It also has the unenviable task of convincing a skeptical public that the leopard's spots are truly changing.

(1993)

You Can Go Home Again

B EING JEWISH NEVER SEEMED ODD TO ME UNTIL I WENT TO
live in Germany for a few years back in 1986. As a kid from New
Jersey, I grew up under the illusion that an assimilated, un-
demonstrative Jew could think he was like anybody else, with the requi-
site sense of normalcy and belonging due any citizen of a civilized
society. Like everyone, I'd heard the occasional tale about a vandalized
Jewish cemetery or hoodlums who beat up "Christ killers," but those
seemed like problems of distant and barbaric places like, say, North Car-
olina or Indiana, which would never affect me unless I went digging
under heavy and wisely placed rocks.

Moving to West Berlin meant disturbing the rocks. The decrepit,
bleach-blonde caretaker of my building, Frau D., gave me a thorough
education before I'd even unpacked. "You have a funny name," she
said upon meeting me (my name means veal in German, a dead giveaway, I was later told). And over the next few months (as I eventually
learned) she carried out a regime of quiet terrorism, secretly removing
my name-sticker from the mailbox day after day so I couldn't receive
mail, leaving little dirt piles in front of my door, and slashing my bicy-
cle tires, until I capitulated and moved out.

Despite growing up in Wakefield, Massachusetts, far removed from

161

1940s Germany, Israel Horovitz, as it turns out, knows the likes of Frau D., as well as the longings behind assimilation, more intimately than any of his previous fifty-odd plays suggested. And *Lebensraum* is, largely because of this intimacy, one of the strongest dramas of his thirty-year career.

The play's premise is diabolically simple: sixty years after the holocaust, in 2005, the Chancellor of Germany awakens from a nightmare and extends a public invitation "to six million Jews from anywhere in the world to come to live their lives in Germany . . . Please, come home." The announcement entices some but horrifies many more and, as we might imagine, sets in motion a series of events resulting in chaos and disaster. With three actors playing forty-three roles in quick-shifting, episodic scenes, the play traces the repercussions of the invitation within the lives of numerous specific figures, including an out-of-work American family that chooses to move to Bremerhaven.

Story apart, though, it is the bizarre comic attitude of *Lebensraum* (Hitler's word for the extra "living space" to which the Germans supposedly had a right), its incongruous buoyant tone, that seizes and holds attention. That tone—more Brecht than Wilder, who has been Horovitz's more frequent ghost in recent years—is its really inspired moment. The actors flit and dash, quickly switching silly half-masks and other emblematic costume bits, at times inserting their heads and arms into faceless portraits that they carry around, talking, like playing cards out of Lewis Carroll. And all this low-budget, lighthearted clowning (directed by Richard McElvain), with its knockabout ease and driving momentum, is what effectively breaks through one's usual defenses against historical meditations on terror.

The first public reaction to the Chancellor is that of a Bremerhaven dockworker named Gustav Giesling (played by a raincoat-clad Scott Richards), who sounds almost reasonable complaining to a reporter about the scarcity of jobs for those already in the country: "Where do we put six million new people, Jews or not? I don't personally care if these six million are Jews or if they're monkeys." The next reaction sinks straight into the murk of unreasonableness, though, as a talk-show host (played by stern-faced Emme Shaw holding up a cardboard TV-frame) spouts classic anti-Semitic bilge: "They will romance our young daughters...Their tears and their knickers will be on the ground in no time!"

This is the Horovitz whose eye for the details of petty cruelty Ionesco so admired. This mischievous author doesn't merely lift rocks; he spends time contemplating, sifting and arranging the lovely worms he finds there. Commenting in a lobby text on his surroundings during his first ever trip to Germany two years ago, which inspired this play, Horovitz is flush with professional admiration: "It was all so shabbily theatrical."

The first "theatrical" casualty in *Lebensraum* is a distinguished professor from Bonn, who is beaten to death after shouting "Heil, Hitler!" during a speech by a colleague praising the Chancellor for attempting to deliver the country from its "sea of guilt." (His crushed head is a tomato squashed over his recumbent body.) The second casualty is a Jerusalem rabbi, who is strangled by an angry congregation member after endorsing the German offer: "We must go. We must do this. We must bring our young people with us. We must reclaim this place for Jews." (His bearded mask is squeezed like a sponge.) The tidiness of the parallel deaths would cloy like a sermon if their presentation weren't so burlesque and they didn't also offer such a convincing picture of the messy thinking that often accompanies holocaust discussion.

More Horovitz mischief: the first to arrive for "Project Homecoming" are a pair of "French queers" who kiss and hold hands and have to be whisked away by the German government before reporters see them ("Jacques and I have been married depuis longtemps"). That is how the American dockworker Mike Linsky and his telegenic American family become the "first" arrivals. With their unassuming ordinariness and sturdy work ethic, they are acceptable media darlings and soon win the public's affection. As more Jews arrive by the hundreds of thousands and claim precious German jobs, however, the national atmosphere sours—all of this just plausible enough to make one wonder at times whether the play might not be a "real" satirical documentary about important news events somehow overlooked.

The scenario of *Lebensraum* is magnificently loaded. And had Horovitz remained true to its darker side, had he stuck with spinning out the bitter comic possibilities of what he knew to be its inherent morbidity, he might have produced a work as nobly and unanswerably "evil" as Brecht's *Baal*, or Sobol's *Ghetto*. Instead, he let his plot grow schematic and sentimental after a point, with a specious Romeo-and-Juliet fable imposing an artificially redemptive ending. Linsky's teenage son Sammy (played with wonderful faux-gangliness by Jeremy Silver) falls in love with Giesling's daughter Anna, as Giesling leads a dockworker's strike to protest the company's Jew-favoring employment policy. When Giesling pulls a gun he is cut down by Jewish militants, and a stray bullet finds Anna lying with Sammy nearby.

Horovitz is no panderer. He obviously convinced himself that this bogus martyrdom might actually help people envision a way out of a basic cycle of hatred that still produces too much real heartbreak. A narrator, speaking of the way Anna's funeral captured the world's imagination, compares her death to that "of another young Anna...Anne Frank." As Cynthia Ozick recently wrote eloquently in *The New Yorker*, however, the meaning of Anne Frank's diary was really hijacked by various editors and adaptors bent on sentimentalizing it by suppressing the young author's unforgiving rage, undomesticable disgust, and specific observations of cruelty. In Ozick's words: "A deeply truth-telling work has been turned into an instrument of partial truth, surrogate truth, or anti-truth."

Similarly, Horovitz does a disservice to his rage-based scenario by letting it slouch toward a vacuously sanguine ending: Jews and Germans, embodied by all three actors, join hands in a Bremerhaven chapel and intone "Nimmer wieder" ("Never again"). The benign and malign channeling of seething, suppressed violence has been one of Horovitz's defining themes his entire career, from *Line* and the other absurdist shorts of the 1960s to *The Widow's Blind Date* and the rest of his realistic working-class plays of the 1980s and 90s. With or without that knowledge, though, one could tell that the character in *Lebensraum* closest to the play's pulse is Maximillian Zylberstein, a Buchenwald survivor who, after sixty years in Australia, returns to Berlin to be hired as personal caretaker for the woman, now indigent, who once betrayed him to the police.

He wants to kill her, has long dreamed of killing her, but he now hits on something better, crueller: to return every day and talk her ear off about everything he remembers. Zylberstein, tormentor of Frau D., is the living heart of this fundamentally aggressive play, regardless of the author's anomalous desire to play peacemaker.

(1997)

Ghosts & The Dead Man

B ERLIN — AT HIS DEATH ON DECEMBER 30, HEINER MÜLLER was widely considered Germany's foremost dramatist. Be that as it may, he spent most of his last decade and a half talking—talking about history, politics, his occasional directing, and, often, the "major" play he wanted to write about Hitler and Stalin when time permitted. According to Berliner Ensemble dramaturg Holger Teschke, this text was never completed, notwithstanding the heralded recent publication and double premiere (in Bochum and Berlin) of *Germania 3: Ghosts at the Dead Man*. Teschke says that *Germania 3*—which lacks the unified tone of Müller's other Teutonic collage works—is really a compilation of material from which the author intended to construct seven different plays, including the one on Hitler and Stalin. His decision to publish the variegated scenes amounted to a hasty response last year to the news that he was terminally ill.

How mordantly piquant, then, that two important German theaters should have fought over the honor and box-office boon of presenting the premiere of this supposedly great, integral, culminating opus. And how perfectly, well, Müllerish that the respectable publisher of the book (Kiepenheuer & Witsch) should now be defending the work's line-by-line integrity in court—slapped with a restraining order barring future sales and a demand for specific textual changes by the heirs to Bertolt Brecht, the author Müller most revered (he quotes him without permission, the heirs say) and whose theater he led at his death.*

It's a grave error to believe that the dead are really dead, Müller enjoyed saying. For one thing, they vastly outnumber the living and thereby dominate history. For another, they colonize our thoughts, coercing, controlling, and luring us into the historical vortices that doomed them. The only possible resistance is to transform monologue into dialogue, as he tried to do in his plays, forcing ghostly potentates into the light where they can be seen and challenged. In *Germania 3*, this applies not only to Hitler and Stalin—whose linked ideological obsessions and mass murders set the premises for the contemporary world, Müller thought—but also to a potpourri of other figures from the GDR, the Third Reich, Croatia, Nibelung myth, Kleist, Kafka, and more.

"What's a ghost? Unfinished business," wrote Salman Rushdie in *Satanic Verses*; presumably, in using this quote in the program at the Schauspielhaus Bochum, the dramaturg didn't intend to reflect unflatteringly on Leander Haussmann's production. "Do it lightly," was Müller's parting comment about the play to Haussmann. The latter's response: a doleful, four-hour, concrete bunker of an evening in which deadly literalism conspires with self-seriousness to immobilize spectators' mental faculties. Unfinished business indeed.

Haussmann seems to have been guided by a principle of plodding fidelity to text not only rare in Germany but also inconsistent with all Müller's theoretical statements about the theater. This author didn't want directorial slaves but rather dialectical conversation partners who understood that trying to freeze a text is like trying to step into the same river twice. It's also redundant: as in the Stalin monologue for which Haussmann finds a Russian-speaking Stalin look-alike, gives him bloody

---

* The revised and enlarged edition of my book *The Theater of Heiner Müller* (NY: Limelight Editions, 2001) contains an appendix describing this legal case, which ended up before Germany's highest court.

hands and spooky backlight, and has others cower before him. And invariably distracting: as in the numerous scenes in which the director uses technical tricks to see how close he can come to making impossible stage directions (a Müller specialty) possible.

Why, when you can gorge visually on headless bodies, skeletons, and innumerable other candied pleasures of sensationalism, should you bother cracking your nut over the historical subtleties of, say, Nazi widows begging a fleeing Croatian SS-man to kill them so they won't be raped by "Asiatic" Russian soldiers? Yes, Müller wrote such gruesome images, but the last choice he would have made as a director was simply to reproduce them physically. Haussmann's single truly original contribution was the addition of a malevolent and unfunny court jester who acts as a colluding chorus and whose motley serves mostly to magnify the play's motley of styles.

The jester's finest moment is also Haussmann's: departing from the text, he grins and introduces three "Brecht widows" by name (Helene Weigel, Elisabeth Hauptmann, Isot Kilian) in violation of an agreement the theater made with the Brecht heirs to keep them anonymous even in the program. When an actor arrives to rehearse a speech from *Galileo*, the bearded women badger him patriarchally with corrections and line readings until he runs off in distraction.

The fictional site of this anti-rehearsal, the Berliner Ensemble, is the actual site of Martin Wuttke's Berlin premiere of *Germania 3*, and one can imagine the backstage discussions of the Brecht-widows scene there. In fact, the staging was more respectful than Haussmann's, with anonymity preserved and the women dressed elegantly in ornate veils and long-trained gowns, but Wuttke's restraint (with people he must continue to work with, after all) ought not to eclipse his extraordinary artistic courage in the production overall. With acute sensitivity to the spirit rather than the letter of Müller's work, this thirty-seven-year-old actor with no previous directing experience (one of the theater's three new leaders) set aside fidelity and homage to begin with, concentrating instead on carving a comprehensible, apprehensible core from an unwieldy mélange.

A raked stage, devoid of furniture, is split into pure black and white halves, each used to frame elegantly crafted tableaux whose visual power is heightened by the stark contrast of the other side. On this essentializing background the action clips along at a pace so snappy that the show ends after an hour and forty minutes. With most plays, such a pace would lighten and clarify, but with material as poetically and referentially laden as Müller's it becomes, oddly enough, its own sort of burden. Hell-bent on lightening up, the actors are nevertheless chained to the gravity of what they must say, and the effort to carry both responsibilities generates an infectious anxiety that follows them like a tin can.

Wuttke's concept might be described as unembarrassed reductiveness, employing seemingly simple oppositional contrasts whenever possible, as if to provide ground beneath the flurry of ideas and anxieties. The theater building, for instance, is papered with black and white posters reading NO ONE OR EVERYONE and THERE ISN'T ENOUGH FOR EVERYONE—slogans from one of Hitler's monologues intended to distill the communist and capitalist mythologies, and hence their justifications for murder. When scenes align themselves clearly under this opposition, the emphasis is helpful, illuminating. When they don't, the inevitable response is suspicion and pique—as when Wuttke, apparently at a loss to fit several scenes into his puzzle, simply seats actors in the theater's boxes to shout overlapping, incomprehensible lines to each other. But the gains far outweigh the losses.

Müller has a chance to come to words in Berlin in ways he is deprived of from the outset in Bochum. Internationally famous actor Ekkehard Schall in a dinner jacket and handlebar moustache, for instance, stands onstage for ten minutes before turning to speak about his nightly angst over the "light sleep" of the dead. His words identify him as Stalin only halfway through his monologue; hence, the audience listens harder than was possible with the look-alike actor in Bochum, possibly even speculating on connections with BE politics that would have made Müller smile.

A similarly light hand is taken with other historical figures, also to make room for the "content" of the current moment—as when one top-hatted figure says to another, gazing about the BE, "the mausoleum of German socialism," eliciting a long laugh from spectators. The figures are supposed to be socialist heroes Ernst Thälmann and Walter Ulbricht, on patrol as guards atop the Berlin Wall, but how many spectators, even from the former GDR, would have sufficient knowledge of those figures to savor the joke? Too few, thinks Wuttke, who leaves them generic in a demonstration not only of good theatrical instincts but also of just the sort of refreshing humor and honesty about self that will be needed to save this troubled ensemble.

"Who knows?" I thought as the lights went down on Wuttke's shrewd production. Maybe Müller-the-ghost will turn out to be more effective than Müller-the-man at ferreting out ghosts among the living. He often said that dictatorship, with all its attendant pressure of censorship and whimsical power, offered better conditions for drama than democracy. Lest we congratulate ourselves prematurely on those pressures disappearing after 1989, we need only ponder the case of the Brecht heirs, who clearly keep the home fires burning, and burning.

(1996)

Press Passes

The following twenty pieces are selected from the 140 theater columns I wrote for New York Press *between the fall of 1997 and the spring of 2001. They are organized by theme, the themes having emerged from the selections and not the other way round. Writing regularly for a newspaper, a critic is necessarily buffeted by the whims and winds of the theater that happens on his watch, and in retrospect what seems to me most interesting about that is the way those winds (the David Mamet and Arthur Miller booms of the late 1990s, for instance) occasionally blew open windows to long dormant thoughts and smoldering obsessions.*

Mameticisms

NEW MAMET CREATIONS CAME THICK AS MANHATTAN STAR-
buckses during this period—play premieres, new novels, films,
essays, not all of the same quality, to be sure, but his sheer pro-
lificness was astonishing. It also ensured that much of the work would be
ignored, or judged hastily by stock expectations. The basic ingredients of
Mamet's drama have always appealed to me—his terse, staccato dialogue, his affection for tricksters, con men, and petty crooks, his gift for
turning the inherent falseness of theater into narrative gold—but I came
away from this bountiful season with renewed admiration for his range
of risk, variety of output, and, most refreshing of all, his utterly un-
ingratiating artistic presence.

American Buffalo, The Atlantic Theater Company

American Buffalo, David Mamet's first two-act play, received mostly
lukewarm reviews when it appeared in 1975. Within a decade—after
several high-profile productions and a film starring Dustin Hoffman—it
helped establish his international reputation. This play and *Glengarry
Glen Ross* (written in 1983) were the works that ultimately changed

Philip Baker Hall as Donnie and William H. Macy as Teach in David Mamet's American Buffalo, *directed by Neil Pepe at the Atlantic Theater Company in New York, 2000. Credit: Mark Douet.*

many people's minds about Mamet, demonstrating that his habitual themes of deception and betrayal weren't merely the crotchets of an angry young Pinter-epigone but rather essential aspects of a coherent artistic vision encompassing American culture as a whole.

I happen to be a Mamet enthusiast. On its own, however, *American Buffalo* would never have won me over. It repulsed me in fact when I first saw it (with Al Pacino in 1981), as have a handful of other Mamet works over the years (in particular *Oleanna*). I didn't make the mistake some others did of confusing the tumid, rhythmic dialogue in *Buffalo* for botched realism; Mamet's stylizations always struck me as refreshing and superbly controlled. The problem was—and still is, in this unusually agreeable revival directed by Neil Pepe and starring W.H. Macy—the narrow frustration inherent in the play's hopeless picture of ignorant inertia, the characters' sheer paucity of self-awareness.

Junkshop-owner Don (Philip Baker Hall), lord of a seedy and cluttered bric-a-brac den in Chicago, plans a burglary with two dim-witted acquaintances: Bobby (Mark Webber), a junkie-kid who is his current protégé, and Teach (Macy), an older, swaggeringly self-doubting hood who may be a former protégé. The mark is a customer who recently bought a buffalo nickel from the store for $90, which convinced Don he'd been ripped off and was thus entitled to steal it back: "I bet it's worth five times that . . . He comes in here like I'm his fucking doorman." The essence of the action is in the flavor of this crime-that-never-happens, in the way the men's blustering about it (driven by their ineptitude) lays bare their perverse inversions of values, their reduction of the American business ethic to a degenerated, greed-based myth that perverts language and ultimately undermines the basis for all genuine connection and loyalty.

This is a beautiful plan for a drama. Unfortunately, the finished work is, for me, nearly devoid of light and air. I've now seen *Buffalo* three times, and each time the obtuseness and pettiness of these nickel-and-dime crooks leaves my stomach in knots. Their dramatic world seems to me hermetically closed, deprived of any humane vantage point from which to appreciate Mamet's subtler purposes, and the same is true, incidentally, of *Oleanna*, with its obtusely arrogant professor and viciously vindictive student pitted against one another in what might as well be a human cockfight. These are not simplistic or uninteresting texts, but they are plays in which Mamet allowed his cynicism to overwhelm his instincts regarding dramatic pleasure.

Waiting for Godot is a good comparison, since it, too, is built around a static non-action. Imagine Beckett stripping Didi and Gogo of, say, the suspicious information they occasionally offer about their pasts ("I remember the maps of the Holy Land. Coloured they were. Very pretty") and their occasional self-conscious references to the performance itself ("This is becoming really insignificant" "Not enough"). The effect would be suffocating rather than, as the final work is, heartbreakingly expansive and liberating. The closest *Buffalo* comes to providing such breezes is Teach's anomalously polemical definition of "free enterprise" in Act 1—"The freedom . . . Of the *Individual* . . . To Embark on Any Fucking Course that he sees fit . . . In order to secure his honest chance to make a profit"—which is quickly swallowed in the general bathos. Mamet's other plays open themselves up through self-conscious role-playing, often introducing some form of it (the real-estate salesmen in *Glengarry* as actors employed to hoodwink customers, the movie execs in *Speed-the-Plow* as cynical dream merchants) that the audience can associate with a general human affliction. If this exists in *Buffalo*, it's so muffled in quasi-realism, you have to work to dig it out.

I'd like to believe that Neil Pepe's production is consciously designed to dig this self-consciousness out, and to let in some humane air. That, however, would imply that the artistic director of the Atlantic Theater (which Mamet co-founded) shares my feelings about the play, which is unlikely. In any case, Pepe's is the lightest, most language-centered and least ominous production of *Buffalo* I've seen. It will challenge the preconceptions of anyone who views the work (as many critics did in the 1970s and 80s) as a *Lower Depths*-like snapshot of sleazy underworld life. None of the three actors seems to care a whit whether he comes off as a believable loser. Indeed, Macy's Teach is so articulate, unmenacing and clean-cut, with his polyester grey suit and neatly groomed moustache, that he can easily lay claim to being the first Teach with whom middle-class spectators might identify.

Whether the play fully supports this is another question. There's certainly a lot of flexibility in the role, more than the previous, thug-like portrayals implied, and Macy (who played Bobby in the original Chicago *Buffalo*) deserves credit for exploring this, and for speaking Mamet's cadences and rhythms with remarkable accuracy and panache. Excellent as he is at conveying Teach's floating anger and diffidence couched in bravado, however, he's not always plausible as a criminal; his violence seems forced and his diction superior to his language gaffes ("God forbid, something inevitable occurs"). Hall, moreover, has the same problem, magnified: he's very good at reciting Mametese, but he never once convinced me, with his wise, smoothly graveled voice and clear-eyed demeanor, that his Don was as thick-headed and resentful as the play indicates. This leaves Webber's Bobby, with his crooked posture and doe-eyed, chip-on-the-shoulder cluelessness, as the only wholly credible performance.

There are obviously many Mamet fans who like this play more than I do, and they may be fascinated by the truly new perspective in this production. The question is whether such a risky, counter-intuitive approach is capable of winning new converts to the work or the author.

(Mar. 2000)

Sexual Perversity in Chicago and *The Duck Variations*, Atlantic Theater Company

Tucked away in one of David Mamet's neglected essay collections (*Make-Believe Town*) is a small gem called "Girl Copy," in which he describes his experience writing for a national men's magazine in the mid-1970s. "I sat for a year in a cork-lined office and looked at photos of naked women. I did it for a living," he writes, explaining that he was paid $20,000 a year to show up occasionally and write fictional letters to the editor, bogus biographies for the photo-spread models, humorous promotional features, cartoon captions, gags, one-liners and more.

Now, many people who know his 1974 play *Sexual Perversity in Chicago*–the work that first earned him wide attention, and the second production (along with *The Duck Variations*) of the Atlantic Theater Company's all-Mamet season–might well hear such a story and say, "It figures." Since its premiere, *Sexual Perversity* has been the supreme campus teaser, the play every angry freshman wishes he had the talent and balls to write, reveling in its torrents of demeaning, macho crudeness and confused rage at women for capriciously hoarding their favors. There's more to the work, of course, but that's not obvious to those still fixated on the sort of adolescent wounds and fantasies that drive it. In any case, the reason the play is of more than prurient interest a quarter century into its prurient career is that it was actually written by a young man who, for all his interest in sex and a steady salary, had seen through the masturbatory desiccation and spiritual devastation of his culture's image-madness.

As he explains in "Girl Copy," Mamet never felt competent at the men's magazine and soon left, although his employers liked his work. He was ultimately bored by the packaged fantasies he was asked to peddle, his superego never allowed him to write about his real fantasies, and the result was what he calls "anomie." Summing up, he cites Kurt Vonnegut: "A young man is admiring the centerfold of some girlie mag. He shows it to an older man and says, 'Look at that woman!' 'Son, that's not a woman,' the older man says, 'that's a photograph.'"

Bernie Litko, the strutting, swaggering centerpiece of *Sexual Perversity in Chicago*, is essentially a clone of Vonnegut's young man. He's a product of the confusion of image and flesh, the preference for image over flesh in a culture that compulsively fetishizes ideal bodies and thus fosters self-hatred and emotional isolation on a mass scale. Acting as a sexual mentor to his friend and coworker Danny Shapiro (although he probably has no more sexual experience), Bernie helps ruin Danny's chances at a satisfying relationship with Deborah Soloman, an illustrator he meets and moves in with. Deborah is able to see through the sick, envious hostility of her former roommate, a poisonously lonely kindergarten teacher

named Joan Webber. Danny, however, is too naive and credulous to recognize that Bernie's cocky stories are implausible and his vision of sexuality has nothing to do with real women ("The Way to Get Laid is to
Treat Em Like Shit"). Danny is also too fearful and unimaginative to rise
above the catch-phrase analysis that passes for thinking all around him.
As Deborah says, bitterly, before they split: "I'm a hindrance. You're trying to understand women and I'm confusing you with information."

Contrary to what some reviewers have said, it's surprising how grace-
fully this truculently youthful, one-hour work has aged. Alexander
Dodge, the designer of Hilary Hinckle's production, knocked himself out
hunting down typical, cheap 1970s furniture for his cluttered and distracting multilevel set (which exiles all the intimate bar scenes to the
lower stratosphere and constantly burdens the actors with a pointless
obstacle course), but the play itself proves curiously indifferent to such
period immersion. Time-bound matters that once seemed central, such as
disco singles bars, sexual permissiveness, and paranoia over first-wave
feminism, now fade to unimportance beside the play's chilling picture of
permanent human disassociation. Hinckle's fine actors (three of them, at
any rate) needed no more realism than Rick Gradone's dead-on period
costumes to bring this picture colorfully alive.

Josh Hamilton finds extraordinary variety in the bleak shallows of
Danny's stunted emotions, his comical stupidity the perfect complement to
Clark Gregg's emptily confident and upbeat Bernie. Gregg also brings a
subtle, winking self-consciousness to his performance, which is risky but
ultimately fruitful, making the action seem rooted as much in the age of
cyberporn and Internet chat rooms as in the heyday of Hefner. Kate Blum-
berg's Deborah is an appealing and vibrant youngster whose earnest aloof-
ness makes it just plausible that she'd hook up with a dud like Danny. The
one casting blunder is Joan, in whom Kristin Reddick finds so little shad-
ing and subtlety that, as an icon of femaleness, her bland, unvaryingly hos-
tile character ends up seeming as reductive and spurious as a porn image.

Interestingly enough, the forty-minute *Duck Variations* (published
with *Sexual Perversity* and often produced with it) lends an air of gravity to *Sexual Perversity* that it doesn't have on its own. This 1971 play is

about two men in their sixties who could be Bernie and Danny decades later. Emil and George sit on a park bench and, for fourteen scenes, speak about ducks, apparently as an oblique way of discussing the fears, disillusionments and regrets in their own lives.

Though they seem to be friends, they decline to call each other that, and their conversation frequently degenerates into captious nit-picking, gratuitous belligerence, and abrupt denial. Each tries repeatedly to seize authority concerning discussion points that are never resolved and seem inconsequential to both. ("Did you know that many human societies are modeled on those of our animal friends?" "Pish." "I beg to differ about it." "Pish foo.") Ultimately, in the same way Bernie and Danny only seem happy when they're "acting" the parts of each other's loyal beaver-hunting buddies, George and Emil seem happy only when they lose themselves in imaginary scenarios, briefly "acting" together as ducks, hunters or (at the very end) ancient Greeks.

John Tormey and Peter Maloney are perfectly adequate as George and Emil, as far as their prodigious character-building talents can guide them. The problem is, a very little acting detail goes a long way in this most Beckettian of Mamet's early works. Tormey and Maloney often come off as doing too much. As in Beckett, these roles require as much attention to the staccato music of the author's chiseled verbal cadences and the sculptural shape of the play's static physical circumstance as to the development of coherent personalities. The embodied reality in this production is poignant and realistic–hundreds of little sighs, eye-rolls, lip-lickings, finger-raisings and so on–but it's also looser and less disciplined than the play needs to remain visually and aurally interesting.

(Jan. 2000)

The Water Engine and *Mr. Happiness,*
The Atlantic Theater Company

David Mamet is not usually thought of as a political playwright. None of his plays deal with topical issues purely for their own sake, and he has reiterated his abhorrence of explicit polemicism in drama on numerous occasions. Now, any definition of political theater that has no room for *Glengarry Glen Ross* or *Speed-the-Plow* (or *Waiting for Godot* or Richard Foreman's *Paradise Hotel*, for that matter) is uselessly narrow to my mind, but everyone understands what is usually meant by the honorific "political" when it comes to theater: it means writing like Brecht's. As it happens, Mamet himself once tried his hand at a Brechtian political parable, tailoring it to his own aesthetic, and the result was a somewhat rough-edged drama of enduring beauty, now receiving a proud revival as the opening show of the Atlantic Theater Company's all-Mamet 15th-anniversary season.

Originally written as a radio play in 1977, *The Water Engine* was adapted by the author into a stage play in 1978. It dates from the period before Mamet first went to Hollywood, when he hadn't yet settled on suspense built around psychological wrinkles and plot twists as an essential feature of his scripts. Subtitled "An American Fable," *The Water Engine* is a melodramatic, almost cartoonish allegory about the American myths of progress and self-invention—a blast at certain depredations of monopoly capitalism that was clearly cooking in his mind during the American bicentennial celebrations and is, if anything, more relevant in today's environment of anticompetitive mega-mergers and out-of-control executive salaries than it was then.

The setting is 1934 Chicago. In his spare time, a punch-press operator named Charles Lang has invented an engine that runs only on distilled water, and he contacts a lawyer named Gross to help him patent it. Gross betrays him to big business (represented by another slimy lawyer named Oberman), which is in league with the police, and these forces try to steal and extort the engine from him. When he resists, he and his sister Rita are hunted down, beaten and killed. As many critics have pointed out, this story, taken by itself, is like a weak parody of 1930s social-protest drama.

There's much more going on in *The Water Engine*, though. The stage, for one thing, is outfitted as a 1930s radio studio, which emphasizes the "acted" nature of even the most realistic scenes, and this histrionic action is itself played out against the background of the Century of Progress Exposition, represented by a Barnumesque "Barker" who occasionally extols technological discovery ("the concrete poetry of Humankind") and then trails off into platitudes ("Much is known and much will *yet* be known, and much will not be known"). Another voice, called "announcer," occasionally speaks scare-tactic passages from a chain letter, warning listeners not to "break the chain," only it's never clear whether that chain is a figure for commerce (seen as a pyramid scheme that excludes Lang), or Lang's sort of heroic individualism which insists that capitalists play by their own rules.

The naive us-them schema of Lang's story, in other words, is constantly complicated by its manner of presentation and the events rushing around it, which suggest that no one is wholly innocent because the system that destroys this man is perpetuated by mythic fictions held dear by him and nearly everyone else. As still another interrupting voice, a soapbox speaker from Bughouse Square, asks at the climax: "What happened to this nation? Or did it ever exist?...I say it does not exist. And I say that it never existed. It was all but a myth. A great dream of avarice... The dream of a Gentleman Farmer."

Director Karen Kohlhaas has captured this atmosphere of blithe complicity with a cool elegance and confidence that smoothes over many of the rough edges. The set designed by Walt Spangler is a sleek, curvy-chrome, art-deco enclosure that (like countless modern environments from certain shopping malls to the New Times Square to the internet) entraps everyone in a nebula of technological optimism. The water engine itself (a wonderfully guileless fantasy whose splendid elemental resonance Brecht would have envied) is operated only in mime while a sound-effects technician, silhouetted at an upstage workbench, provides clanks, ratchets and whirrs. This mime makes the engine read as a trope for creative invention, which, like nearly everything else in the play, then cuts two ways. The *Daily News* reporter whom Lang calls for help, for instance—played with easy, brash suaveness by Josh Stamberg—talks impressively about the role of newspapers in a free society and really does seem to care, yet he also has no problem churning

out logrolling puff to fill a column: "the West is Golden with the promise of prosperity to come."

The rest of the cast is consistently good as well. Steven Goldstein plays
Lang as a stubby little pinion of earnest energy, wisely leaving it to others
to project the ironies that his character doesn't really contain. Similarly,
Mary McCann doesn't overcomplicate the sweet-victim role of Rita, but
manages to give her a refreshingly sensible edge; here she is played as
blind and hence physically dependent on Lang. The play's final scene, in
which the blueprints for the water engine end up in safe hands (like
Galileo's secretly written *Discorsi* at the end of Brecht's *Galileo*), bene-
fits enormously from the performances of Peter Maloney and Carl J. Ma-
tusovich, playing the candystore owner Mr. Wallace and his boy Bernie.
Their poignantly uncomprehending expressions at the final fade-out ensure that no one leaves this production entirely certain that better justice
will prevail in the long run.

We are living today (perhaps you noticed) in a bizarrely self-
narcotized era, when our nation's wealth is being concentrated in the
hands of a tiny minority to a degree that even the last century's robber
barons would've thought unimaginable, but the majority public sits idly
by, docilely content with its crumbs because they're ever so slightly larger
than its parents' crumbs were. We continue to elect real Grosses and
Obermans by the hundreds, convinced of the need to protect billionaires
at our own expense because, after all, each of us might be a billionaire
someday. For these reasons alone, I'm delighted to see *The Water Engine*
given vivid new life by a fine ensemble.

Having said that, however, I hasten to add that I'm also glad that
Mamet bade farewell to the Brechtian parable after this work. The
truth is, this form—whose odor of didacticism can never be quite
purged by complicating ironies—always had more limited theatrical
potential than its advocates claimed, and whatever was left to milk
from it in the media age Mamet realized in this piece. Moreover, his
plays from the 1980s and 90s (and some others from the 1970s) amply
demonstrated that his storytelling instincts are better served by more
truly suspenseful plots and characters of greater psychological com-

plexity; they have allowed him to write about these same American myths with even greater power and insight.

I wish I could report that the curtain-raiser *Mr. Happiness* was as delightful as *The Water Engine*. Unfortunately, this ten-minute monologue by a smug radio host who offers stern paternalistic advice to letter-writers hasn't aged nearly as well as its companion piece. The main reason is that every American today, from the lowly intern to the President, is a potential talk-show host, whereas in 1978 that self-promotional conceit still carried overtones of a weird form of self-congratulation. The performer Bob Balaban is fine as Mamet's nerdy and vaguely Krapp-like phrasemaker, but his acting mitigates none of the dated, flatfooted and obvious aspects of the monologue.

(Nov. 1999)

Boston Marriage, American Repertory Theater, Cambridge, MA

David Mamet's new play, *Boston Marriage*, is magnificent. It's one of the strangest new texts for the theater I've encountered this year and the strangest yet in Mamet's career. Nothing he has done—not the spooky innuendo in *The Cryptogram* or the gaps and disjunctions in *The Old Neighborhood* or the creepy betrayals in the films *House of Games* and *The Spanish Prisoner*—comes close to the leap of faith he took in this witty and unpredictable piece, which extends his new interest in historical period (shown for the first time in *The Winslow Boy*) in a wonderfully nutty direction. There are significant problems in the premiere production directed by the author at the Hasty Pudding Theater in Cambridge (an ART production), but, as with *The Winslow Boy*, the material is so strong that its splendidly odd texture and tone shine through anyway.

The only recent play I know of that compares meaningfully with *Boston Marriage* is *Impossible Marriage* by Beth Henley, which opened in November at the Roundabout Theater to mostly dismissive, and even some contemptuous, reviews. *Boston Marriage* is no less brave or bizarre than Henley's marvelous play, with which it shares major themes and conventions, and in all likelihood it will provoke similar grumblings of discontent and annoyance among startled followers who thought they had the playwright's experimental range more or less nailed down. Interestingly enough, both these playwrights are heterosexuals experimenting in the traditionally gay field of precious wit where ostentation coupled with flamboyance can swiftly annihilate dull conventionalism. Production matters aside, it will be telling indeed if (as the recent *New York Times* review of *Boston Marriage* indicates) the male playwright is treated with more critical respect than the female was when his studiedly artificial play comes to New York.

Boston Marriage is one of those brilliant puzzlers that is so much fun to try to figure out in performance that it seems a shame to give away too much of its plot. Plot, in any case, often takes a back seat to proudly frivolous arguments and crypto-sexual banter spoken by the all-female cast in a heightened and mannered language that sounds drafted by Wilde or Coward but finished by Genet. Wearing exquisite, floor-length turn-of-the-century dresses, the two main characters, Claire (Rebecca Pidgeon) and Anna (Felicity Huffman), occupy a synthetically silly, Dufy-esque painted set (designed by Sharon Kaitz and J. Michael Griggs) that reads "games afoot" before either woman opens her mouth: a pastiche of pastel washes and chintz effects punctuated by serpentine curlicues, red roses behind a robins-egg-blue loveseat, and a striped banner at the proscenium edged by life-saver-shaped ornaments. From the outset, such basic questions as who these women are to one another, and what the real occasion is for their meeting, rush forward, only to recede into the delectation of Mamet's poisonous verbal candy before rising again later.

"I beg your pardon. Have I the right house?" asks Claire upon entering. "What address did you wish?" responds Anna. "Two forty five." "The number is correct in all particulars." "Then it is the decor, which baffles me." "Have you not heard that this one or that, in an idle moment, conceives the idea to redecorate?"

This could be an exchange between Gertrude Stein and Alice B. Toklas, with its intense histrionic familiarity and its ambiguous pronouns that hang in the air. The conversational edges, however, are uncomfortably sharp and grow sharper, and the lesbian innuendo alternates with stories of sex with a man. Anna tells Claire that she has acquired a male "protector," who has paid for her redecoration and given her an emerald necklace (a family heirloom that will figure importantly in the plot). Berating Claire for her "so cruel and prolonged absence," Anna seems to think her friend should be happy about the income "sufficient to support both me *and* you in Comfort," but Claire stuns her with her own surprise announcement: she is "in love" with a pretty young girl. Ignoring Anna's acute jealousy, Claire further announces that she has invited the girl to the house this day for an attempted seduction, presuming upon Anna's "universally known and lauded generosity."

All this may sound perfectly clear, but it is far from straightforward in performance. The dynamic between the women is governed by strict unspoken rules that make it impossible to tell at any point how either really feels. Effete locutions suddenly give way to more typically Mametesque gutterspeak—"You Pagan slut," "Get off my tits"—without obvious cause. "I am sorry I was moved to speak with enthusiasm," says Claire after a minor altercation. At several other points, Claire pedantically corrects factual errors in Anna's conversation, as if Anna were stupid, even though her vocabulary is enormous and she quotes from a daunting array of literary sources. The intensity of the women's involvement with each other does imply mutual infatuation, but the audience is kept constantly off balance by the extremely arch and elliptical nature of the dialogue and by the self-conscious artificiality of the acting (which I'll come back to).

There is also a third character, a Maid named Catherine played with fine feigned obseisance by Mary McCann, who at first seems meek, a violet withered by comically excessive verbal abuse beyond her ken. Anna: "Cringing Irish Terror, is it? What do you want? Home Rule, and all small children to raise geese?" Catherine: "I'm Scottish, miss." Gradually, however, one notices that this maid is unsurprised and unscandalized by all the goings on, and is "acting" her meekness as Claire and Anna are "acting" their classist arrogance. She eventually comes out with openly cheeky and self-aware remarks that make it clear she is in on the elaborate game, itself a fairly obvious reference to Genet's *The Maids* (one of whose characters is named Claire). It's a mark of Mamet's superb control that while one recognizes refined and cynical scheming all along in the vein of *Liaisons Dangereuses*, the use of Genet's more extreme idea of a totalizing playacting ritual (encompassing everything, in retrospect, even the plot's apparent coincidences) comes as a complete surprise.

Mamet has often worked through manipulation of familiar conventions and, as Stanley Kauffmann pointed out in a fine recent review of *The Winslow Boy* in *The New Republic*, one of his favorites is the well-made play. Surprise curtains based on secrets known to some characters but not others, key information imparted in letters and sudden arrivals, tension and suspense built around elaborate schemes (in the third act of *Boston Marriage*, for instance, the women dress in gypsy veils and pretend to be soothsayers): the twin emphases of strict logic and ruthless competition in this 19th-century form make it a perfect vehicle for Mamet's lifelong theme of deception.

But Kauffmann's piece on *The Winslow Boy* pertains to *Boston Marriage* in another way as well; he is one of the only critics I know of willing to talk honestly about the white elephant in the room where Mamet's recent work is concerned. I'm speaking of Mamet's casting of his wife, Rebecca Pidgeon, in prominent roles whose demands she is flagrantly unequipped handle. She lacks the color and range to bring palpable life to such characters as Claire, Catherine in *The Winslow Boy*, and Deeny in *The Old Neighborhood*, and the dulling effect of her narrow repertoire is exacerbated when she appears beside seasoned and resourceful actors such as Huffman and McCann. Guided no doubt by Mamet's notorious preference for "simple directed-but-uninflected" acting (as described in his book *True and False*), both Huffman and Pidgeon devote much more attention to deadpan mugging, rhythmic delivery and hitting the right raised tones of voice than to creating believable emotional connections. Huffman, however, finds rich nuance and enduringly odd suggestion in her actions, whereas Pidgeon merely makes hers seem like deadly exercises in actorly obedience and rote memorization.

Reasonable people can differ over whether Mamet's stiffly controlled directorial style is the ideal means of maximizing the force and resonance of his language, as he thinks. It seems clear to me that the actors who have shown his work to greatest advantage—such as Joe Mantegna, Kevin Spacey, W.H. Macy and Macy's wife Huffman—have allowed themselves wide latitude beyond his eccentrically stringent restraints. *Boston Marriage*, in any case, like all his plays, will be performed in time by many better balanced casts, perhaps even by young boys (as Genet called for in *The Maids*), and regardless who is right about Mamet's current casting and staging choices, those productions will reveal much in his fine work for the first time.

(June 1999)

AFTERWORD

Three and a half years later, *Boston Marriage* arrived in New York with an embarrassing thud. In Karen Kohlhaas's production at the Public Theater, the play seemed inert, repetitive and strained, and most critics drew the straightforward conclusion that the writing was weak. Clearly, *Boston Marriage* is difficult—maybe the most difficult to direct in Mamet's tricky repertory because its playacting aspect is so fluid and variable—but the fault here was primarily the director's.

Kohlhaas's trouble began with her central decision to lean almost exclusively on the style and idiom of Wilde, as if the discovery of that allusion were clever (it is glaringly obvious) and as if the sunny execution of Wildean mannerisms and locutions were a generic cure-all able to sustain audience interest in the most underdeveloped of character dynamics. Dressed in 19th-century finery as posh as Pidgeon and Huffman's and situated in a comically narrow and hot pink but otherwise realistic period drawing room, Kate Burton and Martha Plimpton acted the roles of Anna and Claire like a Gwendolyn and Cecily *manqué*—a pair of spoiled little rich girls trying on arch and sarcastic attitudes like hats and shoes.

Plimpton, at least, vaguely fit the part. Burton's cute behavior was utterly anomalous and forced. One wished the whole time that she would rise suddenly to her grande damish reputation and chuck all the attitudinizing, seize Plimpton by her alabaster throat, and either kill her, make love to her, or both.

The two actresses were so preoccupied with keeping up the manner imposed on them—keeping it the same throughout and the same between them, even to the point of mimicking the moments when each dropped her accent—that they entirely missed the chance to develop a coherent and interestingly varied friendship. They quickly became predictable, and their bitchy, overdone language became suffocating and inadvertently serious. The maid too, played by Arden Myrin, was disastrously one-note, weeping or furrowing her brow in apparently genuine offense at every insult and affront. She was devoid of the inscrutability that makes this deliberately irritating character an interesting puzzle. Even the narrowness of the set (designed by Walt Spangler) seemed to exacerbate the lack of air in this production.

Boston Marriage is a play that lives by keeping the audience guessing about what its game is, and any production that decides too early or too sweepingly on a dominant idiom or style effectively names the game at the beginning. The pleasure of guessing disappears and the Genet-like questions of sexual power-politics and soul-deep roleplaying never meaningfully arise. Wilde's comedy-of-manners world does have a fantastical aspect, but its trappings have been around for so long that, used as drapery as in this instance, they become just another grounded convention. Mamet, bless him, didn't write a grounded play but rather a bizarre experimental escalade. He took, again, a leap in the dark and imagined a place outside his expected field of gravity where the fun entirely depends on never quite getting one's footing.

(November, 2002)

The Unsinkable Avant-Garde

FOR ME, THE TRULY "FABULOUS INVALID" HAS ALWAYS BEEN the avant-garde, not the Broadway theater. Everyone knows, of course, that much of what was once vital and dangerous in American experimental theater is now stale or neutered through co-optation, but only those sanguine enough to frequent unglamorous venues with some regularity are also aware that an indestructible variant of avant-gardism still fuels some of the sexiest and most invigorating theater in New York. This media-era avant-gardism probably deserves a different name, because it has grown awkwardly various, encompassing both savvy veterans and proudly naive youngsters, both new writing and the directing of classics, both a separatist "alternative" ethic determined not to degenerate into a brand and a counterpoised "participationist" ethic based on the clever raiding of mainstream conventions and pop culture. In any case, it's an indispensable body of work, and the body is still clearly breathing.

* * *

The Race of the Ark Tattoo, by W. David Hancock, P.S. 122 Gallery

It's one of those horribly humid New York City evenings and fat grey clouds are gathering above the East Village. I'm late for a performance at the P.S. 122 Gallery, and I just make it in the door, breathing hard, when the rain begins in earnest. Few theater events are more interesting than a really good thunderstorm, I think, as I notice that most of the thirty chairs in the gallery are empty and I join the crowd (five people) milling about tables and racks of flea-market junk in the corner. All this stuff, ostensibly a stage set, is actually for sale, says the balding, hairy-chested man sitting there in paint-stained shorts and a V-neck T-shirt. As it happens, the eighty-minute solo performance that follows, *The Race of the Ark Tattoo,* doesn't so much make me forget the rainstorm as blend in perfectly with it, leaving an impression of a diminutive wonder come upon by chance—a passing distraction that brings flashes of accidental insight and beauty.

Playwright W. David Hancock plays with chance encounters and the numerous grey areas between the authentic and the realistic, evoked through the detritus and bric-a-brac of lives gone under, displayed fetishistically in a gallery. He typically uses a performer of mysteriously uncertain identity, who tells stories about found and cheaply constructed objects belonging to the ostensibly dead. Hancock's writing abounds in radiant twists and sharp unexpected images, but the strangeness of his pieces in performance is more a product of the amateurish, utterly un-polished quality of their presentations, as well as the careful selection of the grimy artifacts.

In his previous piece—the Obie-winning *The Convention of Cartography* (1994)—some spectators left absolutely certain that Hancock (writer and performer in that case) had told true stories about a real artist named "Mike" whose work he had collected (poems on placemats and cigar-box sculptures left in public restrooms, for instance). Other spectators left equally sure that "Mike" was wholly fictional. *The Race of the Ark Tattoo,* performed by Matthew Maher and directed by

Foundry Theatre founder Melanie Joseph, sets similar traps. Programs are passed out only at the end, and I couldn't tell at any point whether Maher's desultory, object-focused stories were fiction or carelessly handled personal history. More to the point of the piece's deliberate maladroitness, I couldn't tell whether Maher himself was embarrassingly inept and confused or performing the most convincing impression of ineptitude and confusion since Ronald Reagan.

Introducing himself as Mr. P. Foster, Maher explains that he was "in and out of a number of foster homes" while growing up (note his surname), was considered unadoptable because of his "violent temper," and was treated with an anti-depressant that caused permanent memory loss. Nevertheless he has fond memories of a period spent at the foster home of Mr. Homer Phinney, a retired custodian, who had a flea market set up permanently in his Cape Cod garage. Foster apparently inherited the stuff after the old man died. Maher loads a bunch of objects into what he calls his "story ark"—a roofless toy Winnebago with a shoulder strap—and asks a spectator to choose one whose story she wishes to hear. The performance, it seems, is random to an extent, since each evening's audience will choose the objects in a different order.

The objects themselves are no more or less strange than any bits of old totemic junk kept on shrine-like shelves in people's garages and basements: a pamphlet on composting, a mayonnaise jar filled with murky water and a plastic crayfish, a crocus corm. The meandering stories attached to them, however, are often haunting and tenacious, as Foster's mind alternates between losing the thread of thought completely and discerning marvelous mystical patterns in the most mundane experiences. He and his girlfriend Jilly, for instance, "were always inventing languages. She had a language of colors and language of license plates. Most people think that a language is to communicate, but it's really to keep strangers out of your head."

A piece of foam rubber reminds Foster of a hole in the seat of Phinney's van, where he hid pennies during long drives that may or may not have included sexual abuse, and this story leads to digressions on autism, herbal concoctions for virility, and skin-dying on Easter Island. A small metal plate supposedly taken from the brain of a dead transient found in a drainage ditch leads to other digressions on maggots, medical implements and Jilly, whom Foster now visits (and still makes love to) in a comatose state after she survived a suicide attempt that was supposed to include him. He intended to jump into a quarry with her but one of his blackouts intervened.

The truth is, none of this information is as clear in performance as even this spotty description (checked against the script) sounds. Related facts are hopelessly scattered, Maher speaks in several voices, imaginary characters take over narrations without being introduced, and the digressions are extremely confusing. Each object supposedly corresponds to a typed, collage-like story-card in a scrapbook kept by Phinney, but sometimes Maher doesn't read the card after selecting it, or he says the right one was lost, or he asks a spectator to read the card and then rereads it imprecisely himself, substituting his own thoughts willy-nilly. He also implies at times that Foster may be dead too.

And the general sense of disorientation is greatly exacerbated by Maher himself, an actor with a real speech impediment that makes him seem indeterminately fragile, to which he adds a realistic Cape Cod accent and a very convincing depressive demeanor. Who *is* he? one continually wonders, as his eyes and attention wander, he forgets his lines, falls asleep, and accidentally spills the disgusting crayfish water on himself. And how seriously is any of it meant to be taken? one thinks—particularly when the stage manager, in full view at a desk to the side, is plainly bored to tears and can't even be bothered finding the right place in the script when Maher confesses he's "blank."

The Race of the Ark Tattoo certainly invites any amount of sober inquiry into its many questions of authenticity and identity. Equally remarkable to me, though, is the fact that a theater artist has been able to make such fruitful use of the flea-market aesthetic that has been a staple of the art world for at least a decade. The tradition of the found object, which harks back to Dada, has entered something like a golden age with such artists as David Hammons, Donald Lipski, Nancy Rubins, Erica Svec and Gabriel Orozco. Lately, Orozco has even taken to videotaping his day-long hunts for precious discards and overlooked "moments" around the city. Then he exhibits the tapes.

Hancock is the only artist I know of, though, who has truly made theater—as opposed to theatrical gallery art—out of this trend, by which I mean that he hasn't only held up for appreciation the objects themselves, or his eye for them, or his ability to transform them, but rather focused on their narrative baggage presented as dramatic action. It's a simple but crucial shift in emphasis. The lure of other people's tawdry treasures has always been strong in the "fallen" modern era. ("If they don't want it, I don't want it," my mother used to say, unconvincingly, as she stepped on the gas.) But Hancock has shown that this lure can also extend to the "other people," the treasures' proprietors, as long as one keeps their authenticity equally doubtful and allows the objects to float free of determinable origins again in the end, as on a mental ark. It's not exactly a rainstorm, but the whiff of the flood is unmistakable.

(July 1998)

Paradise Hotel, By Richard Foreman, Ontological Theater at St. Marks

In the current issue of *Artforum* is a modest proposal by the artist Mike Kelley. It suggests a plan of relief for an American population "so sex-starved, we have created for ourselves a popular culture industry that bombards us continually with a pantheon of fantasy figures of desire." Kelley proposes that the elite class of "stars" who are currently "granted all that society has to offer, yet give back nothing tangible in return" should become real "citizens" by actually providing the social service that "they only hint at presently." That is, they should "be required by law to put in time at government-sponsored sex clinics, where they will be accessible to all." Kelley further proposes that, since the number of celebrities is too small to provide adequate service to all those exposed to mass media, free plastic surgery should be available, enabling anyone to become the "double" of a celebrity of choice—the only price for this

Tony Torn (back to camera), Juliana Frances and Mark Doscow in Richard Foreman's Paradise Hotel, *1999.* CREDIT: PAULA COURT.

operation being "service in the public sexual-satisfaction work force."
Within a generation, people will begin to "construct their own desire free
from the effect of any prefabricated standard" and "sexual repression will
cease to be a major factor as a cause for mental and physical illness."

Because this fine program is unlikely to become public policy, alas, I
humbly propose the following as a more practical substitute: that all 535
members of Congress, plus the guy in the stocks, be required to attend a
performance of Richard Foreman's *Paradise Hotel*. This will force the
most prominent power-brokers in our nation to engage in seventy-five
minutes of dangerously unpredictable thought about American sexual denial, particularly the culture's sick habit of seeing the unruliness of desire
not as liberating but as an opportunity to entrap, exploit and wound.
Some of our esteemed leaders, terrified of what they don't understand in
the play and their loins, will of course cry for censorship. Others, worried
about coming off as philistines, will discover a new fondness for the
avant-garde. Still others, experiencing real sexual epiphanies, will appear
on TV to offer their bodies for state-sponsored prostitution. The whole
episode will strike the public as so pathetic that every last politician will
be replaced in the next elections with someone capable of saying in public something compassionate, intelligent and worldly about sex. The Disney Corporation will ring in the new age by re-recalling all 3.4 million
copies of the animated feature *The Rescuers* it first recalled last week (due
to the appearance of a topless woman for one fifteenth of a second) and
replacing them with enhanced-image copies in which the naked woman
can actually be seen with the naked eye.

We all know the problem, but it takes an extraordinary artist like
Foreman to bring sustenance and inspiration to the sarcasm and irony
that have become every thinking American's shield against frustration
and despair at sexual hypocrisy. Actually, *Paradise Hotel* is itself full of
frustration and desperation—as is every Foreman work, I suppose. This
play, however, seems to me even more impatient than usual with, say,
the impoverishment of language due to our era's enshrinement of ado-
lescence; practically every tenth word in the text is "fuck." Moreover, its
theme of sexual adventure (always implicit in Foreman but now central

and explicit) has the deepest connection possible to his characteristic "unbalancing" techniques. His work is designed to set spectators off balance, make them anxious about the fact that every time their minds pause to mull over a performed moment, several others, equally complex and fascinating, speed by unmulled. If capturing it all is always a futile fantasy, then futile fantasy is the ideal subject matter.

Set in one of Foreman's trademark spaces ritualistically cluttered with bric-a-brac such as striped pillars, strings, plexiglass front panels, clusters of gold-painted dolls, non-functioning clocks, electric candles, blackboards mysteriously draped with cloths, prints of classic paintings pocked with bullet holes, an upside-down gorilla near the ceiling, the show begins with a manic softshoe by the nine-member cast to a scratchy tape-loop ("I'm happy, you're happy, I'm happy, you're happy...") and then this announcement: "All audiences must now be informed that this play *Paradise Hotel* is not, in fact, *Paradise Hotel*, but is in truth, a much more disturbing and possibly illegal play entitled *Hotel Fuck*! We do apologize, ladies and gentlemen—but rather than being disturbed at this revelation—we urge you, please, re-direct your understandable distress—towards an even more potent threat—posed—by yet a third—much LESS provocatively titled play, entitled—*Hotel Beautiful Roses.*"

For the remainder of the action, the five principal actors (four men and a woman—the remaining four are female chorus members) seem in full agreement on the advantages of the presumably illicit Hotel Fuck, which is sometimes personified and which they may or may not ever arrive at. They also seem variously anxious about the encroachment, symbolic or otherwise, of Hotel Beautiful Roses on Hotel Fuck. It's as if the real underlying tension in the play (which contains lots of lewd gesturing and posing, and frontal nudity as well) were between rival images or ideas of sexuality, one brazen and crude, the other furtive and refined, with everyone worried that the latter is merely a pretext for prudery. Leave it to Foreman to set up this conflict—as unresolvable as that between maleness and femaleness—and then sit back and watch as his cool downtown audience cheers for the supposedly paradisiacal crude side while fantasizing about all the humping, crotch-rubbing, spread-eagled actors as if they were Kelley's celebrity "doubles."

Little else in the piece is so readily summarized. The men are dressed in a motley of small caps, striped shirts and suspenders with strange cross-straps. They look like bell-hops from different extraterrestrial hotels, and the choral women, dressed in nearly identical cute black skirts, pom-pom hats and sensible knee-high fishnets, seem like underlings who do the real work. Two characters, Julia Jacobson (Juliana Francis) and Tony Turbo (Tony Torn), are more sexually objectified and eager for multiple partners than the others. She is a leggy, long-haired beauty in wire-rims, side-braids and a hiked-up slip dress who creates consternation when she begs to get "deliciously fucked" by two men at one time: "Mixed up fucking like that, we could end up losing our individual body orientation. Hey!" Tony, by contrast, is a roly-poly, sex-starved pudgeball who stares dumbly (and hilariously) a lot and bends over a table in his "party dress" while Julia holds a target over his butt.

At one point, Julia and Tony have a "girl-girl" fight with sponge-sledgehammers, which soon expands into a mock-violent dance for the whole company. At another point, the characters take turns shooting themselves, as a result (they say) of "selfishness," the threat of beautiful flowers, and other insurmountable pressures. Later, the character Ken Puss Puss (Jay Smith) enters festooned with roses, after which Giza von Goldenheim (Gary Wilmes) walks on, atop cothurni, dressed elegantly as Louis XIV and holding up an enormous striped phallus with a dainty ribbon, and Julia, with uncharacteristic coyness, asks him to adjudicate the question of whether "fucking can always be better with better decoration."

The magic, as usual in Foreman, depends on the sort of acting that treats everything the performer does as "a brilliant decision, especially if it is something stupid" (as he once put it himself). Since his characters aren't coherent personalities with consistent motivations but rather shifting collections of provocative, hysterical and paranoid behaviors that become sites for temporary mental attachment, he relies enormously on such masters of innuendo as Wilmes, Torn, Francis, and Smith, who really can set the mind spinning with just a single silly frozen pose, eccentric locution or tortured glance. For me, the one weak link in this cast is Tom Pearl as Tommy Tuttle, whose one-note belligerence and mafioso accent rather put my mind to sleep.

Near the end of *Paradise Hotel*, as the probably illegal final tableau unfolds onstage, Foreman's recorded voice—which has been heard frequently over loudspeakers throughout the piece—returns one last time, like the afterthought of an impish god. "Here I am," it says. "Oh—here I am again, for the hundredth time, just doing my thing. Just doing my real true thing, for the hundred-millionth time. Again and again and again." And at that moment my ricocheting thoughts bounced from sex to Foreman's forty-odd Ontological-Hysteric Theater productions over the past thirty-one years (things done "again and again") to Rudy Giuliani, whose nose was also tweaked by the scene's nudity. Fuck the Washington crowd if they won't come, I told myself then. Redemptive scandals are where you find them.

(Jan. 1999)

House/Lights, By Gertrude Stein, The Performing Garage

According to a famous myth, Picasso found it impossible to paint a likeness of Gertrude Stein in eighty sittings, but captured it exquisitely months later from memory. True or not, this story has served over the years as a testament to Picasso's genius, to the power of subjective impression, and to the triumph of modernism in freeing artists from slavish dependency on direct observation. The myth also reflects on Stein, though, and suggests a somewhat more current paradigm of the artist who successfully eludes encapsulation, whose work tends to slip further away the closer one stares at it, but who (like Samuel Beckett) seems to invite the very sort of dogged, assiduous scrutiny that conceals her essence. Long cherished as a world-class figure for her stories, sketches and essays, Stein, author of over seventy plays, has remained obscure as a dramatist—partly because of her deliberate abstruseness of course, but also because most directors lack the insight, imagination, and patience to

Suzzy Roche and Kate Valk (upside down) in the Wooster Group's House/Lights, *directed by Elizabeth LeCompte at the Performing Garage in New York, 1999.* CREDIT: MARY GEARHART.

paint her work, as it were, from memory. That's what the plays really require, and that's what Elizabeth LeCompte does best.

A year ago, I wrote that LeCompte's kabuki-inspired production of *The Emperor Jones* with The Wooster Group wasn't merely an interesting adaptation but rather the best production of that O'Neill play I'd seen. Now, *House/Lights*—LeCompte's version of Stein's *Doctor Faustus Lights the Lights*, which has opened for review after two years of development in rehearsal and on tour—is the most inspired production of Gertrude Stein I've seen. It's certainly the only one I've fully enjoyed. LeCompte's instinct for finding classic texts that are indeed freshened and clarified by her explosive multimedia deconstructions is, once again, part of what's impressive. Devoid of the arbitrariness and triviality that plagues so much other multimedia work, her pieces lay bare what was essential and enduring in the original texts and then force that core into intensely revealing interaction with mediated detritus from today's surrounding cultural environment.

Faustus was originally written as an opera libretto in 1938, and it has the reputation of being one of Stein's most accessible dramas, not because it's really any easier to follow in performance than her other work, but because it's rooted in a familiar legend and makes some compromises with chronological time (events in one act actually seem to follow from those in the previous one, and so on). The title character is the inventor of electric light and seems to be a figure for an era that has sold its soul for technology. Faustus complicates this neat picture, however, by arguing with Mephisto over whether he really has a soul to sell and otherwise speaking as if he doesn't consider the deal certain or final. The lights sometimes sing and dance like an inanimate chorus, characters switch sexes and become plural willy-nilly, stage directions and character designations are often indistinguishable from dialogue, and a young woman named "Marguerite Ida and Helena Annabel," who seeks help from Faustus after being bitten by a phallic "viper," becomes a second protagonist. In the end, Faustus longs for darkness and begs Mephisto to take him to hell ("I have sold my soul to make a light and the light is bright but not interesting in my sight"), his final despair in part a reaction to Marguerite Ida and Helena Annabel's progress toward sexual independence.

As one might expect, LeCompte has pumped this old text, with its complicated semantic humor and dense web of classical references, full of her particular frenetically savvy and technophilic energy. The set (by Jim Findlay) is an architectonic thicket of metal frames and railings, seesaw ramps with sliding tables, video monitors, wide banks of bright fluorescent striplights, stools, couches, and numerous incandescent lights of different styles, including several huge bulbs hanging on hinged strips from a mobile pipe overhead. The eight actors dash madly about these obstacles with a surefooted awkwardness that strongly recalls Richard Foreman, with Kate Valk playing Faustus in high heels and a tight grey dress with an odd bulbous ring around the buttocks similar to the one she wore as Brutus Jones. Suzzy Roche is similarly encumbered as Mephisto with badly pencilled eyebrows and little goat-horns on her head. Voices are miked, distorted and punctuated with quacking, ringing and other sounds, and the actors sometimes lip-synch to snippets of music too various to list and assorted video images ranging from attractive static to Desi Arnez to a water ballet to a scene from *Young Frankenstein*. One woman spends much of the action delicately "playing" a laptop computer downstage like a musical instrument.

All of this belongs more or less to the basic Wooster Group vocabulary, however. The really unique and crucial decision behind *House/Lights*, the one that gave it its fascinatingly ambivalent comic texture, was the incorporation of an inadvertently brilliant sexploitation film from 1964 called *Olga's House of Shame* (directed by Joseph Mawra). Perceiving the Steinian qualities in an obscure film like this and knowing how to apply them was what I meant before by painting from memory. The film is narrated by a cheery, newsreel-style male voice that tells of a rash of retaliatory violence against female underlings committed at an abandoned mine by a ruthless international crime boss named Olga. The footage itself, however, is always explicitly titillating and seems to mock even this alibi-narrative by concentrating on "torture" scenes in which pretty, deadpan Olga (in high-fashion clothes) seems about as dangerous as a stuffed animal, all the violence is ridiculously phony, and the real action seems to be about consensual bondage games. Olga takes a while to acknowledge her lesbian inclinations openly, and this is one link with Stein and the slow coming-of-age of Marguerite Ida and Helena Annabel. Another link, though, is the film's flat, affectless atmosphere and sense of disjunction between words and intentions, words and actions, and actions and reactions. The parallel of this flatness, or deliberate phoniness, is far more compelling to me than the strained plot parallels LeCompte suggests by giving all the *Faustus* characters secondary names from the film.

Stein thought this sort of disjunction ("syncopation" was her word) was implicit in theater and tried to make it explicit in her plays, but LeCompte improved on the idea, using it not only to emphasize the famous "continuous present" but also to reintroduce danger to this self-mocking play. Every time a conspicuously unfrightening torture scene from the film is also acted out live, for instance (as happens several times), the live actors behave in a noticeably more violent manner than the filmed ones, reminding the audience of the presence of and risk to live bodies in this wild play about damnation. Similarly, whenever one of the live actors poses on a stool to duplicate a salacious breast- or crotch-shot from the film, the play's somewhat abstract connection between plural identity and female degradation becomes suddenly and jarringly concrete.

Fortunately, LeCompte is above easy political positiontaking, obviously aware that the whole spirit of this show depends on maintaining the irresolvable rift between sincerity and insincerity. She consequently has no qualms about letting the entire second act (which deals with Marguerite Ida and Helena Annabel's "curative" encounters with Faustus and other male figures) become a wonderfully hammy set-piece for Valk. Valk sits center stage the entire time, poised between pillows and framed by metal poles, talking by turns neutrally, snidely and conspiratorially in a dewdrop Betty-Boop voice to a microphone outfitted with a viper's head, the viper speaking back to her in the hilarious, ventriloquist-dummy voice of John Collins.

Doctor Faustus Lights the Lights, as it happens, has been something of a rite of passage among American avant-gardists: Robert Wilson directed it in 1992, Richard Foreman in 1982, Larry Kornfeld in 1979 (with the Judson Poet's Theater), and Judith Malina in 1951 (the first production of The Living Theater). Unfortunately, I saw none of these versions. I have, however, seen eight or ten other Stein productions (including Wilson's *Four Saints in Three Acts* and an expensive German version of *Faustus*), most of which were unbearably tedious, providing me many hours to ponder why this author's particular playfulness is so hard to get right on-stage. Stein's ideas and insights about language and theater are no more or less difficult to apprehend, in the end, than those of any other fiercely idiosyncratic modernist, such as Joyce, Beckett or Artaud. The problem, I think, is the blandness and sleepiness in her writing, rooted in her sing-songy nursery-rhyme cadences and simple reiterative vocabulary, which was always controversial and hasn't aged at all well in the info age. The deadliest equation, in my experience, is Stein paired with a director (such as Wilson) who tries to superimpose a differently faux-naive performance idiom and ends up with a mixture of two flavorless liquids. The best, as LeCompte brilliantly demonstrates, is the director whose street-smarts tell her when to walk away and where to go.

(Feb. 1999)

Automatic Earth, by Kevin Cunningham, Signature Theater

The theater has a troubled relationship to new technology. Not that most of its practitioners are particularly conservative, quite the contrary, but there is an abiding conservatism in the form itself. The technical advances theaters have incorporated over the centuries, such as steel rigging, gas and electric light, hydraulic lifts, have invariably enhanced the art as it already existed. They didn't change its basic anthropocentric, language-based storytelling nature, and the same is true of most of the practices coopted from the avant-garde through this century.

The marvels of the media age are completely different, though: video and digitally altered image and sound, large-screen projection and holography, to name the most obvious examples. Like an Elvis look-alike at a bar mitzvah, such accoutrements tend to take over the theater experience, asserting themselves over all mundane human content. As Marshall McLuhan warned more than three decades ago, new media don't merely carry messages but tend to displace them. They're like robotic egomaniacs that resist being used merely to supplement or embellish stories enacted by living people in real time, despite the existence of a few brilliant exceptions, such as Elizabeth LeCompte and The Wooster Group, who understand the intricate tightrope game of balancing live and mediated humans.

The prevalence of multi-media theater groups today has less to do with public demand than with the fact that new technology has become a winning grant-application strategy. The dominant "Oh, wow!" school of reviewers also stands ever-eager to hail anything electronically mediated as "cutting edge." The quick celebrity often afforded mixed-media artists—and art critics are greater culprits on this score than theater critics—conveys the impression that human-scale storytelling skills, usually honed over years in the past, are no longer necessary at all as long as the expensive electronic toys are themselves entertaining enough. Besides, no one in the information age has time for apprenticeships. This is why it sometimes seems as though there's an abundance of work of the caliber of The Wooster Group out there when, actually, there's almost none.

I go avidly to see John Jesurun's pieces whenever they appear, because he always seems capable of achieving the tricky balance just mentioned, usually falling just short. Most often, though, I come across vacuous and self-important spectacles of carts pulling horses, such as GAle GAtes' *Tilly Losch*, Robert Lepage's *Elsinore,* and La Fura dels Baus's *Faust 3.0* (performed at last year's Lincoln Center Festival)—to mention only a few recent banquets that neglected to provide real food. Such events always remind me of weekend novelists with expensive computers but nothing to say, or kids who can't pass algebra walking around with calculators capable of fifty advanced math functions.

3-Legged Dog is a New York-based multi-media theater company founded in 1994 by Kevin Cunningham, Mike Taylor and Jill Szuchmacher. I haven't seen their work before, and I try not to prejudge anyone.

I did grow pretty skeptical, though, after reading in the program to *Automatic Earth* that the company considers line-production of (*not* participation in) the New York State Governor's Conference on Art and Technology to be one of its major credits. It also didn't help to learn (from a 1998 article in *The Villager* supplied with the press materials) that the origin of the company's name is a mishap suffered by Cunningham's pit bull Sid, who lost a leg while chasing a car. Sid's accident might strike some people as a sign that the dogged pursuit of technology can be harmful. Cunningham saw it rather as "a metaphor for the artist, and what's needed... persistence in the face of adversity."

Happily, *Automatic Earth*, written by Cunningham and directed by Rick Mordecon, isn't entirely vacuous. It has an interesting premise, snatches of lovely writing, at least two excellent actors, and captivating sixteen-by-twenty-four-foot video images that actually illuminate the enacted story at times. Those times, alas, are much too fleeting and scattered to save the images from seeming arbitrary and trivially rooted in science-envy (fast-action weather-satellite pictures, for instance, and transmuting graphics supposedly based on chaos theory). The well-written speeches (spoken mostly by a brain-damaged central character) are surrounded by thudding clichés and glaring narrative oversights.

The first live tableau, which follows contemplative pre-show footage of rushing clouds and the sound of wind, is savagely comic: a man (P. J. Sosko) quivering on the floor with a pitchfork through his head. This is Vining, victim of a horrible farm accident, who is taken to an upstate New York mental hospital where callous doctors, thug-like attendants and a crowd of inmates who mill about, occupied with various bizarre and disgusting obsessions, erase with triteness whatever interest the harsh comedy had to begin with. Vining is (of course) a poetic soul whose complexity the institutional yahoos can't fathom, but as he slowly regains language—incessantly writing and then speaking in aphasic jumbles reminiscent of the patients in Arthur Kopit's *Wings* and Susan Yankowitz's *Night Sky*—he briefly connects with a fellow inmate named Cabid (C. P. Thornhill), a pathological "biter." Then he's thrown out into the cold, cruel world.

The show establishes a parallel between Vining's journey (from accident to recovery to post-hospital wanderings) and the development of a category five hurricane, from the belch of a cannibalistic frog in Mali to various air currents it affects to continent-sized cloud-swirls and tornado-force winds. Trouble is, the often stunning weather footage and scientific graphics, some beautifully altered, are described and discussed exclusively by an anomalous, techno-babbling female narrator (Vera Beren) who strips down to ever sexier clothing while perched on a spiral staircase to the side. She seems much less intent on clarifying causes or principles than on proving that she too has a poetic soul (after all, she's wearing a slip!). At one point, for instance, she speaks of the hurricane's "harsh spirals of auto-cannibalism along its inner eye wall," a facile, undigested reference to the frog's and Cabid's cannibalism (it seems), which clunks inertly like the dozens of other wooden nickels she drops.

With the hospital inmates remaining inexplicably onstage the entire time, Vining has a short affair with a drifter and former stripper named Chester (Sara Parry) whom he meets on the road—a sequence so touchingly acted by Sosko and Parry that it briefly made me think the whole show-offy, half-understood science pageant might actually transform into a play. Then the plot utterly degenerates, as Chester leaves him, he befriends a stereotypical junkie-artist named Jerry (Stephen Payne) in Houston, and almost finds Chester again. A manacled Cabid is seen receiving copies of Vining's cryptic poems. The ending is a digressive hodgepodge of hand-wringing by Chester and Jerry and a long, impossible-to-follow monologue by Vining about a perfect landscape. No question of patching things up here with revising and editing. The very basic problem is that Cunningham never really thought through how all his nifty weather videos, digital effects and technospeak formed a meaningful backdrop to any volitional human journey.

The playwright Max Frisch once quipped that "technology . . . [is] the knack of so arranging the world that we don't have to experience it." For two and half millennia, good playwriting has been the knack of so arranging stories about human life that even the most thick-skinned can't help but experience them. The battle lines have long been drawn, and the enduring multi-media artists, like all successful mediators, will be those who listen respectfully and imaginatively to the demands of both sides.

(July 1999)

A *Streetcar Named Desire,* by Tennessee Williams, New York Theater Workshop

Two years ago, the Belgian director Ivo van Hove burst brazenly onto the New York scene with a production of an unfinished Eugene O'Neill play that was one of the most intelligent, magnificently erotic, and profoundly theatrical events of the season. His *More Stately Mansions* featured a stage divided into emotional territories rather than realistic locations, nude wrestling during what would otherwise have been a trite husband-wife spat, and superbly controlled animalistic snarling, hissing, and barking that cut to the rich psychological core beneath O'Neill's ambivalently realistic surface. It was a stunningly physical, unforgettably immediate production, as flattering to O'Neill's memory as The Wooster Group's *Emperor Jones*, even though public discussion of it was enfeebled by an inane controversy over the ethics of reviving the work.

Now van Hove is back with *A Streetcar Named Desire*, written by an equally sacrosanct American theater icon, and since this play certainly was finished for production, and since the classic script is more or less intact here, no Williams protectors are likely to protest. The director's concept, however, is every bit as aggressive and perceptive as the one used for O'Neill, featuring the same cavalier disregard for realistic surfaces and emotional definition of space, and even more nudity. If the result is somewhat less stunning overall than *More Stately Mansions*, it is nevertheless extraordinarily interesting—a clear-sighted and disturbing view of a work whose enshrinement within its original performance style has often circumscribed it as a harmlessly pretty perennial. (I haven't seen the recent opera adaptation of *Streetcar*, nor has it yet played in New York.)

Designed by van Hove's frequent collaborator Jan Versweyveld, the set is a broad expanse of plain, rough planks with a working bathtub to one side and an impressive array of musical instruments (played by Chris Cochrane and Avram K. Fefer) arranged along the black rear wall amid hanging metal rods, a spring stretched between metal barrels and a strip of pale purple light. This could be one of Jim Findlay's constructions for The Wooster Group, except that the actors almost never interact with the instruments and metallic objects, only with the bathtub, a few non-descript chairs and, once, an electric guitar. Hand props and furniture are scarce, there are no walls, even of the diaphanous sort popularized by *Streetcar*'s original designer Jo Mielziner, and the actors never bother with mime to clarify place or intention (turning doorknobs, say, or dealing cards, or raising drinking glasses). References to such practical details aren't cut, but they're treated as quaint archaic verbiage, to be rushed through dismissively (often at the expense of Williams' celebrated lyricism) on the way to the real substance beneath: a cruel battle for love, security and existence itself (partly set to clangorous background music) in which social veneers are merely survival strategies.

This battle is incipient even in the preshow action, which omits the famous bellowing for Stella and other introductory material before Blanche Dubois arrives. As the house lights dim, Elizabeth Marvel as Blanche smokes and paces upstage in a see-through negligee as a stern-faced black woman (later identified as the neighbor Eunice, played by Saidah Arrika Ekulona) sits inscrutably to the side. Cacophonous, clanking music rises, Blanche strips naked, puts on long lace gloves and a tight summer dress as if girding for a fight, and then she grimly walks downstage to meet Eunice. A traditional Blanche modeled on Jessica Tandy or Vivien Leigh would assert herself at this point with inflated airs and an exaggerated accent; instead, Marvel slumps unattractively, speaks in low, measured, reasonable tones about the problems of her trip, and submits patiently to what seems like an aggressive interrogation from Eunice ("I think she said you taught school...And you're from Mississippi, huh?"). Thus begins the most original ingredient in this willfully unconventional interpretation: Blanche isn't portrayed as a flighty and fragile ditz but as the only character in the play with any common sense, wit or charm.

For van Hove, apparently, *Streetcar* isn't a sentimental tale about the final destruction of a hypersensitive misfit; it's rather the horrifying spectacle of a benumbed and bedazed social group callously purging itself of a nonconformist who is by far its most appealing member. The nudity, for instance, cuts through the dated pretenses that usually make Blanche seem out of touch while keeping the audience acutely aware of the ruthless judgements our society visits on women's aging bodies (no less today than when the play was written in 1947). The thirtyish-looking Jenny Bacon, who plays Stella, and the fortyish-looking Marvel are constantly undressing and dressing again in various 1940s period costumes, inviting appreciation and comparison of their different physical beauties. According to the play, Blanche is in a panic over her diminishing attractiveness to men, to whom she has compulsively (and ineffectually) attached herself for protection. Marvel's chain-smoking but self-possessed Blanche, however, never treats this panic with full seriousness. She seems more impatient than frightened, more exhausted with the charade of femininity than trapped by it. It's as if she had come to her sister's home to find real sympathy and companionship at long last, or else to expire in a wholly conscious endgame.

The quality of consciousness in the show is its saving strangeness. Van Hove is the enemy of subtext, it seems, revealing it explicitly again and again through peculiar vocal deliveries and atextual physical action. Bruce McKenzie as Stanley Kowalski, for instance, chugs three beers in quick succession upon entering, deliberately ignoring Blanche as she sits primly on the chair beside him. Then, in the following scene, his suspicious search for the tin box of papers about Belle Reve consists not of rifling through Blanche's suitcase but of groping her body up and down—his alpha male's privilege to intimidate and violate her asserted firmly and quickly.

Bacon's Stella, for her part, moves through much of the play in a stupor of selfish cupidity, pawing and draping herself over Stanley whenever possible, hungrily kissing his disgustingly greasy hands, even writhing in pleasure as he fondles her during the lonely birthday party for Blanche when Mitch (nicely played by Christopher Evan Welch) stands her up.

The only breach in this Stella's total loyalty to Stanley is a brief interlude of feline furiousness that interrupts one of their carnal embraces during the discussion of the Napoleonic Code—a sudden furiousness (conceived more musically than rationally) that is soon turned on Blanche as well. Both Bacon and Marvel deserve medals for the variety and rich depth they bring to a performance style that seems built on a theory of predominant surfaces.

Which brings me to the chief reason why, for all this production's admirable clarity and fabulous physicality, I think it nevertheless lacks the deep, emancipatory heat that all its stripping, stroking, splashing, dancing and raving imply it should have (and that *More Stately Mansions* did have). The problem is a sorely miscast Stanley. A sharp-featured, sandy-haired actor of medium build, McKenzie plays this famously seductive role with a humorlessly quarrelsome, coldly menacing manner that never warms or cracks into believable softness. Worse, he comes off as smart and savvy, never endearingly dopey or ignorant—more the hit-man-detective Killer Joe than the animalistic nature Williams conceived. In scene after scene—when ranting and quivering like an epileptic on the floor ("wasn't we happy together...till she showed here?"), for instance, or breaking up a party he doesn't like by mauling and then smashing an electric guitar—he fails to invest Stanley's violence and insensitivity with credible sensuality, and the result is a gaping hole in the erotic center of the show.

Another problem, also substantial, is conceptual. In Elia Kazan's frequently quoted director's notebook for the first production of *Streetcar* is a lucid discussion of the 19th-century "tradition"of female behavior to which Blanche sticks, even though in her time it "is an anachronism which simply does not function" anymore to make a woman feel secure. The poignance of Blanche as Williams wrote her resides in her belief (in the face of massive evidence to the contrary) that this tradition continues to grant her status, position, and even heroism. To play her, as Marvel does, as such a pillar of strength, sensibility and modernity that all her references to the tradition are plainly strategic is to eradicate that poignance. Such conspicuous contemporization (especially as played against Versweyveld's generically technological set) also renders many details of the play's southern milieu windy and irrelevant. At least one entire scene—Blanche's aborted seduction of the paper boy—makes no psychological sense whatever for the character as played by Marvel, who never seems carefree enough to flirt in a conniving or reckless manner.

Still, the production is too dense and intelligent to be ruined by even such big blemishes. The ending, for instance, is very moving and memorable, as van Hove removes the certainty that Blanche is actually raped or crazy, substituting the harrowingly present-tense spectacle of a woman we have admired, utterly stripped of self-respect, crawling about the stage for at least ten minutes like a toy with a dying battery. "Don't say I lied to you," she says in a culminating line to the uncomprehending Mitch, who, like everyone else, never recognizes that her transparent fantasies were a preciously realistic gift in their own right.

(Sept. 1999)

Arthur Miller
and the Barbecue Grill

———

A T AGE 87, MILLER IS BEYOND DEBUNKING. HE HAS BEEN through so many cycles of the celebrity roller coaster that its shocks can't possibly faze him anymore. More than that, he is as much icon as man, a beloved sage and a monument to a less fragmented time when people, problems, and dramatists could still be widely accepted as quintessentially American. Unfortunately, one trouble with entering a pantheon is that the public starts taking you on faith, which for an artist is tantamount to living death. Whenever I've written on Miller, I've tried to pay him the compliment of looking and listening closely, but I've sometimes felt that the light of such scrutiny is harsher than he thinks appropriate in the trick-booth of the theater.

Death of a Salesman, Eugene O'Neill Theater

Death of a Salesman keeps on going and going. At fifty years old, on its third Broadway revival, it still draws tears, cheers, standing ovations and intemperately enthusiastic reviews. As much a national myth as a play, it has proudly outlasted its many prestigious detractors, its emotional weight nullifying its logical problems in hundreds of productions from New York to London to Moscow to Beijing, its unobtrusively moralistic tale of the everyman-martyr Willy Loman practically defining mid-century liberalism for two generations of Americans. Respect and attention must be paid to a cultural icon of this magnitude, regardless of one's taste or politics. And truly, one would have to be a stone not to be moved by this powerful production from Chicago's Goodman Theatre, starring Brian Dennehy and directed by Robert Falls.

Falls seems to have taken his main cues from the concept of a mind-scape envisioned by Miller when he originally titled the play *The Inside of His Head*. The paradigm of Joe Mielziner's widely imitated set for the Broadway premiere, for instance—a small cutaway house dwarfed by a backdrop of expressionistically slanted high-rises—has now been discarded, replaced by a clunky collection of blue-grey screens and various rolling units backed by an impersonal bare wall and an empty area for cold sky-projections (design by Mark Wendland). With the rolling units—two rooms of a house, a door, an exterior wall, for instance—frequently sliding off and leaving the stage empty except for actors and light, this environment stresses the desolation of Willy's particular mental interior and also reflects, perhaps, the greater corporate sterility in today's popular conception of business callousness.

Falls cleverly introduces hints of what might be called exteriority, or worldliness, and then blends them quickly into the aching ordinariness of Willy's experience—dangling theatrical effects before us, so to speak, the way Willy perceives other people dangling comforts and business success before him. Rather than the sentimental flute melody Miller called for in the play's opening, for instance, the action begins with the sound of cars rushing along a highway, after which an ominous drumbeat rises along with an insistent brass melody that builds and climaxes with a blast of light in the audience's eyes. The blast frames the hulking silhouette of Dennehy like a film noir villain—a showbiz conceit that ought to irritate but doesn't because it's obviously a shrewd way of injecting some self-consciousness into the famous image of the tired salesman stooped over his sample cases (by now a visual cliché). The moment is a gently wry reminder that most people regard Willy as essentially unthreatening.

Dennehy, for his part, plays the role as a sort of pillar of ineffectuality. Not for him the profusion of idiosyncratic mannerisms and mutterings and dashings about that made Dustin Hoffman's diminutive Willy seem like the tip of a psychological iceberg. (The key line in Hoffman's performance was: "I am not a dime a dozen!") Always consummately believable, Dennehy's character is precisely what he seems: a simple, truly common man with a resplendent smile he mistakenly thought was a passport to riches, who has stuffed himself full of patently empty fantasies and demanded that his family sustain them. That candid clarity, that modest sufficiency of identity, is the production's main source of emotion. Whether talking to himself over a milk bottle or shushing his wife ignominiously or spouting his delusions to his sons or swaggering in front of his neighbor, he comes off as entirely, heartbreakingly, fathomable. The character's tragedy in Dennehy's incarnation is not merely to fail and perish without recognizing his mistakes but to live as a figure wholly *known* by others.

Standing often with his hands in his pockets, for instance, Dennehy never gets them in past the knuckles, and this results in a diffident, stiff-elbowed, hunched-shoulder posture that falls just short of caricature. One gets no sense of a complex neurosis, or of an elaborate insecurity perversely allowed to fester, but rather of fundamental, unalterable weakness. Interestingly enough, Dennehy (who often has his sleeves rolled up) doesn't have very muscular forearms (for all his bulk that recalls the original Willy, Lee J. Cobb), and when Biff (Kevin Anderson) starts pummeling him in the penultimate scene, his whimpering, timid reaction—hiding his face behind open palms—is not only wrenching in its own right but also a jarring reminder that Willy is in some ways an *atypical* American male, because his violent impulses are directed wholly inward.

Two superbly individualized characterizations provide flattering foils for Dennehy's uncomplicatedness. Howard Witt acts the Lomans' neighbor Charley with unusually acute grace and compassion, his

endearing gruffness and facetiousness coming off as strategies for handling a deeply felt friendship with Willy that requires tricks to get him
to accept help. Still more impressive is Linda—long considered one of
the theater's consummate thankless roles—who becomes an anti-hero
in her own right as played by Elizabeth Franz. Full of sunshiny grins
that linger much longer than the mood justifies, and possessed of thin
lips that tremble in response to all good and bad news, she is a sort of
post-feminist vision of an inveterate "enabler" whose ability to let absolutely anything slide off her back if that will support her deranged
man counts as a mighty victory over despair. Biff is extraordinarily
vivid as played by Anderson, and most of the rest of the cast is sharp
and strong as well.

In the end, though, it's clear that *Salesman* has also aged in ways that
even this talented company can't cloak, and at times, the smoothness of
the production even exacerbates the problem. Biff's spiteful grudge
against his father after catching him in an affair, for instance, has always
loomed too large in the plot, but previous productions made this seem
less of a problem by using the complexities of Willy's character, the details of the set, and other attractions as constant distractions. (I once saw
a production that transformed the insufferably trite character of Uncle
Ben into a fascinating eccentric whom the audience adored, for instance.)
In Falls's deliberately simplified construction, Miller's naive clumsiness
soon grows tiresome, since all the references to Willy's betrayal in the
first act (rosily juxtaposed with flashbacks showing exaggerated jock-
worship of Biff and the innocent, cartoonish pride of both boys in their
dad) come off as nonsense that delays Biff's real confrontation with
Willy about the destructiveness of his demand for fantasies.

To me, there are also problems with some of the period detail itself.
Happy's desire to "outbox that goddam merchandise manager" for
whom he works; Biff's theft of a fountain pen from Bill Oliver, the former employer he deludes himself into regarding as a potential benefactor; Willy's longing "to own something outright before it's broken": all
this can't help but seem reductively quaint in a wealthy, self-satisfied,
media-savvy America like ours, which wants to believe that the Lo-

manesque lower middle class is either fading away or already gone. Wannabe urban "players" in our day don't box but rather outmaneuver; and they don't commit petty theft when they can plot grand larceny. Furthermore, one hears little nowadays about planned obsolescence because the very act of throwing away has become pleasurable, with legions of ingenious marketers plying us with wonderfully dispensable packaging and indispensable "upgrades."

Let me be clear that my point is not that the figure of the salesman—with his delusory ideology of ingratiation and his wall of denial to keep the pain of humiliation at bay—has become any less germane to the American character than he was in 1949. On the contrary, the main problem in producing Miller's classic today is that supersalesmanship is really the more relevant paradigm. The dreams of this production's current audience, for instance, aren't merely of paid-off mortgages and the privilege of wearing slippers while conducting $200-a-week in business over the phone from a hotel room, as Willy Loman's are. This audience's dreams have to do with, say, thirty-room mansions in Fairfield County, reserved executive parking spaces for Lexuses, and making killings on big deals like Bill Gates (that real-life Uncle Ben), or more to the point, like the unscrupulous real-estate salesmen in Mamet's *Glengarry Glen Ross*. Recently, *The New York Times* ran a photo of *Salesman*'s opening night on its front page, followed a day later by a notice within the paper that ticket sales were going extremely well, and this was a perfect illustration of the changed environment in which the play operates. No one today buys into the old tripe about being "well liked" because we're all too cynically invested in the new tripe about being "well promoted" and dispatched on the happy road to celebrity and super-wealth.

Death of a Salesman is the crowning achievement of what Kenneth Tynan once called the American drama's "mission of martyrology"—the line of plays dating back to Anderson, Odets, Rice and Hellman that are built around heroes as victims of societal injustice—and because of this it is bound to keep slipping further out of style in an America tired of both hard- and soft-sell moralizing. My guess is, though, that the play will continue to be as popular overseas as it has been for decades, because its brilliantly naive concept of the common-man martyr who is everyone's father, uncle and brother allows the whole world to weep for a beleaguered Individual while congratulating itself on being able to see through the American dream. The work is a triumph of packaging, and that is not a trivial point. Somewhere on the globe, almost all the time, Willy Loman will be dying for us, and as Nietzsche said: "When one *does away with* oneself, one does the most estimable thing possible: one thereby almost deserves to live."

(Mar. 1999)

The Ride Down Mt. Morgan, Public Theater

Seeing a new Arthur Miller play is like quarreling with your neighbor over the backyard fence. You think he'll say something new and thrilling to show you a side of life you've never seen before, give you a glimpse into the profundities of the suburban mind, but, alas, you finally realize your mad hopes have been dashed once again on the pillory of the barbecue grill.

The Ride Down Mt. Morgan—which is receiving its New York premiere seven years after its world premiere in London—is unlikely to change anyone's mind about Arthur Miller. In his native land, this author has long been a litmus-test: either you're a dewy-eyed, leftishly patriotic defender of the "common man," for whom Miller's international popularity is an immutable trump card, or you're a cold-hearted, cerebral snob who decries his flat-footed language, murky political symbolism, and tendency to exaggerate the mythic potential of thoroughly ordinary stories. These groups might as well have separate sections in restaurants.

A play like *The Ride Down Mt. Morgan,* however, is one of those classic Miller tales that tests everyone's affiliations afresh. Like *Death of a Salesman,* it has yawning logical holes but can be extraordinarily moving nevertheless because of its charmingly flawed central character. And, like *The Crucible,* it stretches topical allegory to the limit of plausibility (the topicality in this case including parallels with Monicagate all the more startling since they predate Clinton's presidency), and then it successfully distracts attention from that strained topicality with memorable aphorisms on capacious themes.

One of the most interesting features of *The Ride Down Mt. Morgan* is that its main theme happens to be *the* favorite among authors of big, self-consciously "fin-de-siècle" plays over the past decade or two: the fate of the human social animal faced with the worship of ego and individualism. We've seen this in dramas as disparate as Tony Kushner's *Angels in America*, David Edgar's *Pentecost,* and Rolf Hochhuth's *Wessies in Weimar*—all of which are themselves part of a broader tradition of millennarian inquiry reaching back to Brecht and the canonical modern dramatists. That Arthur Miller has now weighed in on this question isn't exactly surprising—many of his past works, notably *All My Sons* and *After the Fall*, have had similar concerns—but it does make one listen with keen attention.

The plot of *The Ride Down Mt. Morgan* centers on a wealthy and seductive fiftyish businessman named Lyman Felt (another classic Miller pun, like Loman), played by Patrick Stewart in this production (with hair! or is it felt?), who is the head of his own insurance company and a small-plane pilot. For nine years or so, Lyman has used his extraordinary personal freedom to maintain two marriages, one in Manhattan, the other in Elmira, New York—each with a household, a local leisure life, and a child. When he is hospitalized due to a road accident on the mountain of the title, his bigamy comes to light because his wives and grown daughter meet in the hospital waiting room.

The newspapers run with the story, endangering his career (there's the Clinton parallel, along with Lyman's insistence that it's okay to lie sometimes, even to his nine-year-old son). His wives demand explanations and that he make a choice between them. One is a primly beautiful, slightly nagging Episcopalian named Theodora whom he met in college, played with properly humorless dignity by Frances Conroy, the other a much younger, Jewish, sexually confident insurance colleague named Leah, played a bit too nervously and at times falsely by Meg Gibson. Lyman spends most of the play trying to come to terms with the past

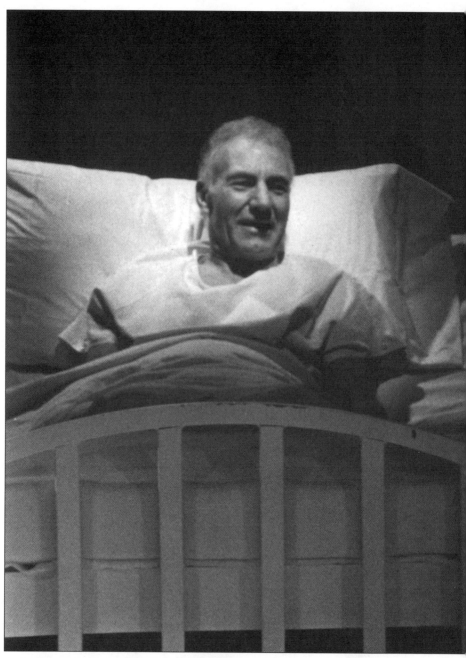

Patrick Stewart as Lyman Felt and Frances Conroy as Theodora in Arthur Miller's The Ride Down Mt. Morgan, *directed by David Esbjornson at the Public Theater in New York, 1998.* CREDIT: MICHAEL DANIEL.

while moving through his troubled present. Half Albanian, half Jewish, he's something of a successful, non-suicidal, tragicomic counterpart to Willy Loman—notwithstanding his seemingly suicidal accident, which turns out to be a result of haste due to jealousy.

The play makes use of the same non-naturalistic technique Miller has employed for decades, featuring cinematically cross-faded scenes that blend present into past and fantasy into reality, and at first this seems ideal for a bigamous fantasy (as it was in Bruno Barreto's film *Dona Flor and Her Two Husbands*). Very soon, though, it becomes clear that the technique is just as problematic here as it has been before in Miller, displaying the same drawbacks as the German Expressionism from which it sprang. That is, the play's claim to examine a single subjective point of view, with everything else serving as illustrations of the way that mind works, justifies any and every fudged plot connection and half-baked characterization. Lyman's assessment that both his wives were never happier than during his bigamy, for instance, is treated as truth even though it's uncorroborated by either woman. Daughter Bessie, played by Kali Rocha, is a stick figure whose stiff indignance carries zero weight because we never learn anything substantial about her or her relationship with her father. And Lyman's claim in the end to want both his wives makes no sense because everything he's said about Theodora is unflattering.

There's nothing wrong with suggesting that the action takes place entirely in one man's imagination, of course. It's only because Miller doesn't follow through with this approach that so many narrative loose ends are left conspicuously trailing. That's just the problem with Miller: he makes you feel you're watching a deeply compassionate play about your father, then lets you down in the details. As I watched Lyman beg Leah not to have an abortion, for instance, I found myself wondering how a sexually voracious man who is already a father could forget that the arrival of a baby would mean the end of his sexual idyll. And when Leah then capitulated (after he offered marriage), I wondered how his proposed part-time presence in Elmira squared with her adamant refusal to be a single mother.

The script is certainly pleasant on its own, but that any director could turn it into an actively funny and modestly thoughtful show is surprising. (There really ought to be special directors' awards for saving authors from themselves.) Stewart is a big factor as Lyman—solid and endearing, his famous, half-swallowed, back-of-the-throat intonations casting an amusing classical veil over the insurance exec's glib humbug. It's the director David Esbjornson, however, who establishes the atmosphere of suave humor in which such acting can loom large.

Aided by a tastefully restrained set by John Arnone that delineates discrete acting areas with light, hospital curtains and sliding metal-grid panels, Esbjornson is terrific at creating the seamless flow between real and imagined action necessary to cover for Miller's failure to think through the transitions. The director also has a knack for identifying subtle emotional moments that bear amplification (such as Lyman on his cell phone in Elmira reaching out to Theodora to fill his post-coital emptiness and finding her unequal to it). Esbjornson adds effective humor whenever possible (Lyman feigning grogginess to avoid conversation, for instance, or squatting on his pillow and beaming as his wives lie together chatting on his hospital bed). And several times the production risks opening up the humor into the farcical or absurd (an exploding bed; a floating tableau of people and furniture; Leah and Theodora discussing cooking while standing like wedding-cake ornaments behind cutaway dress-sculptures atop ornate plinths).

Esbjornson's pretention-thwarting talents aside, though, I suspect that what most people will take away from *The Ride Down Mt. Morgan* are memories of its epigrammatic lines, which are as numerous as they are dubiously connected. "Boredom is a form of deception." "Insurance is basically comical, isn't it?" "Why does anybody stay together, once they realize who they're with?" "A man can be faithful to himself or to other people—but not to both." "Taste to me is what's left of life after people can't screw anymore." "The truth is always embarrassing or it isn't the truth!" We're all capable of enjoying such piled-on aphorisms, and have done so before with this author. Now as ever, alas, they stand in stark contrast to truly coherent plays of ideas.

(Nov. 1998)

The Price, Royale Theater

I missed the premiere of Arthur Miller's *The Price* in 1968, due to pressing obligations in fourth grade, but in 1979, I saw a production of it that still gleams in memory. It moved from the tiny Harold Clurman Theater to the larger, now defunct Playhouse Theater on West 48th St., where I saw it, and starred a wonderful, ancient Yiddish theater actor named Joseph Buloff as the wry, old furniture dealer Gregory Solomon. Buloff was unforgettable in this role—an hoary, sweetly acerbic, philosopher-businessman-cum-cuddly-grandpa whose clownish antics never seemed like mere cold calculation, always like subtly brilliant compromises between cold calculation and compassionate attempts to rescue lives.

I've always been grateful to this production, both for its own beauties and for introducing me to a Miller work that I could genuinely like. Miller's major plays invariably move me, but after carrying me along on their carefully arranged emotional journeys, they just as inevitably let me down. As soon as my mind starts to engage the process of "second-think," I recognize the shaky social analysis and all the problems of implausibility, moralizing, technical gimmicks, and unjustified mythic conceits that serve as buttresses for the emotional edifices. But here, in contrast, is a play as tightly woven and ineluctably pitched as a classical tragedy, with a story about recrimination and redemption between two estranged brothers that rises almost effortlessly to universality largely because of its humble particularity. Miller never wrote better than in *The Price*.

The setting is the cluttered attic apartment of a brownstone that was once the home of Victor and Walter Franz and their father—marvelously conceived, in this occasionally powerful but ultimately disappointing new production directed by James Naughton, as a gigantic Ionesco-like exaggeration of compression and accumulation, with tables, bureaus, lamps, rugs and more piled densely, twenty feet high in every available corner, and flanked by an expressionistically distorted ceiling and rear windows (design by Michael Brown). After the father went bust in the 1929 stock market crash, he languished and moldered in this place, surrounded by relics of his lost wealth, and Victor—played here by Jeffrey DeMunn with an effectively punchy combination of no-nonsense factuality and inadvertent sensitivity—gave up his dream of a science career to care for him, eventually becoming a policeman.

Meanwhile, Walter—played with a keen sense of patrician entitlement by Harris Yulin—went to medical school and became a wealthy surgeon, and when the play opens, the brothers haven't spoken in sixteen years. Victor's grudge about his missed opportunities has festered into a noxious inertia that now threatens his marriage, and he and his alcoholic (and possibly unfaithful) wife Esther—played with superb intensity by Lizbeth Mackay as a nervous soul yearning desperately for a reason to be loyal—await Solomon, who has been called to bid on the furniture because the building is scheduled for demolition. Walter walks in just as a deal is being finalized (probably to Victor and Esther's great disadvantage), and his entrance changes the terms and spirit of the whole negotiation. Suddenly the proper valuation (the "price") of everything—not just the furniture but the whole overbearing past it palpably represents, as well as the characters' current lives—is the real subject under discussion.

There is schematism and a strong whiff of cliché in Miller's characterization of these brothers and their antagonism. His triumph, however, lay in transforming a simple and ordinary transaction into much more than the crisis point in a family drama. *The Price* is as much an allegory of quintessential American selfishness and selflessness as *Death of a Salesman* is, but far less forced and therefore stronger and more convincing. This is partly a result of the single pressurized setting (the play is classically structured, with a single location and an action that takes no longer than the time elapsed onstage) and partly of Miller's refusal to choose between the brothers. He declares no moral victor, as he loudly does in, say, *The Crucible* and *All My Sons*. Each of the characters is equally necessary to the searing, tragicomic conclusion, including Esther, whose life hangs in the balance as much as the men's, and crusty old Solomon (note his name), with all his evasions and manipulations, offers the only guidance the audience will get in serving as judge. "Good luck you can never know till the last minute, my boy," he says at the end—the same grimly purgative sentiment Sophocles inserted into the last line of *Oedipus Rex*.

As Buloff beautifully demonstrated, this crucial seriocomic judicial or advisory role is why Solomon must be played with the greatest possible breadth of soul, and it's also why Naughton's production, in which so much is impressively shrewd and right, can be so badly damaged by a single casting blunder. For one thing, Bob Dishy looks and acts too young and hearty to play Solomon. With his bearish physique and brawny growl, he never communicates real vulnerability or decrepitude; he seems a contemporary of the brothers. When he comes puffing up the stairs, his exhaustion seems like a put-on. For another thing, his thick accent sounds much less Yiddish than German, and the difference between Yiddish and German is the difference between funny and unfunny, mellifluous and sinister. This Solomon is far too bitter, sharp-edged and calculating to read as a clown; when he eats his egg and his Hershey bar, he is simply eating, not performing impromptu vaudeville vignettes. He seems like an old Nazi imitating a Jew, prompting laughter only at the character's expense. When Victor speaks at one point of "people fall[ing] in love with you," it seems like an irrelevant delusion.

Happily, the play's still powerful central speeches about the age of disposability and the fear lurking behind ambition and specialization are too strong to be ruined. The irony is that, in the mouth of such a weak Solomon—who is the heart of this play in which Miller finally transcended tendentiousness—the speeches sound vaguely tendentious.

Those who swear by Arthur Miller as America's greatest playwright (and by *Death of a Salesman* as our greatest play) typically believe that the most important test of a drama is whether it is a powerful expression of collective conscience. His fans appreciate moralists, and consider him one of the greatest. They compare themselves—or their fathers, uncles and brothers—with his downtrodden heroes, feel bad about the social and family circumstances that humiliate and undo them, and leave the theater feeling righteous about the profundity of their feelings and, hence, the solidity of their positions as mainstays of America's presumably shaky conscience.

This has always seemed to me one of the most counterproductive approaches to drama possible in a land where evasion of social responsibility begins in the cradle. Americans can't be preached to from the stage because they all feel innocent, and they won't sit still while some smart-aleck dramatist sells them ideas they don't want to buy because they've had enough of that in their daily lives. This is where Brecht, who diagnosed the problem very accurately, got the solution just as wrong as the Millers and proto-Millers of his time. Brecht's ostensible theater of free choice was really for the most part a theater of preachy parables. As Oscar Wilde wrote in *The Picture of Dorian Gray*, "conscience makes egotists of us all."

(Dec. 1999)

Musicals and Other
Broadway Blandishments

———

T HOMAS MANN ONCE SAID THAT A WRITER IS "SOMEONE FOR whom writing is more difficult than it is for other people." I sometimes think of a theater critic as someone for whom writing about Broadway is more difficult than it is for other reviewers. An extra modicum of mental toughness is certainly required to write well about contemporary Broadway, not because there's never anything good there but because of the elaborate smokescreen that producers set up to make the promotion of art, rather than the art itself, the main object of public discussion. The angriest letters I received at *New York Press* were never about my opinions per se but rather about the assumptions behind my Broadway reviews, my refusal to accept the promotional smokescreen as normal, my tendency to describe the blockbuster game as crass and beside the point. After my *Ragtime* review (reprinted below) appeared, for instance, one patriot actually took time to write that I was welcome to "go review plays in Cuba or Vietnam" if I didn't like the show's promo campaign. I count that letter among my most precious tributes.

*　　*　　*

The Lion King, by Elton John, Tim Rice, and Julie Taymor, New Amsterdam Theater

Here's the highest compliment I've heard Julie Taymor receive for *The Lion King*: my five-year-old son Oliver, asked after attending with me whether he preferred the movie or the play, instantly replied, "the play!"

Awash like most kids in Disney's saturation advertising, Oliver insisted on seeing the animated film when it came out in 1994, and since then he has withstood many a judgemental frown to be able to watch the video over and over. Okay, show me the parent who avoids Disney altogether and I'll show you a cave dweller or a control freak. Taymor, for her part, leaves me grateful, both for the stunning inventiveness of her work and for making the difference between art and mental junk food obvious to a five-year-old.

There are two marvels in this project: Taymor's exuberant art—as director, costume designer, and puppet-maker, she's the principal creative force—and the fact of the tyrannical Disney organization having ceded so much control. Despite the advance reports of an exception in the making, one had reason to expect less than nothing. Publicists, after all, will say anything, and *Beauty and the Beast*, Disney's previous foray on Broadway, was merely a cynical effort to squeeze a few more millions out of an existing "marketing property." Watching that grimly literal and vulgarly overproduced show, I felt like a biology specimen pressed between the pages of a quarterly report. It was hard to believe that such a producer would have any more qualms this time about insulting everyone who still considers theater a place for original creativity and discovery.

Amazingly, someone seems to have had qualms. As philistine as Disney continues to be in general—the massive sentimental distortions and insipid sanitizations of perfectly vivid and viable myths in *Hercules*, for instance, will take a generation of inspired teaching to undo—praise should be given when it's earned. If the Medici of this world aren't acknowledged for their occasional nods to humanism, why should they bother trying to rise above greed and barbarity? *The Lion King*, shockingly, is not an exercise in mechanical recognition of corporate trademarks but rather a genuinely open invitation to fully human children of any age to see and think for themselves.

The first ten minutes are unforgettable, a scarcely credible cataract of activity. As the baboon-shaman Rafiki (Tsidii Le Loka) begins the song "Circle of Life" by triumphantly "calling" the sun (a giant folded-paper disk) from the horizon, the stage slowly fills with an increasingly improbable menagerie of human-animal hybrids. A nine-foot-wide elephant, operated by four actors (one inside each leg), collapses to thirty-four inches to make its way up an orchestra aisle. Two giraffes walk on with stately clumsiness—actors with neck extensions and long, hoofed stilts on their hands, short ones on their legs. Clusters of sleek dancers in striated leotards leap balletically, each bearing three gazelles, two attached to their arms, one to their heads.

It's an explosion and celebration of imagination, delimited only by the fantastic tapestry of Africa that Taymor sees in her mind's eye. And the staging, on Richard Hudson's marvelously free and joyous setting, is as replete with inspiration as the costumes and puppets. Pride rock, for instance, the lion king's equivalent of a throne, juts magnificently upward like a granite corkscrew out of a flat stage. The impression of a drought is created by sucking a giant blue floor-cloth down a small hole, its gorgeous water-like bunching patterns slowly disappearing against dessicated grey planks. Grass and other jungle plants are played by actors who react hilariously to the character's lines. One worries briefly that the invention will exhaust itself too early, but then each new scene introduces yet another burst of inspiration suggesting that Taymor's wellspring of imagination, particularly concerning human-puppet interaction, is unfathomably deep.

The effect of a hyena's malevolent, slothful slouch, for instance, is created with a thin, hairy strip that continues the line of the human backbone forward over the head and down, with a laughing mask hooked on at chest level, controlled by the actor with one hand. A carved lion mask hovers on a wire support above the actor's painted face, inviting meditation on the dual expressions, except in moments of ferocity when the mask slides forward as if suddenly swallowing the human underneath. Zazu, the dodo bird employed as king's gofer, is a man (Geoff Hoyle) in a blue clown out-fit, smeared whiteface and a bowler who uses a long curved rod to control, with uncanny specificity, a three-foot bird puppet sitting atop his hat. These combinations send the mind spinning in a hundred directions no one could anticipate—not even Taymor, let alone a Disney executive.

It's a testimony to the strength of suggestiveness in her inventions, in fact, that the shortcomings of the story—which largely follows the film—seem unimportant. Some new songs (all pop pulp, like most of the old ones) and plot-padding were added as the seventy-five-minute cartoon became a two-and-three-quarter-hour musical, but nothing altered the text's basic formulaic cautiousness. It's still *Hamlet* bleached of all inter-esting intricacies and ambiguities in order to accommodate the one bland coming-of-age tale Disney knows how to tell. For those in caves or with-out kids: the evil Scar murders his brother, the lion king Mufasa, seizes his crown with the help of goosestepping hyenas, and convinces his son Simba that the cub caused dad's death; Simba then runs away, grows up, and returns to reclaim his kingdom.

That Taymor accepted one-to-one correspondence on this level also worried me to begin with—much dialogue and all the jokes are lifted from the film verbatim, as in *Beauty and the Beast*—but then Oliver's re-actions purged most of my remaining disquiet. "What do you think of Pumbaa and Timon?" I asked him, referring to the clownish warthog and meercat that are the only puppets Taymor copied literally from the cartoon. "That guy in the green suit with the green face and green hair was *so* funny!" he said, speaking not of the ungainly brown-and-white meercat puppet but of the actor (Max Casella) who holds it in front of him while playing Timon with wonderful assertive nervousness. Oliver, in other words, looked right through the damn Disney icon, too fasci-nated by the humor and mechanics of the live performance to be drawn into a nostalgia trip about a toy image from yesteryear. (Love that kid.)

Disney hardly has a monopoly on loathsome marketing to children, of course. Twentieth-Century Fox's *Anastasia*, for instance, has the most offensive premise I've seen in a performing artwork since *Miss Saigon*: the Russian revolution as a demonic curse, objectionable because it deprives a pretty girl of elegant parties. What makes Disney especially disgusting is its unabashed imperialism, its success at popularizing the notion that the colonization of young minds is wholesome and patriotic. Its animated features such as *The Lion King, Snow White, Cinderella,* and *The Sword and the Stone* even demonstrate something like a fixation with portraying monarchy as normal and beneficent. Taymor really tip-toes round such issues, adding self-conscious quips by Zazu that adver-tize her independence but never get too specific: "This wasn't in the film!" "It looks like a shower curtain from the Guggenheim."

Perhaps, however, she does more than tiptoe from one angle. The lions, presumed to be rightful rulers of the jungle, are the most human-looking of the beasts. They carry no cumbersome puppets that impede agility, their faces are usually visible beneath the masks, and the cubs Simba (Scott Irby-Ranniar) and Nala (Kajuana Shuford) are played by children without masks. During one heart-to-heart between Mufasa and Simba, dad puts his mask on the floor and lets their animal natures drop away entirely for a time. The point is, this central design decision by Taymor eventually cre-ates the impression of a species that, despite its nominal bestiality, must earn its right of governance through exemplary humane behavior.

Not a bad lesson for children, or for Disney, I thought, watching pride rock twist toward heaven for the last time. As someone wrote in one of those books that kids flip through when the videos get boring: "From those to whom much is given, much is expected."

(Dec. 1997)

Ragtime, by Terrence McNally, Stephen Flaherty, and Lynn Ahrens, based on the novel by E.L. Doctorow, Ford Center for Performing Arts

After considerable mulling, I've concluded that I'm of two different minds about *Ragtime,* and that they shouldn't be reconciled. Forcible reconciliation is the stuff of politics, not criticism. The truth is, I enjoyed this blockbuster musical, cheering for the heroes, booing the villains, shedding a tear with every heaving bosom. But the other truth is, I was also disgusted by it, chiefly due to the facile, at times mercantile patriotism in which much of it is wrapped. Unusually for me (at least with Broadway), neither of these feelings seems to want to give way to the other, so I'm left explaining why my ambivalence might be interesting. First, the disgust.

Nothing less than America is on sale at the spanking new Ford Center for Performing Arts. Easy love of America. "The Livent Gift Shop" in the lobby (Livent is the name of Canadian producer Garth Drabinsky's company, which renovated the building) offers "American Dream Tea" in red, white, and blue "Ragtime" mugs, designer American-flag pins, flag-and-liberty-torch "Ragtime" sweatshirts, as well as copies of Drabinsky's autobiography and capitalist manifesto, *Closer to the Sun*. A central character in the musical runs a successful business manufacturing flags, bunting, fireworks and other patriotic paraphernalia, and the appeal of that merchandise has been bleached of the irony novelist E. L. Doctorow and playwright Terrence McNally gave it. Here it is used to package and sell the whole show. The second-act curtain is a giant, tinselly pastiche of Childe Hassam's American Impressionist paintings of Fifth Avenue bathed in flags.

"Brilliant marketing," you could say, and you'd be right. The second-act curtain was reproduced in *The New Yorker* two weeks prior to the play's opening. And a densely illustrated article on *Ragtime*'s advertizing campaign—*not* the show, but the promotion—appeared in the December *American Theatre*. What was one to expect from so much crowing about superfices but an attractive, well-made souvenir? And *Ragtime* is a massive souvenir. Strangely enough, it also sometimes jolts the mind awake by grasping at complexity, and astonishes by reflecting seriously on history and democracy. It's a bit like America in the 19th and 20th centuries, awesome and repulsive by turns, so vulgar in its marketing that the very idea of substance beneath often seems preposterous.

A walloping three hours long, this show is muscular and well-oiled from start to finish, and a major reason is the affinity of the material for adaptation. Doctorow's tale works better in some ways as a musical than as a novel. The novel seemed innovative when it appeared in 1974, interweaving three turn-of-the-century American family stories (New Rochelle WASP, immigrant Lower-East-Side Jewish, and Harlem black) in a syncopated ragtime-like design—the 70s was the decade of the Scott Joplin revival—and wryly setting them in broader context by way of "coincidental" interactions with historical figures such as Henry Ford, Emma Goldman, Harry Houdini, J.P. Morgan and Evelyn Nesbit. But other novelists such as Don DeLillo went on to ply this technique more adroitly, and in retrospect some of Doctorow's coincidences look less like playful efforts to lighten weighty events than shortcut solutions to knotty plot problems.

In musicals, though, a quotient of improbability is always expected, even cherished. It doesn't seem contrived onstage for Tateh, the immigrant Jew who scratches together a living cutting out paper silhouettes on the street, suddenly to reinvent himself as the filmmaker "Baron Ashkenazy" and turn up at a posh Atlantic City hotel. And it isn't psychologically implausible that the WASP Mother (the whole family has titles instead of names) falls in love with and then marries the "Baron" after Father dies conveniently on the Lusitania. Singing people who look longingly at one another should end up together, and that's that. And McNally capably supplies the minor adjustments necessary to ensure this effect (onstage Tateh confesses his beggarly heritage to Mother, for instance), even adding some whopper coincidences in the name of narrative efficiency (anarchist leader Emma Goldman is now Tateh's street buddy).

Equally interesting is that the syncopated storytelling—which qualified as newfangled in the novel and was then celebrated as an ideal vehicle to narrate the burgeoning "American century," with its complex admixture of themes and energies—comes off as thoroughly conventional in the musical. Indeed, syncopation *is* the basic structure of modern musicals, and *Ragtime* simply calls attention to one historical root, as have other musicals such as *Funny Girl* and *Cabaret*. Truly remarkable, though, is that the show sometimes uses this sugar-coating to accomplish the historically elusive goal of getting American spectators to think about history itself.

One of the first song sequences is a good illustration. As Father (Mark Jacoby) leaves for a year to join Peary's expedition to the North Pole, Mother (Marin Mazzie) sings a splendid protofeminist lament (*not* a sorrowful love elegy) called "Goodbye, my Love": "Tell me how to be someone whose heart can explore while still staying here." Then Father on his outbound ship sings in tandem with Tateh on an inbound one, each aggressively apostrophizing the other with contrasting visions of the American dream. "A salute to a fellow who hasn't a chance, journey on," cries the smug explorer, stuffed with the fruits of liberty that he both dangles and takes for granted. "He's a fool," says the fiercely ambitious immigrant about Father, unable to conceive of a valid reason to leave the "best place" on Earth once one is in. These are pearls of juxtaposition, forcing spectators to feel their big emotions by way of *thought* about such unsentimental issues as the sustenance of American vigor by immigrants, and the challenge to crude models of freebooting by newly enfranchised women.

And there is more to admire. Director Frank Galati has used the New Rochelle family's Little Boy (Alex Strange) to marvelous effect, for instance, planting him downstage as a clairvoyant proxy for the audience, and letting his earnest outbursts add unpredictability to many scenes and his inexhaustible wonderment stand as a reproach of his uninquisitive father. Stephen Flaherty's music is lusty and resolute, creating an environment in which the performers (strong vocalists every one) are always sensually present. And McNally manages to fit more of the novel into this script, preserving a taut kaleidoscopic coherence, than anyone would think possible who saw Milos Forman's politically and narratively oversimplified 1981 *Ragtime* film.

Still, this musical contains its own timorous simplifications that I'm surprised no one has yet protested. Most egregious is the story of Coalhouse Walker, the black pianist who turns militant after his car is vandalized by white racists and who is stonewalled attempting to find legal justice, which is Doctorow's boldest and most provocative conception. Knowing the frustrating and painful struggles that the rest of the century will bring, the reader almost wishes that a band of black nationalists really had barricaded itself with hostages inside the Morgan Library in 1912 and made international headlines. The musical turns this story-line into a bowdlerized fairy-tale, using the mollifying, anti-agitational ideas of Booker T. Washington as a leitmotif, and presenting Walker as a physically unimposing, feebly pathetic malefactor who drops his gun as soon as Washington wags his paternal finger. (Actor Brian Stokes Mitchell has a nice baritone but never shows that he truly comprehends Walker's rage and monumentality.)

What America is this a picture of? I wondered, watching Mitchell being attractively "machine-gunned" near the end with a fireworks-barrage of lights. An America that's not supposed to scare tourists, obviously. Had the makers of *Ragtime* dared to scare them just a bit more, however, they might have had a masterwork on their hands rather than merely an exceptionally powerful machine painted red, white and blue.

(Feb. 1998)

Marie Christine, by Michael John LaChiusa, Vivian Beaumont Theater

Amadeus, by Peter Shaffer, Music Box Theater

All theater involves cheating, to some extent. There is mini-cheating, as when information that ought to be obvious to those speaking is imparted solely for the audience's benefit, or when antics, hysterics or exaggerated costumes are used to cloak actorly ineptitude, or when Nazi salutes are used to add meaningless ballast to weightless *Hamlet* productions. And then there is big cheating, as when superficial conflicts are aggrandized with monumental music and settings, or when specious arguments are patched over with swatches of milky sentimentality. No reliable rules govern these matters, of course. A popular play—in this and every other millennium—is simply one whose tricks the public doesn't catch on to, or else one whose cheating it decides to overlook because it feels it has gotten enough pleasure in return.

A great play, by contrast, is one whose cheating is earned, relevant to the action and necessary to the play's eloquence—as when Euripides's child-murderer Medea (conceived in 431 B.C.) escapes the scene of her crimes in a dragon-drawn chariot, offering not only a marvelous spectacle in itself but also a stunning reminder of how much larger and more unfathomable she is as a moral phenomenon than the mortals around her have comprehended. This is the sort of thing Aristotle had in mind when he said sagely that, in drama, "one should choose events that are impossible but plausible in preference to ones that are possible but implausible." Imagine the loss of scale had Medea gotten away by, say, bribing her guards, or slipping through a hitherto unmentioned tunnel beneath her house.

Marie Christine, John Michael LaChiusa's musical version of *Medea* set in the antebellum Creole society of 1890s New Orleans, certainly has the blush of popularity about it. Its music is moving, excitingly propulsive, and complexly varied (with Carribean rhythms side by side with ragtime, tuneful R & B, dissonant Weill-like ballads, and much more)—by far the strongest and most original new score in the past several Broadway seasons. The show's story follows the outline of the ancient legend with minimal contrivance. And the lead actress, Audra McDonald, a force of nature apparently incapable of uttering a sound that isn't richly musical, pulls it all together with her luminous presence and glittering voice.

In the end, though, *Marie Christine* is really a study in cleverly veiled cheating. It's enjoyable partly because it is mired in the "possible but implausible," which prevents it from rising to any truly transcendent or harrowing level of experience. The title character, for instance, is a voudon "healer" displaced to Chicago (Medea was a barbarian sorceress displaced to Greece), but all her voudon posturing is on the level of ribbon-waving mumbo-jumbo, threats and incantations grounded in fully explicable psychological suggestion. This supposedly "dark" religious tradition, in other words, remains unmysterious and unmagical, with the result that Marie is never really frightening or monstrous. She is a likeable, human-scale character who, distracted by jealousy or not, simply would never do to her children what the plot says she does.

LaChiusa's prodigious composing talents notwithstanding, he'd have been wise to collaborate with a real writer on this project, someone capable of inventing at least a powerful speech or two to make Marie seem compellingly strange and foreign beyond readily explicable and schematic social politics. The proud, mixed-race Marie—betrayed by her white lover Dante Keyes (Anthony Crivello) when he needs to get respectable in order to run for city office—is diminished by her violent act of revenge. She chooses it petulantly over several perfectly acceptable alternatives, which reduces her to mundane criminality. (The whole show is a flashback from prison, where she has been sentenced to die the next morning.)

Interestingly, in an article in the house magazine *Lincoln Center Theater Review*, the inmate-celebrity Wilbert Rideau, a perceptive journalist and filmmaker, hinted at some of these problems between the lines of his praise for LaChiusa's work: "In real life, you would not likely find a Marie Christine among the nation's murderers. Her peculiar pathology could exist only in a fable.... Unfortunately, *Marie Christine* is ultimately about destructive relationships." What Rideau cannot have seen, however—unless he was released from the Louisiana State Penitentiary to see a performance, which I doubt—is how LaChiusa, McDonald and the director Graciela Daniele were able to make all the compromises seem trivial for two and a half hours. The surging production, with its pounding rhythms and the slightly pandering mania of an African drummer perched on a sky-high platform, its rush of black-clad choral prisoners swirling around the confessing Marie, whose singing voice could cure anyone's despair—all this and more pulled the audience along with card-sharp efficiency on the play's modest emotional journey. Only later, in the fullness of afterthought, did the deficiencies of scale and plausibility seem important.

Peter Shaffer's *Amadeus*, on the other hand, is a famously popular play that cannot sustain its clever cheating until its final curtain. It begins with several good, serious ideas speculating about the death of Mozart and the homicidal envy of his lesser rival Antonio Salieri. But even in this slick production directed by Peter Hall (who also directed the original London and Broadway productions in 1979 and 1980), its nearly three-hour length seems about twice what the drama requires.

Unlike the 1984 film directed by Milos Forman, the play *Amadeus* focuses on Salieri and his need to confess to the audience (which presumably shares his mediocrity, as underlined by the huge upstage mirror in Hall's production). The film's dominant portrayal of Mozart as a boorish, obscene child is also a major part of the play, but the thrust is on Salieri's need to explain his hostility toward Mozart in many more words than the screenplay (also by Shaffer) could tolerate. Salieri's quarrel, as he explains in a long monologue at the end of Act 1, is really with God, who made him competent but unexceptional despite his hard work, and chose "spiteful, sniggering, conceited, infantile Mozart!—who has never worked one minute to help another man" as "his preferred Creature."

This is an interesting dispute that raises fascinating questions about society's glorification of mediocrity and the moral neutrality of genius. The problem is that, as a dramatic knot, it's inert, because one of the major parties to the conflict, God, has nothing to say in response, and since Shaffer (like LaChiusa) demonstrates unequivocally, early on, that he isn't up to the task of painting a truly larger-than-life figure. Mozart's silly infantilisms get old very fast. Shaffer asks good questions but then leaves himself nothing to do in his second act but plod grimly through a catalogue of Salieri's carefully concealed cruelties and thwartings of Mozart, all of which demonstrate precisely the same point about God's indifference to the sort of worldly recognition he enjoys at Mozart's expense.

In the end, Shaffer patches together a complex-seeming conclusion by tossing together old and new loose ends, but it won't wash. There's a trite reunion of Mozart with his shallowly drawn wife, for instance, and a botched suicide attempt by Salieri, after which he suddenly and inexplicably anoints himself as holy confessor: "Mediocrities everywhere— now and to come—I absolve you all." Both playwright and character seem to think Salieri has become an immortal creation at this point, and his snickering claim to have rescued himself from historical oblivion by whispering his name as Mozart's assassin reflects unflatteringly on Shaffer as a pathetic, last-ditch appeal to cheap notoriety.

Still, for the pleasures of this play's deft cheating in its first act we should nevertheless be grateful—particularly since its swift and sumptuous establishment of the 18th-century Viennese court constitutes high historical ambition compared to everything else currently on Broadway, and since Salieri's self-consciously "scandalous" need to confess provides clever sugarcoating for some important ideas about art and morality and the value of complexity in entertainment. The tricks of the play are indeed amusing for an hour or so: the convention of hearing Mozart's music over loudspeakers while he or others read his manuscripts, for instance, and the artificial suspense (which no one believes, including Salieri) created by dozens of whispering offstage voices. David Suchet is a surprisingly amiable Salieri, generating sympathy for his character through what seems, strangely enough, to be genuine affection for Mozart's music. And Michael Sheen is impressive as Mozart, inasmuch as consistent childishness and sweaty, anxious exertions can substitute for the depths Shaffer couldn't fathom. Neither actor can rewrite the play, alas, which leaves both of their characters huffing and puffing on a dubious treadmill.

(Jan. 2000)

Dame Edna: The Royal Tour, by Barry Humphries, The Booth Theater

Few spectacles are closer to the American heart than that of the professional famous person. Celebrity-worship is our culture's vernacular faith, and (as the sociologist C. Wright Mills once said) our star-system is the inevitable result of making a fetish out of competition. We venerate people who *have* done remarkable things, of course, but we don't let the scarcity of such people deprive us of the pleasure of venerating. Perpetually inventing stars out of thin air (and thereby degrading heroism) gives us the illusion that gloves-off competition really is a stimulus to community, not just to rapacity and isolation—that the few lucky winners in our winner-take-all game really can bring us meaningfully together, and perhaps reflect starlight on us, if we just seize the precious opportunities to take proper notice of them.

I remember feeling inchoate disgust, even as a child, at this sort of manufactured general reverence that presumed to include me—at "applause" lights, laugh-tracks, the empty-headed, face-lifted losers posing as winners on TV shows like *Truth or Consequences* and *Hollywood Squares*. The show that most clarified my feelings on this score recently, though, was on Broadway—Sandra Bernhard's *I'm Still Here Damn It!*, which ran at the Booth Theater last year.

Not yet face-lifted (I assume), the notoriously angry Bernhard—her legit acting career uninspiring since *King of Comedy*—is a talented singer, as demonstrated in *I'm Still Here* and her previous solo show *Without You I'm Nothing*. Unfortunately, she lacks the original sparkle, or perhaps the dedication, to become a big recording star despite her unperfect looks (read: big nose), like Barbra, and she has consequently taken aim at an ersatz stardom of spite. Using her perceived professional rejection as comic material, she now presents herself as a sneering, standup critic of the system that purportedly hurt her—an utterly false and pathetic pose that tries to pass off crypto-gayness as cutting-edge feminism and squanders her fine intelligence on bitchy little backbiting gossip about celebrities whose acquaintance she's obviously proud of.

When I first saw the pretentious, self-satisfied 'tude in the press releases for Barry Humphries's *Dame Edna: The Royal Tour*, now playing at the Booth Theater—"It is well known that Dame Edna is arguably the most popular and gifted woman in the world today..."—the pang of nausea I felt was familiar. Here, it seemed, was an Australian Bernhard in drag trading on the same pseudo-intellectual, trend-conscious spite-comedy conceived as vengeance for the slights of youth, serving up the same sad, self-cannibalizing triviality posing as savvy culture-critique.

How pleasant to find out that Dame Edna isn't disgusting. There are Bernhardish elements in her, and I'm not convinced she's as profound as John Lahr makes her out to be in his 242-page 1992 book *Dame Edna and the Rise of Western Civilization* (which I picked up and read with pleasure after the show). But I was unexpectedly drawn in by her poise and the extent to which she relies on skillful negotiation of dangerously unpredictable audience interaction. Name-dropping is added here as spice, almost as an afterthought. Edna is, thankfully, a precise and polished clown act that—no matter what you may think of her jokes or lightweight politics—convinces you that Humphries is actually famous for a reason.

Dame Edna is the most prominent of Humphries's many alter-egos. She has been a pop-culture icon in Britain and Australia since the 1950s while remaining relatively obscure in the United States. (A previous show, *Housewife/Superstar*, closed quickly Off-Broadway in 1977.) To help the New York audience get hip fast, *Dame Edna: The Royal Tour* begins with video clips dating back forty years that first show the dowdy housewife-character he originally invented to ridicule the dullness and ignorance that nearly suffocated him as a child in Melbourne. Then the clips progress to the garishly glamorous, utterly self-absorbed matron he currently plays, with her double-chin, butterfly glasses, and lavender bouffant hair, holding court in an astonishing array of prestigious and exclusive places while rubbing elbows with the likes of Robin Williams, Sean Connery, Roseanne Arnold and Charlton Heston.

Meanwhile, an announcer prepares the audience for Edna's special brand of mock-infantilization by offering absurdly basic explanations of what to expect during the evening: "Dame Edna attracts a nice type of person, whereas other Broadway shows may not... Actors are sometimes obliged to perform when they can't obtain work in television." These statements imply that anyone who would come see Edna is probably a hopeless couch potato, which hints at the double-edge of her aggressive charm. At once thoroughly malicious and unfailingly gracious, she's such a perfect hostess that most people don't care that they're being insulted.

There is no story-line to the show (for this reason it's "perfect for senior citizens," she says, "no plot you can lose"). She simply enters onto the elegant stage—an ornate, curving stairway beside a white piano with a huge flower arrangement, set into receding cutouts of giant, bejeweled crowns—and visits with the audience for two and a quarter hours. "I feel bonded to you," she says, "I don't think of you as an audience. More like a focus group." Occasionally she sings, dances like a football player, and tells stories, but mostly she asks questions of selected spectators and riffs scathingly on their responses. The sharpest barbs are followed with statements like, "I mean that in a loving, caring way." At one point she adds, "I was born with a priceless gift: the ability to laugh at the misfortunes of others."

Thus, the spectators in the balcony are "paupers" who are ever so nicely told not to expect more eye contact from the star than their ticket price justifies. Those in box seats who speak back to her are dubbed "parakeets," those who don't "mutes," and both groups are abused mercilessly from then on. The night I attended, a woman in the orchestra said she lived in a rowhouse in Astoria and was then asked: "Are you sure you're in the right seat?" Another woman, nicely dressed, was invited up to the stage with her friend for a meal (a real one) and greeted with: "Napkin, I think. We don't want any more stains on that frock." The "guest" never smiled again, to the audience's immeasurable amusement.

Some jokes obviously inserted for New York did leave me wondering whether Edna's political edge is sharper when she appears in London or Melbourne. "Who came by taxi?" she asks, for instance, calling for a show of hands: "Lovely, you must know the Arabic for 'Booth.'" The oriental sequin-dress she wears in the second act is "a tribute to Woody Allen's mother-in-law. [Pause for effect.] Think about that for a moment." Occasionally, in other words, one senses that she thinks her political incorrectness is more dangerous and hard-hitting than it is. Moreover, there's conspicuous evasiveness in the fact that all her live targets are women or the elderly. (Perhaps, it occurred to me, Humphries fears that swipes at the vanity of younger men might provoke unfunny aggression, rooted in homophobia, and this might be dangerous for Edna, or might force her to respond directly, possibly threatening her mass appeal. In any case, says Lahr, Humphries isn't gay.)

There are enough jokes that do hit home, though. Edna's good friend the Queen, for instance, keeps getting the theater's name wrong: "the Oswald Theater ... the Hinkley Theater ... the Squeaky Fromme." Anyway, what ultimately holds one's attention is less the content than the meticulous delivery—the low falsetto voice with its occasional dulcet belches, the priceless twisted-mouth grimaces that accompany every punch line, the leggy stances, extravagantly clumsy hopping dances and horrisonant crooning that turn all her songs into fantastically odd spectacles of maladroit virtuosity. Dame Edna, in the end, is a deserving celebrity who is unthinkable apart from the tradition of empty celebrity—a picture of pure competitiveness dressed up as loving mother, who allows us to laugh off our rapacious cynicism or stare it in the berouged face, depending on our inclinations.

(Nov. 1999)

Voices in the Dark, by John Pielmeier, Longacre Theater

Thrillers are one of America's favorite forms of psychological junk food. Everyone knows they don't offer real sustenance, but we nevertheless pride ourselves on that degenerate expertise that enables us to make distinctions among the cheap thrills. No predictable climaxes or carelessly laid clues for us; we know when the pickles are missing from a Big Mac. And even when all the twists and chills have been properly arranged, we know the compulsory pop-psychology sauce also has to be right—that plain-mayonnaise coating without which terror-concoctions aren't considered fun in our age. We're connoisseurs, whose specialized knowledge gives us the illusion that our media-saturated minds aren't really waterlogged.

Commercial producers say they're always on the prowl for good thrillers but rarely find them. My guess is, the problem has more to do with the quality of writers attracted to the form than with its inherent difficulty, or maybe we really have grown too sophisticated for some of our most cherished humble pleasures. In any case, the last thriller to make serious money on Broadway was *Deathtrap*, which opened in 1978 and ran five years. The recent revival of *Wait Until Dark* was a misguided celebrity-gamble that collapsed under the ineptitude of Quentin Tarantino's acting and the quaint datedness of its 1966 script.

And now *Voices in the Dark*, a play originally written in 1991 by John Pielmeier (author of *Agnes of God*) that steals shamelessly from *Wait Until Dark* and half a dozen other famous shockers, is Broadway's newest candidate for Scare of the Year.

Let me refrain from making towering predictions. I've been too often wrong about the reaction of the bridge-and-tunnel crowd and the tourists to purely commercial fare. I find it hard to see, though, how this instantly stale and absurdly overprocessed dish could have even mass-market appeal.

Here's the setup. Lil (Judith Ivey), a popular, dial-a-shrink radio host whose marriage is on the rocks, travels to an Adirondack cabin to patch things up with hubby, but is snowed in there and terrorized by a psycho who had previously called into her program. The psycho remains a distorted phone-voice until the second act, but Pielmeier's "wink wink" dialogue and ostentatiously derivative, secluded-cabin circumstances make every male in the cast immediately suspect. There's the husband (who missed his plane), Lil's gay agent (who leaves early on), the two sex-starved locals who run errands for her (one older and fat, one younger and nerdy), a chronically irritated detective, and a wrong-number caller who earns her trust by saying he's a cop attending a nearby convention. Also mixed into the stew are: gruesome use of a jacuzzi, possible cannibalism, a Cuisinart, a conspicuous high-voltage power-line (installed so Lil can broadcast from the cabin—yeah, sure), and lots of gratuitous waving of kitchen knives.

Ivey is perfectly serviceable as the tough, cigar-smoking yet endearingly needy therapist. Her TV experience (*Half a Dozen Babies, The Shady Hill Kidnapping, Frogs*) has well prepared her for Pielmeier's quippy dialogue, and her easy confidence maneuvering through its clever peaks and banal valleys makes her appealing. She even gets one chance to act (as opposed to quip, whimper, and scream) in an "on the air" scene at the beginning in which a suicide-caller is talked down from a ledge ("Hi! Welcome to 'Last Resort!'"), but none of the other, good actors gets such an opportunity and the juicy public-therapy situation never returns. Nor is the interesting early suggestion that the terror will be Lil's comeuppance for trivializing people's real mental illnesses as entertainment meaningfully pursued. Instead, Pielmeier settles for a formulaic patchwork of self-conscious thieveries and clichés, garnished with psychobabble about multiple personalities couched in the same sort of spitfire harangue that passed for psychotherapy in *Agnes of God*.

The biggest problem with *Voices in the Dark* from a popular perspective, though, is its inability to maintain suspense. (Remember Gene Wilder in *Willie Wonka & the Chocolate Factory*: "The suspense is terrible. I hope it'll last.") This is no sophisticated postmodern work in which all the quoted bits are cleverly worked into the mystery but rather a clumsy attempt to generate the comfort of assembly-line familiarity with the unintended result of ruined surprise. You might be startled by the leap in the dark by this play's left-for-dead villain, for instance, but (whether you saw *Wait Until Dark* or not) you'd have to be pretty naive not to know it was coming at some point after the electricity goes out. Similarly (whether you saw *Sorry, Wrong Number* or not), all the play's phone and phone-answering machine scares feel reheated, and all the ominous innuendo, particularly from the gawky locals, feels mechanical and tired.

Voices in the Dark has a badly confused attitude toward the relationship of fear to audience foreknowledge, epitomized by the scene in which Lil, a worldly, modern woman with substantial cooking experience, repeatedly shoves her fingers six inches into a food processor and then acts surprised when she's injured. Also symptomatic is the ridiculously elaborate hunting decor of David Gallo and Lauren Helpern's setting (animal-hide upholstery, dozens of stuffed trophies), a wildly expensive conceit that apparently exists for the sake of a single early gag line ("Welcome to Eddie Bauer's clubhouse").

The thriller, like the mystery, has always had great literary potential because its popularity is rooted in genuine interest in death. It's not the public's fault that the genre has mostly been exploited by hacks whose formulaic repetition of proven effects does little more than reassure audiences that the world will always remain essentially the same, give or take a grey hair or two. In a way, the anemia of a knockoff amusement-park monster like *Voices in the Dark* is vaguely reassuring, because the very complacent plebeian connoisseurship its makers thought would sustain it turns out to be more demanding than they anticipated. Sometimes real imagination, after all, and not just quick fixes, rushes in to fill the vacuum left by worn out old tricks.

(Aug. 1999)

The March of the New

N EW PLAYS ARE THE LIFEBLOOD OF THE THEATER. GOOD
or bad, though, they rarely get their critical due when they first
appear. To some extent, this is a consequence of the twin occupational hazards of regular reviewing: a jaundiced eye from sustained
exposure to mediocrity and a tendency to overpraise when something
decent does come along. Getting the tone and terms really right in a new
play review, so that they stand up to scrutiny long afterward, is the brass
ring, and anyone who publishes a criticism collection is evidently under
the impression that he snatched it once in a while.

Wit, by Margaret Edson, MCC Theater

Times past, people didn't have the sterile institutions we have to bar-
ricade them from the reality of death, and they created great plays,
poems, paintings and other artworks in their attempt to apprehend its
awesome presence and power. Not so in our discouragingly functional
era. Violent death and its aficionadoes aside, the more typical obsession
today is with pathology, specific processes of disease and deterioration,

which tend to be ghastly rather than awesome and thus stimulate art whose aims are relatively mundane.

The dramatic appeal of patients dying of explicit causes in hospitals has been proven again and again. We've seen this used as an occasion for sentimental stories about bitterness and reconciliation (*Terms of Endearment, Longtime Companion, One True Thing*), as a platform for legal and political argument (*Whose Life Is It Anyway?, As Is*), and (probably most often, on the tube) as a scarcely covert means of glorifying medical institutions and justifying docile submission to them.

The truth is, though, the clinical specificity we think we crave in the name of realism usually stands in the way of real rumination on mortality. How much easier it is to focus on arrangements of IV tubes, shades of skin pallor, and details of hair loss than it is to ask, say, what death itself might have to teach us about our moral and social self-image—or more pointedly, whether we're really ready to settle for the byte-size place in the universe that technology is mapping out for us.

On the surface, Margaret Edson's *Wit*, an unassuming jewel of a play about a prominent literature professor dying of ovarian cancer, would seem to be part of the problem. Professor Vivian Bearing's condition is discovered so late that her only hope is to submit to an experimental, uniquely arduous, eight-month regimen of chemotherapy. Being a tough and deliberative researcher herself, a specialist in the "holy sonnets" of John Donne, she sees merit in the pure acquisition of knowledge, and spends much of the 105-minute action describing her condition and treatment in duly particularized monologues. The medical apparatus is more dehumanizing than she anticipated—even her own doctors seem more interested in writing a paper on her ovaries than in her recovery or humanity—and her chief weapon of self-defense is wit, her own tempered by Donne's.

The blatant schematism (and hence functionalism) of this setup promises nothing, and that turns out to be precisely the author's point. This first play by Edson, a Georgia elementary school teacher who once worked in a cancer ward, is a disconcertingly restrained conception that offers no hint for a long while of the emotional intensity its intellectual rigor will generate. Its very obviousness (seeming obviousness, of course) is the source of its strength in the end—coupled with a fierce and mercilessly precise performance by Kathleen Chalfant (as Bearing) that is among this remarkable actress' best.

Wearing two hospital gowns and with her head shaved beneath a bright red baseball cap, Chalfant enters through the audience, wheeling an IV stand like a dog on a leash, and says "Hi. How are you feeling today?" with marvelous mock geniality. Tough and sinewy yet tenaciously curious and buoyant, she immediately wins affection and respect. ("'How are you feeling today?' I am waiting for the moment when someone asks me this question and I am dead.") At the same time, some spectators may not realize that this affection is based on a paradox: a woman who has long lived mostly inside her fine head, and is further isolated by her disease (the false solicitude of medical workers being the least of it), now reaches for communal contact in the guise of an amiable theatrical narrator commenting on herself.

The whole upbeat spirit of the play depends on maintaining this ticklish contradiction, which Chalfant does with panache. She's witty but never self-pitying ("What's left to puke? You may remark that my vocabulary has taken a turn for the Anglo-Saxon"), and is adept at addressing the audience confidentially without falling into tones too chatty for us to accept as the professor's second self. At times in this production directed by Derek Anson Jones (first staged last year at Long Wharf Theater in New Haven), Chalfant's narrator seems like the sympathetic teacher that Professor Bearing says she never could be (perhaps judging herself too harshly).

In any case, the main reason apart from Chalfant that the play gathers such emotional steam is that Edson has pared the story down to essentials. Bearing receives no visitors until she is past coherent conversation in the penultimate scene. "That won't be necessary," she says when her doctor (played by Walter Charles) offers to contact someone. We meet her father, her mentor, and her students in flashbacks, but no unfinished business with relatives or friends complicates the present-tense action, and no eleventh-hour love interest threatens to turn it pseudo-tragic. Bearing eventually accepts some tender ministrations from a kind-hearted nurse (played movingly by Paula Pizzi), but apart from that and her witty remarks to the audience, she is a wholly isolated figure whose every movement and decision therefore takes on a figural flavor.

To what extent, Edson seems to ask without answering, have we all sacrificed crucial bits of our humanity by accepting insularity and fragmentation (in scholarship and elsewhere) as normal aspects of modern life? On the one hand, if Bearing really was as austere and rigid a teacher as the flashbacks depict, she is indeed the literary counterpart to Jason Posner, the cloddish young medical Research Fellow (played by Alec Phoenix) who thinks his required course in bedside manner was a "collosal waste of time." On the other hand, when we finally see Bearing give a lecture ourselves (on "Holy Sonnet 9"), we come to doubt the veracity of the flashbacks, since she is captivating and insightful in ways that reflect on the rest of the play and beyond.

For instance, she says Donne juxtaposes "aggressive intellect" and "pious melodrama," staking out contrasting self-dramatizing positions in an ongoing, extraordinarily disciplined effort to articulate his anxieties about salvation. Similarly, one might add, Bearing approaches the end of her extraordinarily disciplined life and remarks with good humor that life has grown "corny" (she's been given a popsicle by a nurse who calls her "sweetheart"). For Edson, as for Donne, such corniness can't be corny in any cheap sense because it's the spontaneous, humane counterpressure to mechanical and "aggressively" heaped up clinical information. Acts of kindness in such contexts (including a late scene in which Bearing's old mentor arrives and reads not Donne but the children's book *Runaway Bunny* to her barely conscious protégé) count simply as facts, like steps in the pathology of a disease.

One contemporary work that does compare meaningfully with *Wit* on this score is Sherwin Nuland's *How We Die*, which won the National Book Award in 1994. As a physician, Nuland too understood that no one would listen to a word of his wisdom about mortality unless he couched it in accurate and up-to-date clinical information. Hence, in offering the information, he grafted his prodigious compassion and rage about it onto his descriptive prose, figuratively thrashing certain diseases with switch-strokes of indignant adjectives and burying others beneath torrents of aggressively veracious, depictive words. Regardless of whether Edson knew Nuland—*How We Die* is quoted in some of *Wit's* press material—the obvious affinities between the works amount to high praise for a debut play.

(Sept. 1998)

Oedipus, by Dare Clubb, Blue Light Theater

"What do I know of man's destiny? I could tell you more about radishes," wrote Samuel Beckett, one of the few latter-day playwrights willing to deal with the thorny subject of man's fate. This was a favorite subject of the Greeks, and it's surely timeless, but contemporary American playwrights have stumbled over it, as their many clumsy attempts at classical adaptation can testify. Worried about coming off as retro or snooty if they dwell on anything that smells too much like philosophy, our writers have tended to focus instead on such "radishes" as contemporary reference, updated metaphor, and hip language, regardless of their real underlying interests. Not Dare Clubb, whose four-hour *Oedipus* confronts the knottiest and most unfashionable questions of fate and free will with disarming frontality, canniness and zeal—and hipness as well, I might add.

Clubb's *Oedipus* is an original play, not a modernization of Sophocles, and it has its problems. The sheer ambition behind the project, however, as well as the quality of this production directed by the author, are extraordinary. Clubb has obviously been through intense mental wrestling not only with himself but with the whole canon of modern drama. Ibsen, Strindberg, Büchner, Chekhov, Pirandello, Beckett, and Brecht are only the most obvious voices in his dense web of allusions. But details aside, it's simply refreshing to see thinking worthy of the name preside unabashedly on an American stage. And it's inspiring to see such a heady project lure so many excellent actors away from flourishing film and TV careers: the twelve-member cast includes Frances McDormand, Billy Crudup, Jeffrey Donovan, John de Vries, Kevin Geer, and Carolyn McCormick.

The basic difference between this *Oedipus* and most other dramatic versions of the myth (including Sophocles's and Cocteau's), is that Clubb's protagonist doesn't try heroically to elude his horrific fate but rather rushes headlong to embrace it, possessed by the idea that such self-actualization (as we might call it), even if disgraceful to some humans, is the only way to honor himself in the eyes of the gods. Twenty years old and played gently, reflectively, and with marvelously intelligent diffidence by the lanky Crudup, Oedipus becomes a criminal in the name of "divinity" in the first act, then embarks on a fantastical, would-be epic journey to the limits of his mind in order to figure out what he really knows about who he is and, therefore, what he's destined to do.

The action opens not in Thebes (as most versions have it, with Oedipus as a king, husband and father) but rather in Corinth, where the young man still lives with the rulers Merope and Polybus he takes for his parents. On a set consisting of rough, sawdust-lined planks backed by generic classical flats that look disassembled for storage (design by Narelle Sissons), McDormand enters as Merope, in severe emotional distress. She confesses an inappropriate, Phaedra-like passion for Oedipus and engages in a fascinating and startlingly blunt debate with her servant Periboea (Johanna Day) about the nature of her feelings and rationalizations. Merope: "It's just love, Periboea...Not violence. Not hatred. I'm speaking of affection. Of the desire to bestow kind gestures on a loved one. Gifts. Tokens of esteem." Periboea: "You use love to justify doing whatever you want without considering anything except your own unrestrained desire."

More memorable than either woman's ideas about morality, however, is McDormand's magisterial nervousness, which establishes a heightened emotional ground on which the remainder of the production rests. Anyone who knows this actress only from her Oscar-winning portrayal of the pregnant sheriff Marge Gunderson in *Fargo* ("you betcha!") is in for quite a surprise. Ferociously ardent, dangerously overwound, stomping barefoot from place to place as if caged yet always centered and sonorous, she seems to channel energy from beneath the raw stage boards as Merope. And this earthy, fleshy fact, her rooted, warm-blooded presence, returns continually to mind during all the chilly and complex talk to come about fate and the destructive power of words.

Words turn out to be Clubb's other main obsession. "Speaking is an action," says Periboea; it can bring reality into being. Hence, to utter an oracle (understood here as one's presumption about the future) can have disastrous consequences—both because people tend to be fallible listeners and because they're also often obtusely literal. ("You're so literal" is the most biting insult in the play, and it returns again and again, boomeranging on the author in the last act—a point I'll come back to.) Oedipus, returned from the Delphic oracle, marches in to kill Polybus after Merope tells him he mustn't question the gods, whereupon she shouts, "You simpleton! You missed the point!" It seems she was referring only to the bit about coupling with mom, but they have sex anyway, after which she floats an absurd Miss Julie-like plan for them to run away together.

What Clubb does next with all this grave silliness reflects better on him than any other decision in the work. After the first of two intermissions, the classical flats are cleared off and Oedipus (having callously departed after learning that Merope wasn't his mother) finds himself in a wholly imaginary plane, on a nearly bare stage, akin to the distorting-mirror world of *Peer Gynt*. The dialogue had suggested earlier that time and space were flexible, when the young Oedipus was described as vanishing in a field at Colonus, where blind, old Oedipus died. Now, accompanied initially by his friend Teiresias (whom Donovan plays as a sneaker-wearing, nihilistic smartass reminiscent of Büchner's character Valerio in *Leonce and Lena*), Oedipus moves through scenes that have all but no temporal fixity, each providing a different twisted reflection of him whose implications he fails to heed.

The herdsman who rescued Oedipus as an infant, for instance (played by Lawrence Nathanson), is a spluttering madman obscenely fixated on the memory of Merope's pulchritude; he refers to the baby as "the little pile of crap." Teiresias and Oedipus (who is always insisting that his isn't "a common experience"; "My fate's not the world's fate") next meet a loquacious hunter (played by de Vries) who serves ludicrously epicurean dishes such as "peeled rabbit eyes in wild melon soup" and thus seems to stand as an enlargement of the inherent pettiness of obsessive self-actualization. Finally, Oedipus meets up with his grown sons Eteocles (Alex Draper) and Polynices (Geer)—although none of them recognizes the relation—and they turn out to be freebooting bandits feeding off a war they have no stake in, their squabbling and mutual annihilation a seriocomic reflection of the empty circularity of Oedipus's moral reasoning.

Not all of the play is as lucid or efficient as I've made it seem. Each section contains bursts of beautiful language, but the classical milieu does sometimes come off as a pretext for overwriting and gratuitous reference. My most significant complaint, however, has to do with the last act, when Oedipus finds his real parents, Laos (Jonathan Fried) and Iocaste (McCormick). Much of this—and in particular the climactic encounter between Oedipus and his real mother—amounts to a disappointing retreat from the liberating realm of discursive fantasy that had so marvelously broadened and elevated the play's thought.

There are parallels here too with some of Clubb's sources. Ibsen's Peer returns to his Solveig in the end, as Goethe's Faust returns to his Gretchen. Neither of those endings, however, reads as a retraction of the courageous mythic symbolism that went before because neither author ever really relinquishes the supernatural context that had allowed his drama to take off. The symbolism Clubb employs in his last act (Oedipus is nailed to a rocky cliff like Prometheus, arms out like Christ) seems tacked on, because the prime energy is spent on a formulaic harangue by Iocaste about Oedipus's selfishness. She harps on his cruelty without ever adequately explaining why she so cruelly left him to die as a baby, and feeds him sententious advice about "self-questioning," "gratuitous generosity," and "unthinking kindness." Such reductive summarizing pales beside the far more sophisticated and articulate discussions during Oedipus's journey.

The mundane realistic point is clear, I suppose: some things you just have to hear from your (hypocritical) mother. Who wants explanations, though, when you've just had poetry?

(Oct. 1998)

Corpus Christi, by Terrence McNally, Manhattan Theater Club

Impossible Marriage, by Beth Henley, Roundabout Theater

As scandals go, the one surrounding *Corpus Christi* is a bust. Lately it has been given political substance by association due to grave events such as the homophobic murder of Matthew Shepard in Wyoming and the NYPD's use of excessive force against a peaceful Manhattan demonstration protesting the murder. Scandals, however, if they aren't always fun themselves, are at least supposed to be parasitic on fun, conducted in the wake of illicit fun. Oscar Wilde once said that "scandal is gossip made tedious by morality." How exceptionally tedious, then, to find the object of scandal in this case, Terrence McNally, feeding the flames of banal morality himself.

Nothing would please me more than to be able to launch a laudatory broadside about *Corpus Christi* at the ignorant and vicious homophobes who have protested outside Manhattan Theater Club and threatened violence against the author and the theater. MTC was wrong to cancel this show, brave to reverse its decision. And as the pamphlets shoved into my hand out front demonstrate (none based on a reading or viewing of the work), the protesters' motivations are certainly censorial and therefore base, whatever their piety. Sadly, though, it turns out that this supposedly offensive play, which seemed to promise some substantial unconventional argument about the nature of Jesus, largely mirrors the constricted and simplistic world view of its attackers.

The title *Corpus Christi* refers to the town in Texas where McNally

grew up and to the Christian holiday, associated with plays and pag-
eantry in the middle ages, that celebrates the sacrament of the Eucha-
rist. Since (as everyone knows by now) the play deals in part with the
gay sexuality of its Christ figure, named Joshua, the title's literal meaning, "body of Christ," is also a deliberate provocation. Staged by Joe
Mantello on a polished-wood platform with benches atop a faux-
concrete slab in a raw workshop space stripped of proscenium and
masking (set by Loy Arcenas), the action merges the Texas of McNally's
youth with the Roman-occupied Judaea of Jesus and real time in the
theater itself.

At the opening, one of the thirteen male actors, all incredibly charming and suave, announces that we will hear "an old and familiar story"
that has "no suspense and fewer surprises" but nevertheless "bears re-
peating." Another man referred to as John (Michael Irby) then baptizes
his companions, mentioning each actor's real name before christening
him after one of the apostles: "I bless you Christopher Fitzgerald. I bap-
tize you and recognize your divinity as a human being. I adore you,
Chris. I christen you Thomas." And at this point everyone has ex-
changed his street clothes for the apostolic garb of a neat white shirt and
khakis. Mild jokes about the theatrical circumstance aside ("I hope that's
not the same water we used in the last performance"), the grinning,
cultish earnestness of this sequence, and of much of the rest of the play
as well, calls to mind nothing more strongly than the demeanor of the
glazed-eyed, weak-kneed army of the pious outside on the street (all of
whom I'm sure are charming at home, too).

The play goes on to tell a version of the Jesus story adapted to fit the
sketched out life of a gay Catholic kid growing up in 1940s and 50s
Texas, but McNally never abandons his adherence to the most deaden-
ingly conventional notions of faith and worship. Joshua is born in a
cheap motel rather than a manger. Men bearing free room service stand
in for the three kings: "We're telling you this child is the son of God."
"Hell, every mother feels that way." Scene after scene, in other words,
sticks to the same facile attachment to the received story patched up with
droll modern references (most *not* connected to gayness), leaving the au-

dience to do the hard work of figuring out what the hell the superficially applied American milieu has to do with anything.

The apostles briefly describe the ordinary Texas lives they gave up in order to follow Joshua—one was a lawyer, one a doctor, one a hustler, and so on—but, with a couple of exceptions, this information is put to no further use. Joshua (Anson Mount) is a polite, conventionally handsome, intellectually clueless boy who keeps a picture of James Dean under his bed, says "yes sir" and "no sir," and seems so detached from independent thought that his speeches taken from famous biblical passages come off as canned platitudes. Worst of all, Judas (Josh Lucas) is portrayed from the beginning as the archetype of trite evil (or should it be evil triteness?): a predatory tough with a permanent sardonic sneer, who likes to say shocking things ("I've got a big dick") and who initiates Joshua into boy-boy love at the senior prom by kissing him in the bathroom. That more than half the play dwells on Joshua's high school years seems a result of McNally's decision to rely only on knowledge about Jesus that every high-schooler possesses.

The sheer unimaginativeness of *Corpus Christi* is the true shocker. Why not provoke real thought, for instance, about the difference between love and skin-deep attraction by playing Judas as handsome and self-secure and Joshua as homely and needy? McNally can't even be bothered thinking through the implications of his anachronisms (how, exactly, is a curfew for the kids at "Pontius Pilate High" analagous to the Roman Prefect locking the city gates?). The presentations of Joshua's miracles (healing an HIV positive man with a hug, turning one fish into five for a beggar-woman with kids) sidestep all consideration of changes in scientific and social thought since Jesus's age.

I kept waiting for McNally's take on the coming out tale of Jesus at twelve in the temple among the "doctors," to see if he could write himself out of this hole of banalities. Needless to say, he wasn't up to it. Most of his scenes and nearly every secondary characterization remain flimsy sketches (a madman is a guy who can only say "fuck you," for instance), seemingly because he's just impatient to get back to the serious business of slavishly imitating the gospels.

McNally didn't arrive at this troubling pass of narrowness out of nowhere, of course. His 1994-95 Broadway hit *Love! Valour! Compassion!* was a magnanimous and appealing plea for inclusion—inclusion of certain unflamboyant gay lives within the culture's collective image of normalcy. *Corpus Christi*, far from the first work to associate Jesus with homosexuality, is really a continuation of the same impulse: a passionate plea to include gay men (earnest, clean-cut ones, at any rate) in the club of ordinary, suffering human beings—just like those regular guys Jesus and his apostles. There's nothing wrong with this impulse; if anything, it's relatively modest. The author simply discredits it when he emulates the willfully oblivious posture of those least worthy of solicitude: fundamentalist know-nothings.

Would that wonderful Beth Henley—who has never received what I think is her critical due, despite her Pulitzer Prize—commanded a fraction of the attention for *Impossible Marriage* that McNally received before most people even knew what he'd written in *Corpus Christi*. This is the first new Henley play to open in New York in many years, and to date it's been greeted mostly with dim-witted dismissals by reviewers unprepared to appreciate anything but her usual idiom of standard American realism. The production directed by Stephen Wadsworth does have some bumps, but this play is a brave and marvelously wacky departure from Henley's past work, containing immeasurably more wisdom and original thought about, say, the divinity of love than McNally's imitative holy tale.

The action takes place in the lush garden of a Savannah country estate where Kandall Kingsley (Lois Smith) is preparing to host the wedding of her gamine of a daughter, Pandora (Gretchen Cleevely). Pandora's older but scarcely more earthbound sister Floral (Holly Hunter), who is to all appearances nine and a half months pregnant even though she later reveals that her extremely handsome and solicitous husband Jonsey (Jon Tenney) never makes love to her, has decided that Pandora's engagement is inappropriate and determines to stop the wedding. Floral has never met the fiancé, a well-known novelist named Edvard Lunt (Christopher McCann) whom she presumes is too old, and much of the humor and poignance over the intermissionless hour and forty minutes stem from the fact that both she and her mother (whose marriages have been disastrous) assume they are better judges of marriage than flighty and callow Pandora.

Also key to the story are a too easily overlooked minister named Jonathan Larence (Alan Mandell), who has been away in Nigeria, and Lunt's angry, maladjusted son Sidney (Daniel London), whom Lunt doesn't recognize at first. Explaining how these two figure in, however, would give too much away. The compelling strangeness of the work is partly due to its pairing of seemingly inappropriate lovers, and partly a product of its deliberate staginess. Characters enter and immediately state their personal philosophies to others they barely know, or melodramatically confess their actual motivations to those they think are adversaries, eliciting startlingly sensitive responses.

Everyone pauses for poses, epigrams, and arch, over-rehearsed line readings that ought to annoy but instead create rich questions about collusion and trust. And it is all a perfect frame for another delightfully capricious performance by Hunter, who fills out Floral (as she has so many other Henley characters) with a superbly idiosyncratic repertory of weirdly evocative little dances and private twisty faces.

My quibbles with the production have to do with imbalance in the cast. McCann's mortician-like solemnity as Lunt, for instance, seems reductive when compared with Hunter and Smith's much greater complexity as Floral and Kandall, and this ends up preventing the play's humor from finding a consistent ground. London also plays Sidney too stiffly for the character to rise above its nerdy cliché. None of this, however, dampened my admiration in the end for this singularly courageous comeback by one of our best playwrights.

(Oct. 1998)

Acknowledgements

The following is a list of sources not specifically mentioned in the text.

"The Death (and Life) of American Theater Criticism: Advice to the Young Critic," "The Last Biography?", "Documentary Solo Performance: The Politics of the Mirrored Self," "The Gospel According to Billy," *Theater* 33:2 (2003), 28:2 (1998), 31:3 (2001), 31:3 (2001).

"The Critic in Extremis," "Stardust Melancholy," *American Theatre*, Sept. 2001, Jan. 2003.

"The Critic as Humanist," *Plays, Movies, and Critics*, ed. Jody McAuliffe (Durham and London: Duke Univ. Press, 1993).

"Krap's First Tape," "Susan and Bob in Bed," "To B.E. or Not To B.E.," "Ghosts & The Dead Man," *Village Voice*, June 20, 1995, Jan. 4, 1994, Aug. 24, 1993, July 16, 1996.

"Suffering Fools," "Send in the Clown," "Dayzed," "You Can Go Home Again," *New York Press*, Dec. 2-8, 1998, Oct. 25–31, 2000, July 21–27, 1999, Oct. 22–28, 1997.

"Robert Wilson's 21st-Century Academy," *New York Times*, Aug. 13, 2000.

"Marathon Mensch," *Salmagundi*, Fall 2002.

Index